# JOHN AMONG THE GOSPELS

# JOHN AMONG THE GOSPELS

## The Relationship in Twentieth-Century Research

### D. MOODY SMITH

*Fortress Press*

*Minneapolis*

JOHN AMONG THE GOSPELS
The Relationship in Twentieth-Century Research

Diagram by Frans Neirynck from *Jean et les Synoptiques: Examen Critique de l'Exegese de M.-E. Boismard*, BETL 49, copyright © 1979 Louvain University Press. Reprinted by permission of Peeters Press, Louvain, Belgium.

Excerpt from *Eusebius: The Ecclesiastical History*, ed. Kirsopp Lake, J. E. L. Oulton, and H. J. Lawlor (Cambridge, MA: Loeb Classical Library, 1926–32).

Excerpt from *The Ante-Nicene Fathers*, vol. 10 (Grand Rapids, MI: William B. Eerdmans Publishing Co., 1986).

Excerpt from *Jean et les Synoptiques* by Mgr. [Bruno] de Solages (Leiden: E. J. Brill, 1979).

Excerpt from "B. W. Bacon on John and Mark" by D. Moody Smith from *Perspectives in Religious Studies* 8:3 (1981): 201–18. Reprinted by permission.

Excerpts from "John and the Synoptics" by D. Moody Smith from *Biblica* 63 (1982): 102–13. Reprinted by permission.

Biblical passages are author's translation, unless otherwise specified.

Interior Design: Karen Buck
Cover Design: Eric Lecy

Cover illustration: St. John the Evangelist, adapted from a Strassbourg/Johann Reinhard Gruninger Bible (German, 1485) in the rare books collection of the Burke Library at Union Theological Seminary in New York.

---

Library of Congress Cataloging-in-Publication Data

Smith, D. Moody (Dwight Moody)
    John among the gospels: the relationship in twentieth-century research / D. Moody Smith.
      p.    cm.
    Includes bibliographical references and index.
    ISBN 0-8006-2530-7 (alk. paper)
    1. Bible. N.T. John—Criticism, interpretation, etc.—History—20th century. 2. Bible. N.T. Gospels—Criticism, interpretation, etc.—History—20th century. I. Title.
BS2615.2.S623   1992
226.5'06—dc20                          91-44739
                                               CIP

---

The paper used in this publication meets the minimum requirements of American National Standard for Information Sciences—Permanence of Paper for Printed Library Materials, ANSI Z329.48-1984. ∞™

---

Manufactured in the U.S.A.                                     AF 1–2530

96    95    94    93    92    1    2    3    4    5    6    7    8    9    10

To Franklin Woodrow Young

# Contents

# Abbreviations

| | |
|---|---|
| ATANT | Abhandlungen zur Theologie des Alten und Neuen Testaments |
| BBET | Beiträge zur biblischen Exegese und Theologie |
| BETL | Bibliotheca ephemeridum theologicarum lovaniensium |
| *CBQ* | *Catholic Biblical Quarterly* |
| *ETL* | *Ephemerides theologicae lovanienses* |
| FRLANT | Forschungen zur Religion und Literatur des Alten und Neuen Testaments |
| *HTR* | *Harvard Theological Review* |
| *JBL* | *Journal of Biblical Literature* |
| JSNTSup | Journal for the Study of the New Testament—Supplement Series |
| *JTS* | *Journal of Theological Studies* |
| NovtSup | Novum Testamentum, Supplements |
| *NTS* | *New Testament Studies* |
| *RB* | *Revue biblique* |
| *RSR* | *Recherches de science religieuse* |
| SANT | Studien zum Alten und Neuen Testaments |
| SBL | Society of Biblical Literature |
| SBLDS | SBL Dissertation Series |
| SBS | Stuttgarter Bibelstudien |
| SNTSMS | Society for New Testament Studies Monograph Series |
| *ThR* | *Theologische Rundschau* |
| *TLZ* | *Theologische Literaturzeitung* |
| TU | Texte und Untersuchungen |
| *TZ* | *Theologische Zeitschrift* |
| WUNT | Wissenschaftliche Untersuchungen zum Neuen Testament |
| *ZNW* | *Zeitschrift für die neutestamentliche Wissenschaft* |
| *ZTK* | *Zeitschrift für Theologie und Kirche* |

# *Preface*

The differences between John and the other Synoptic Gospels were viewed as a problem in the ancient church, so that already at the beginning of the third century Clement of Alexandria offered a classic explanation for them: John, in some contrast to the other evangelists, wrote a spiritual gospel. The problem of their relationship has frequently been a source of fascination for exegetes and for the past decade and a half has stood at the center of my attention. For reasons that I hope will become clear in this book, it has a tantalizing quality, because evidence seems to point in contrary or opposite directions at once.

In taking stock of the problem and attempting to assess the evidence, I have tried to see how and why John's dependence upon the Synoptics was generally acknowledged at the beginning of this century but began to be challenged, particularly between the World Wars, so that by the last third of the century John's independence was more widely asserted. More than a decade ago, however, the older position that John knew and used the Synoptic Gospels, which had never been abandoned by some renowned scholars such as C. K. Barrett and W. G. Kümmel, was already finding new defenders.

In this situation my own interest was stimulated, and I began to study the problem afresh, becoming distinctly aware as I did of the shifting ground of scholarly opinion beneath my feet. When I set about to write, it seemed proper to begin with a *Forschungsbericht*, which at that time would have concluded in the late 1970s. Yet two factors or developments continually enveloped and threatened to defeat me. First, I became increasingly aware of the scope of the problem and the amount of scholarly work already expended upon it. Second, even as I worked and wrote, colleagues continued to publish works dealing with or bearing upon the problem, so that I had a sense of at once swimming against the stream and being borne away by the flood. The renewed interest in John and the Synoptics was indicated by the nearly 150 scholars who attended the 1990 Louvain Biblical Colloquium, which was devoted entirely to that subject.

Through the generosity of the Center of Theological Inquiry, I have had a summer and a semester to resume my writing. In doing so, I turned first to this *Forschungsbericht*, revising and enlarging it. In the process I soon found that I had produced a chapter of several hundred manuscript pages. In reading it, I was pleased to discover that it had an integrity and direction of its own, imparted not so much by me as by the shape and course of scholarship. This chapter seemed to be a book in itself, and I have thus decided to publish it as such in the hope that it will be helpful to others, students as well as scholars, who are interested in this ancient and important subject. Knowing where scholarship has been is important in determining where it should go.

Although this book cannot claim to be comprehensive, I do hope and believe that it is accurately representative of the shape and emphasis of scholarly work on the subject during the twentieth century. Obviously it was not possible to mention every relevant work, and I have doubtless made some mistakes and omissions. There is a bibliography of the important and pertinent works, most of which are described or mentioned in the book. The reader will notice that in-text quotations from literature in German or French have been translated. In the footnotes the original languages have generally been allowed to stand, but in a few instances, which are noted, I have offered translations.

For indispensable support, without which I could not have brought the project to this point, I thank the Center of Theological Inquiry, and particularly its chairman, Roland Frye, who early on took an interest in my work and has continued to encourage me. Daniel W. Hardy, the Center's director, has unfailingly supported our work, presiding over a community of scholars in which a nice balance between sharing and individual endeavor is struck. Friends and colleagues have offered me more encouragement than they know as I worked and puzzled over this project, notably Raymond E. Brown, R. Alan Culpepper, J. Louis Martyn, and Franklin W. Young. Robert Kysar, now of the Lutheran Theological Seminary at Philadelphia, kindly read the manuscript at an earlier stage and made important suggestions for improvement. Of course, I assume full responsibility for the book in its present form and particularly for any errors it may contain.

The dedication of this book to Franklin Young is a token of recognition of what I owe him for his friendship, colleagueship, and encouragement. In 1977–78 he resumed the directorship of graduate studies in religion at Duke in order that I might take a sabbatical leave to begin work on this project. All along he has read pieces that I have produced and has encouraged me to work at the problem. Moreover, in similar fashion he has stimulated and helped many students and younger scholars, who, I am sure, would want to join me in expressing appreciation and thanks to him for his interest and generosity.

Mrs. Frances Parrish, head of Duke Divinity School's secretarial pool, has generously put her staff at my disposal, even in my absence, and Ms. Sarah Freedman has indefatigably worked over a manuscript partly typed, partly handwritten, at best marginally legible, and has successfully transformed it by means of a word processor. I am grateful also to them as well as to Mark Matson and Andy Wakefield, doctoral students at Duke University, who have in several significant ways assisted in the production of this book.

My friend John Hollar of Fortress Press set me on this course and encouraged me to keep at it. I learned of his untimely death the day he was to have returned to his office from the Frankfurt Book Fair, when I had called the Press to tell him of my leave at the Center and my hopes for resuming work on this manuscript. Of course, Jane Allen Smith has for decades supported me in this, as in many other undertakings and endeavors, which I could never have dreamed of fulfilling or accomplishing without her.

D. Moody Smith
*The Divinity School*
*Duke University*

# 1

## John among the Gospels: The Problem and Its Earliest History

The problem of John among the gospels is chiefly the question of the relation of John to the Synoptic Gospels. For the obvious reason that John and three other gospels are now found in the New Testament, attention has centered on their relationship, and rightly so, for these gospels are historically and theologically most important, in the sense of being most widely used or read, in the early church. Yet perhaps even the first century and certainly the second saw the writing of other gospels or gospel-like documents, and this fact must not be lost from view. Hence we prefer to speak of John among the gospels rather than John and the Synoptics. At the same time, discussion, both ancient and modern, has naturally centered on the relationship of John and the Synoptic Gospels, so our attention also will be focused primarily there.

Accordingly, it will be helpful to ask, first of all, what the problem of John and the Synoptics is. At one level, it is quite analogous to the synoptic problem, that is, the problem of synoptic relationships. How does one explain John's differences from the Synoptics while taking account of its similarities to them? Thus it is a problem of literary and historical relationships. Behind it stands the question or concern of how these different Gospels relate to the history of Jesus that lies behind them and to the theology and proclamation of the church that lies, so to speak, in front of them. That is, how do they relate to the church's understanding of its mission and message as it seeks their authorization in the Gospels. These last questions are not the subject matter of this book, but they can never be far from view. The literary and historical problem has elements or aspects that modern criticism is well aware of but that should be noted briefly at the outset. Further, the problem of John's differences from the Synoptics did not go unnoticed or unexplained in antiquity, a fact we modern critics should acknowledge. Therefore we shall describe briefly how the problem was perceived and explained then.

## THE ELEMENTS OF THE PROBLEM

John is a gospel like the other gospels. It is arguable, of course, that only Mark and John are truly gospels, while Matthew is, for example, a manual of discipline and Luke is an ancient biography. We shall, however, stick with the churchly and commonsense definition of all four as gospels, that is, narratives of the ministry of Jesus.[1] John is as much such a narrative as the others. It begins the account of Jesus' ministry with the familiar story of his encounter with John the Baptist, continues through a public ministry and an extended narrative of his death, and ends with resurrection appearances of the crucified Lord to his disciples. The story of Jesus' passion is narrated in a way similar to that of the Synoptics, and at the center of his public ministry appear accounts of his feeding five thousand people, walking on the sea at night, and receiving the "messianic" confession of his disciple Peter. In all four Gospels it is taken for granted that Jesus was the expected Messiah of Judaism, the fulfillment of Israel's hopes. As such he taught, healed the sick, and finally was crucified and died. The general similarity of the Johannine and synoptic accounts is impressive.

Moreover, there are specific points of comparison where the similarities are real. In discussion of the synoptic problem, verbatim agreements in wording and the order of events or episodes play a significant role. Matthew and Luke frequently agree with Mark in both respects, and where they depart from Mark, they usually do so separately. So one finds threefold agreement of all the Synoptics, and agreement of Matthew or Luke with Mark but not, as a rule, agreement of Matthew and Luke against Mark. (Admittedly, there are some minor verbal agreements of Matthew and Luke against Mark that cause a problem for the Markan hypothesis of critical orthodoxy.) The synoptic narratives and the actual wording of the synoptic texts have such strong resemblances and points of agreement that it is meaningful to talk about the one narrative or text *departing* from the other in wording or order. Gospel

---

[1] On the use of the term "gospel" *(euangelion)* for written documents and the difficulty of establishing a single literary genre, see Helmut Koester, *Ancient Christian Gospels: Their History and Development* (Philadelphia: Trinity Press International, 1990), 1–48, esp. 24–31 ("Why Did Written Documents Come to Be Called 'Gospels'?").

parallels are published in which the closely related texts appear side by side, even if the fact that sometimes clearly parallel passages occur in different places, or in a different order, has to be indicated to the reader. When, however, John is introduced into such an arrangement, the Johannine column more often than not is blank, so different and diverse is this Gospel in sheer content.

Nevertheless, there are some verbatim agreements as well as striking agreements in the order of events. In *The Four Gospels: A Study of Origins*, B. H. Streeter singles out six striking verbatim agreements of John with Mark, which he thinks amply demonstrate the fourth evangelist's knowledge of the Second Gospel (Mark 6:37 = John 6:7; Mark 14:3, 5 = John 12:3, 5; John 14:31 = Mark 14:42; Mark 14:54 = John 18:18; Mark 15:9 = John 18:39; John 5:8–9 = Mark 2:11–12).[2] There are a number of others. What is more, despite the remarkable absence of most Markan material from John, particularly in the public ministry, wherever John has Markan episodes he usually presents them in the order in which they occur in Mark. As in the case of the synoptic problem where Matthew's or Luke's agreements seem to be through or with Mark, John's agreements in wording or order with the Synoptics seem to be principally agreements with Mark. This is a matter deserving closer scrutiny, and there may be some exceptions, but for the moment it suffices to observe that, with respect to order of events, where John agrees with the Synoptics he agrees with Mark. By the same token, the preponderance of John's verbatim agreements with the Synoptics are agreements with Mark. It is perhaps not surprising that the fact that Matthew's wording is very close to Mark is reflected in John's verbatim agreements with Matthew, as well as with Mark, being much more numerous than his agreements with Luke. The points of agreement with Luke often have to do with historical data or perspective. For example, in Luke as in John, and in these Gospels alone, Jesus is portrayed as feeding a multitude only once. In John and Luke only, there is no formal trial or conviction of Jesus before Jewish authorities. Only in John and Luke does Pilate three times declare Jesus innocent. Only in John and Luke is there no cry of dereliction from the cross. And only in these two Gospels does the risen Jesus appear to his disciples as they are gathered together on Sunday evening in Jerusalem. In fact, John and Luke alone depict the risen Jesus appearing to disciples in Jerusalem.

Despite the remarkable character of many of these agreements, it must be emphasized that they are scattered. It is not as if John were following one of

---

[2] B. H. Streeter, *The Four Gospels: A Study of Origins* (London: Macmillan & Co., 1936; originally published 1924), 397–99.

the other accounts, as Matthew and even Luke so often seem to be following Mark. The striking verbatim agreements between John and even Mark represent only a very minor fraction of the text of either. Even where the two Gospel accounts are obviously narrating the same event (e.g., the feeding of the multitude or the arrest of Jesus), the amount of verbatim agreement is relatively small when compared with that among the Synoptic Gospels. (Strangely, this lack of agreement with the Synoptics seems to be paralleled in the so-called apocryphal gospels, insofar as we know them.)

Finally, the total presentation of Jesus and his ministry in John is vastly different from what one finds in the other, Synoptic Gospels. Each of the Synoptics has its own perspective and point of view; but when they are compared with John, their similarities to each other stand out. John's differences and distinctiveness can be summed up accurately, if somewhat simplistically, under three heads: ministry, miracles, and message.

The ministry of Jesus in John differs significantly from the synoptic version in its geographical locality and its temporal span. (There are also, of course, contradictory data, as when John dates the crucifixion on Nisan 14 rather than 15 as the Synoptics have it.) The traditional three-year ministry of Jesus assumes the distinctive Johannine chronology, in which there are three Passovers (John 2:13, 23; 6:4; 11:55) rather than the synoptic, according to which there is only one. In John, Jesus is much more frequently in Judea and Jerusalem than he is in the Synoptics, in which he goes there only once, at the very end. John creates the impression that Jesus worked mostly in Jerusalem or Judea. The model Beloved Disciple seems to join him there. Perhaps he was a Jerusalem disciple. For Luke too, Jerusalem was of very great importance, but his itinerary of Jesus' ministry is much closer to Mark's than to John's.

The presentation of miracles and Jesus' attitude toward them are again much different in John than in the Synoptics. The very terms used are suggestive. According to the Synoptic Gospels, Jesus accomplishes mighty works (*dynameis*), effecting healing and deliverance for those afflicted by sickness or demons. When accosted by any who are seeking a sign from heaven to test him (Mark 8:11; cf. Matt. 12:38–39), the Jesus of the Synoptics reacts quite negatively. (Admittedly, it is not certain that such a "sign from heaven" is a miracle, yet such an understanding of it fits Jesus' whole demeanor in the Synoptics, where he seems to retire in the face of public acclaim.) On the other hand, in the Fourth Gospel miracles are from the outset called signs (*semeia*), as it is simply assumed that their purpose is to point to Jesus and to signify who he is. Occasionally the other view of signs seems to break through (John 2:23–25; 4:48), but the difference from the Synoptics is nevertheless real and significant. In addition, the number and type of miracles are different. In John, Jesus exorcizes no demon and cleanses no leper—typical forms of Jesus' activity in the Synoptics. No Markan healing narrative is recounted, at least not in recognizable form. By way of contrast, most of the Matthean and Lukan healing narratives are clearly based on the Markan. In the light of this fact it is less surprising that the only miracle story recorded in all four Gospels is the feeding of the five thousand. Luke omits the walking on the water that occurs immediately following the feeding in the other Gospels. Luke and Matthew share with John the story of Jesus healing a centurion or ruler's servant or son at a considerable distance, but this episode is not found in Mark. Given the fact that all the Gospels present Jesus as a miracle worker, it is all the more astonishing that the divergences between John and the Synoptics are so great.

Jesus is a teacher and preacher in John as well as in the Synoptics, but the content of his message is quite different in the one and the other. (Although the verb "to preach" used of Jesus in the Synoptic Gospels is not found in John, Jesus is several times portrayed in John as "crying out.") Aside from the fact that the typically synoptic parables and epigrammatic sayings are largely missing in John, where Jesus engages in sharp debate and utters long discourses, the content of what Jesus has to say differs in ways quite familiar to readers of the New Testament. In the Synoptics, Jesus announces the imminence of the kingdom or rule of God and through parable or specific command calls for obedience to God's will as it can be known by common sense in the light of Scripture. In John, the kingdom of God fades into the background as Jesus speaks and debates about his own messianic status or, particularly, his relationship to God and the role he has been given to accomplish. In John, Jesus debates Christology with his opponents and teaches his disciples Christology as well as eschatology. Although he commands that his disciples should love one another, he speaks only in symbolic terms (for example, washing the disciples' feet) of what that love should consist.

Closely related to these differences in Jesus' message is a distinct difference in theological-ethical vocabulary often found on the lips of Jesus.[3] For example, the Greek words for love (*agapē*), truth (*alētheia*), knowing (*ginōskein*), and world (*kosmos*) are anywhere from twice to ten times as frequent in John as in the Synoptics. By the same token, typical synoptic terms for kingdom

---

[3] C. K. Barrett, *The Gospel According to St. John: An Introduction with Commentary and Notes on the Greek Text,* 2d ed. (Philadelphia: Westminster Press, 1978), 5–6, presents a convenient tabulation of significant differences in vocabulary.

(*basileia*), miracle (*dynamis*), parable (*parabolē*), and preaching (*kērussein*), among others, occur infrequently, if at all, in the Fourth Gospel. Not coincidentally, the vocabulary of the Gospel of John, and of the Johannine Jesus, is much closer to that of the Johannine Epistles than to the Synoptic Gospels. The difference of vocabulary is a good measure of their difference in theology.

The problem of John and the Synoptics is, then, how to account for John's extensive differences from the other Gospels within a generally similar overall framework. These differences embrace content and style and include major aspects of their respective portrayals of Jesus. In principle, the problem of John and the Synoptics may not be different from the synoptic problem, but in fact the problem is exacerbated by the extent of the divergences of John from the Synoptics. Their portrayals of Jesus are symptomatic. One can without great difficulty speak of the synoptic Jesus, based on Matthew, Mark, and Luke. Whether the synoptic Jesus and the Johannine Jesus present a common front or can be brought together only by main force and awkwardness or theological legerdemain remains a question.

## THE EARLIEST PERCEPTION OF THE PROBLEM

In all probability the problem of John and the Synoptics lurks somewhere behind the emergence of the Fourth Gospel on the stage of church history. The evidence is less than explicit, but there was during the second century a kind of reticence or obscurity about the Fourth Gospel. We cannot be sure that this reticence was due to John's differences from the Synoptics. Certainly such differences were not the sole factor affecting the acceptance of the Fourth Gospel in the church. On the other hand, it is clear that serious questions about the relationship were raised, so that answers had to be given, and the problem of John and the Synoptics was perceived as such by the end of the second century.

Evidence of knowledge of the Fourth Gospel in the early church may be discernible as early as Ignatius of Antioch in the second decade of the second century, for at times he seems to reflect John's distinctive language (e.g., *Magnesians* 8.2). At mid-century Justin Martyr seems to know, and even quote, John (*I Apology* 61), but he does not cite it by name as one of the memoirs of the apostles. In Irenaeus of Lyons in the final quarter of the second century we finally have an early church authority who knows and cites the Gospel of John, putting it on the same level as the others. From Irenaeus's own use of John, however, it is quite clear that he was not the first to draw upon or to cite it as authoritative. Earlier, gnostic exegetes had known and interpeted this Gospel, albeit erroneously, and therefore Irenaeus was at pains to set forth a proper exegesis of the prologue (*Against Heresies* 3.11.1–9). (Moreover, Origen's citation of his predecessor Heracleon, who wrote a commentary on John at mid-second century, suggests the widespread use of John among gnostic Christians.) Irenaeus's insistence upon the necessity of four gospels can be construed as an effort to gain support for a four-gospel canon, which was only then being disseminated in the church. The problem would have been the Fourth Gospel rather than the other three. Perhaps some conservative Christians were uneasy about John precisely because it was popular and widely used among gnostic Christians and others deemed heretical.

Just such a man, Gaius, an elder in the Roman church, and apparently by his own lights orthodox and conservative, opposed the use of the Gospel of John. Although he may have resisted the Gospel because it gave aid and comfort to heretics—in this case, Montanists, who claimed possession by the Paraclete promised in John—he apparently grounded his objections on the fact that John differed so obviously from the other, Synoptic Gospels, which were already being accepted as authoritative and, in effect, canonical.[4] Against him, Hippolytus, another elder of the Roman church, wrote a *Defense of the Gospel and Apocalypse of John* that is no longer extant. Quite possibly Irenaeus presents the usage that is establishing itself in the Roman church. Gaius protests against it in the name of an older conservatism, and Hippolytus attempts to deliver the coup de grace to this now obsolete position.

Residual reservations about the Gospel of John are perhaps reflected in the famous statement of Clement of Alexandria, perhaps a quarter of a century later than Irenaeus: "But that John, last of all, conscious that the outward facts had been set forth in the Gospels, was urged on by his disciples, and divinely moved by the Spirit, composed a spiritual Gospel" (*apud* Eusebius, *Ecclesiastical History* 6.14.7). This famous statement, which seems to capture so well the essence of the Fourth Gospel vis-à-vis the others, continues to be quoted as an apt characterization of the distinctiveness of that Gospel. Clement speaks in an entirely positive way, but it is not difficult to see in his statement a defense of the Gospel of John against the charge that it differs so markedly

---

[4] Recent research suggests that the case against the Gospel of John was based on its differences from the Synoptics, whatever the actual motivation may have been. See J. J. Gunther, "Early Identifications of Authorship of the Johannine Writings," *Journal of Ecclesiastical History* 31 (1980): 413–15, and especially Joseph Daniel Smith, Jr., "Gaius and the Controversy Over the Johannine Literature" (Ph.D. diss., Yale University, 1979), 289–92, 384–412. Smith argues that the Roman presbyter's opposition to the Fourth Gospel was motivated by its use among Montanists, whom he opposed (p. 426).

from the Synoptics: John wrote a spiritual gospel, intentionally and purposefully different from the other three. Clement also makes clear that John knew and approved of the others.

A century later Eusebius of Caesarea acknowledges the problem of John and the Synoptics but offers another version of why John wrote as he attempts to explain the existence of this rather different Gospel, which stood now in church usage alongside the other three:

> John, it is said, used all the time a message which was not written down, and at last took to writing for the following cause. The three Gospels which had been written down before were distributed to all including himself; it is said that he welcomed them and testified to their truth but said that there was only lacking to the narrative the account of what was done by Christ at first and at the beginning of the preaching. The story is surely true. . . . Thus John . . . relates what Christ did before the Baptist had been thrown into prison [John 3:24], but the three other evangelists narrate the events after the imprisonment of the Baptist. If this be understood, the Gospels no longer appear to disagree.[5]

Interestingly enough, Eusebius states this not so much as his own view as a plausible opinion widely held. Perhaps he saw that the obvious overlap between John and other gospels renders it inadequate as a comprehensive explanation. Certainly Eusebius's statement indicates that the problem of John and the Synoptics, as we style it, had been the subject of continuing discussion, apparently even after John was being read as an authoritative book.

Just such prosaic, somewhat historicist, solutions as Eusebius describes were, however, strongly resisted by another exegete who nevertheless accepted the authority of John. Thus the great theologian and biblical scholar Origen, in his *Commentary on the Gospel of John*, espoused a totally different way of making sense of John and the Synoptics. Origen was well aware of major discrepancies between the Johannine and synoptic accounts of Jesus' ministry, and of early efforts to deal with them, but saw no point in trying to resolve them historically. Rather, he let them stand and interpreted John anagogically or mystically. Commenting on the problems created by John's chronology of the beginning of Jesus' ministry, which cannot be satisfactorily reconciled with that of the Synoptics, he writes:

> Those who accept the four Gospels, and who do not consider that their apparent discrepancy is to be solved anagogically [by mystical interpretation], will have

---

[5] Eusebius, *The Ecclesiastical History* 3.24.7–13, eds. K. Lake, J. E. L. Oulton, and H. J. Lawlor, Loeb Classical Library (Cambridge: Harvard University Press, 1926–32).

to clear up the difficulty, raised above, about the forty days of the temptation, a period for which no room can be found in any way in John's narrative.[6]

After enumerating additional problems, Origen concludes:

> There are many other points on which the careful student of the Gospels will find that their narratives do not agree; and these we shall place before the reader, according to our power, as they occur. The student, staggered at the consideration of these things, will either renounce the attempt to find all the Gospels true, and not venturing to conclude that all our information about our Lord is untrustworthy, will choose at random one of them to be his guide; or he will accept the four, and will consider that their truth is not to be sought in the outward and material letter.[7]

The latter alternative was, of course, consistently followed by Origen.

To give another example, in commenting on the cleansing of the temple, which occurs at the beginning of Jesus' ministry in the Gospel and toward the end in the others, Origen remarks: "I conceive it to be impossible for those who admit nothing more than the history in their interpretation to show that these discrepant statements are in harmony with each other" (*Commentary* 10.15). Accordingly, Origen argues for the necessity of his mode of interpretation by insisting on the impossibility of the alternative of historical harmonization. Again we may infer that he knowingly departs from an accepted, and probably dominant, mode of exegesis, by means of which the problem of John and the Synoptics was being dealt with. Doubtless Origen was swimming against the stream, but the acumen of his critical remarks was unmatched by his contemporaries. He saw clearly that the commonsense effort to harmonize John and the Synoptics made no critical sense at all. Nevertheless, the resolution of the problem of John and the Synoptics that Origen so vigorously rejected quickly became the accepted one in biblical exegesis in the church. An awareness of the seriousness of the discrepancies and the weight of the kinds of objections Origen raised had to await the rise of historical-critical exegesis. And even then efforts to see John's Gospel as somehow compatible with, or a supplement to, the Synoptic Gospels did not die out. Indeed, they continued down into the twentieth century and survive, if in qualified form, today. This century has, however, seen serious challenges to this traditional view, as it has to many positions long regarded as sure or settled.

---

[6] Origen, as cited in A. C. Coxe, ed., *The Ante-Nicene Fathers: Translations of the Writings of the Fathers down to* A.D. *325,* vol. 10. (Grand Rapids, Mich.: W. B. Erdmanns, 1986).

[7] Ibid. For this and the preceding quotation, see Origen's *Commentary* 10.2.

As John became part of a generally accepted fourfold Gospel canon, it was regarded as an apostolic writing, the work of John the disciple of the Lord, the son of Zebedee. That it had been composed in full cognizance and affirmation of the other three was scarcely doubted. Until about a century ago, the view that the Gospel was the work of the apostle still had strong and numerous defenders, and few thought to doubt its positive relation to the Synoptics. All that was to change. Rejection of its apostolic origin was already fairly common at the beginning of the twentieth century, and questioning of its relation to the Synoptics was not far behind.

The twentieth century has, in fact, more than once witnessed the dissolution of a consensus on the relationship of John to the Synoptic Gospels. At the beginning of the century John's knowledge and positive use of the Synoptic Gospels was widely, if not universally, granted. Even so self-consciously critical a scholar as Benjamin W. Bacon took this consensus as his beginning point. It remained for Hans Windisch to question whether the fourth evangelist's attitude toward the Synoptics was actually positive and for Percival Gardner-Smith to question his very knowledge and use of them. In the light of their proposals and the exegetical work of such prominent scholars as C. H. Dodd and Rudolf Bultmann, the earlier consensus that John knew and used the Synoptic Gospels crumbled and was replaced by a consensus that represented almost the opposite point of view. John did not know the Synoptic Gospels in their present form, or, if he did, they existed only at the periphery of his consciousness and purpose. Perhaps he became familiar with them only after his own work had basically been completed. Most commentaries on the Fourth Gospel written since World War II have followed this line. In the last quarter of this century, however, the ground seems to be shifting once again. Not that John's independence lacks proponents or defenders, but now the older view that John presupposed and used the Synoptics is being revived. Ockham's razor is invoked against the unnecessary multiplication of entities—in this case hypothetical sources—as one speaks of redaction-critical interpretation of the Fourth Gospel against the backdrop of the Synoptics. This significant problem affords an interesting example of the convolutions, as well as the evolution, of New Testament scholarship in this century.[8]

---

[8] The earlier history of the problem in modern research is treated by Hans Windisch, *Johannes und die Synoptiker: Wollte der vierte Evangelist die älteren Evangelien ergänzen oder ersetzen?* Untersuchungen zum Neuen Testament 12 (Leipzig: J. C. Hinriches'sche Buchhandlung, 1926), 1–40. For the period up to the mid-1960s, see now also Josef Blinzler, *Johannes und die Synoptiker: Ein Forschungsbericht,* SBS 5 (Stuttgart: Verlag Katholisches Bibelwerk, 1965). For the last decade and a half, see Frans Neirynck, "John and the Synoptics: 1975–1990," in the proceedings of the 1990 Louvain Colloquium, *John and the Synoptics,* ed. A. Denaux, BETL (Louvain: Louvain

University Press, 1992). Note also the *Forschungsbericht* of Jürgen Becker, "Aus der Literatur zum Johannesevangelium (1978–1980)," *ThR* 47 (1982): 279–301, 305–47, esp. 289–94, as well as Robert Kysar, *The Fourth Evangelist and His Gospel: An Examination of Contemporary Scholarship* (Minneapolis: Augsburg Publishing House, 1975), 54–66. Cf. also Kysar's "The Fourth Gospel: A Report on Recent Research," in *Aufstieg und Niedergang der römischen Welt*, ed. H. Temporini and W. Hasse (Berlin: Walter de Gruyter), II.25.3 (1985): 2389–2480, esp. 2407–11, and his "The Gospel of John in Current Research," *RSR* 9 (1983): 314–23, esp. 315–16. For the first half of this century there is the somewhat broader survey of W. F. Howard, *The Fourth Gospel in Recent Criticism and Interpretation*, rev. C. K. Barrett (London: Epworth Press, 1955), 128–43.

# 2

# The Development of the Independence Theory: From Bacon to Gardner-Smith

## THE CONSENSUS OF NINETEENTH-CENTURY CRITICISM

The position of critical scholarship at the end of the nineteenth century and in the early part of the twentieth, that John knew and used the Synoptics, is reflected in the standard introductions of Adolf Jülicher and James Moffatt as well as in the more conservative introduction of Theodore Zahn. "It is almost universally regarded as certain," Jülicher writes, "that John was a later production, because the Synoptics are all utilised in it."[1] Moffatt is more cautious: "That the Fourth gospel presupposes the general synoptic tradition may be taken for granted; the real problem of literary criticism is to determine whether it can be shown to have used any or all of the synoptic gospels." Yet he concludes: "The Fourth Evangelist, like his two immediate predecessors, thus bases on Mark's narrative, but diverges from it repeatedly; these divergencies are in some cases accidental, in others due to a preference for Matthew or Luke, or for both combined, and, in other cases, again, the result of some independent tradition."[2]

The case for Johannine dependence upon the Synoptics is argued more extensively by Zahn. Like Moffatt, Zahn maintains that John assumes knowledge of the Gospel material on the part of his readers; the question then

---

[1] Adolf Jüdlicher, *An Introduction to New Testament*, trans. Janet Penrose Ward (New York: Putnam's, 1904), 396. Jüdlicher grants that the differences from the Synoptics are far greater than the agreements but nevertheless maintains that John's dependence is self-evident.

[2] James Moffatt, *An Introduction to the Literature of the New Testament* (New York: Charles Scribner's Sons, 1914), 533, 546.

becomes whether he derived this knowledge from oral tradition or from books. Church tradition and a sound critical judgment favor the view that John knew Matthew, Mark, and Luke. Zahn maintains that John "throughout his Gospel . . . utilises the synoptic narratives, sometimes by connecting his own account directly with the same on the presupposition that they are known, sometimes by taking for granted that some event there recorded had happened which he does not repeat, sometimes by guarding the readers against possible misunderstanding of the synoptic accounts, or by informing them for the first time of details which had become effaced in these accounts, or by correcting slight inaccuracies which had crept into them."[3] Here we have a succinct statement of the traditional view that John wrote to accompany, to supplement, and to some extent also to correct the Synoptic Gospels. One recognizes in Zahn particularly a modern recension of the ancient and traditional view of John's relationship to the Synoptic Gospels.

Despite some questioning voices, Hans Windisch could in 1926 rightly claim that "for most scholars today it is a foregone conclusion that John knew the Synoptics."[4] When more than a decade later, Percival Gardner-Smith addressed the same subject, he too took as his beginning point the commonly held view, which he represents as well-nigh universal (as it was in the English-speaking world of the time), that John knew the Synoptic Gospels and wrote with full cognizance of them.[5] In the English-speaking world this view could by then claim the support of B. H. Streeter, who regarded it as certain that John knew Mark and as probable that he knew Luke as well.[6]

Streeter's work, *The Four Gospels*, claimed an almost canonical authority in English and American scholarship. His magisterial espousal and exposition of the evidence favoring Markan priority and the four-document hypothesis was

---

[3] Theodor Zahn, *Introduction to the New Testament*, trans. M. W. Jacobus et al. (Edinburgh: T. & T. Clark, 1909), 3:264; cf. 254–98.

[4] Windisch, *Johannes und die Synoptiker*, 43. In this connection, Windisch cites the third edition of B. Weiss's introduction as well as Moffatt's. Typical also would be the position of the German scholar H. H. Wendt, *The Gospel According to St. John: An Inquiry Into Its Genesis and Historical Value*, trans. Edward Lummis (Edinburgh: T. &. T. Clark, 1902), 33: "He must have known our three synoptic Gospels. . . . He also assumes an acquaintance with the synoptic tradition in his readers." Similarly, in Great Britain F. W. Worsley, *The Fourth Gospel and the Synoptists: Being a Contribution to the Study of the Johannine Problem* (Edinburgh: T. & T. Clark, 1909), 24: "First of all, we have seen that the contact with the first and third Gospels is comparatively slight. It is sufficient, I think, to show that the fourth evangelist was acquainted with these Gospels, but we shall see in the next chapter that the points of contact with the second Gospel are definite and deliberate."

[5] Percival Gardner-Smith, *Saint John and the Synoptic Gospels* (Cambridge: Cambridge University Press, 1938), vii: "There is virtual unanimity in the view that St. John, the latest of the evangelists, was to some extent indebted to the work of his predecessors."

[6] Streeter, *The Four Gospels*, 393–426. The original (1924) edition espoused the same position.

with some reason regarded as a benchmark of synoptic scholarship. Streeter's broad learning, together with his obvious balance and good sense, not to mention his fecund imagination, lent great weight to his judgments. It is not surprising, then, that his opinion on the question of John and the Synoptics not only reflected the already current viewpoint but influenced subsequent opinion in the English-speaking world. Streeter's conclusions seemed unequivocal: "The above comparison of John and the Synoptics leaves on the mind the impression that besides Mark and Luke (or conceivably Proto-Luke instead of Luke) John used no other documentary source."[7] Yet already Streeter saw a problem in the widely held position he had just espoused: "A standing difficulty of New Testament scholarship has always been to explain why the author of the Fourth Gospel goes out of his way, as it were, to differ from the Synoptics on points having no theological significance."[8] Thus, while Streeter enunciated the dominant view in a convincing way, he also raised a troubling question that would later cause problems for it.

## BENJAMIN W. BACON

If one were to select a scholar to represent the dominant position and perspective on the question of John and the Synoptics in the first quarter of the century, the choice might better be Bacon than Streeter. Streeter set forth the evidence that made John's use of Mark and Luke seem to him and most others an inevitable conclusion. But Bacon elaborated and expanded upon such evidence to trace John's hand in the appropriation of synoptic material. Bacon, an important and influential American scholar who taught at Yale in the last decade of the nineteenth century and the first quarter of the twentieth, was a classic representative of a fearless biblical criticism aligned with a liberal, evangelical theological perspective. While he maintained the traditional view that John knew and positively embraced the Synoptic Gospels, he had rejected Johannine authorship and indeed the value of John as a historical source alongside the other Gospels. In his 1910 volume, *The Fourth Gospel in Research and Debate*, he set forth his views boldly and succinctly.

Anyone who will take the pains to verify the evidence, as presented in the footnotes we here subjoin, can see for himself the general method of the fourth

---

[7] Ibid., 416–17.

[8] Ibid., 417. Streeter undertook to resolve this problem by suggesting that the fourth evangelist, a person of considerable authority in the church, would have felt free to alter the accounts of Mark and Luke (his principal sources), neither of whom were apostles.

evangelist in dealing with Synoptic material. (1) Matthew is practically ignored; (2) Mark is made the basis; (3) supplements and changes are made with large use of Luke both as to motive and material. The formative principle determining the entire construction is, as we have already made clear and now reiterate, the "spiritual" gospel of Paul. It is this which forbids any such mere transcription as that which characterizes our first and third evangelists in their combination of Mark and Q.[9]

Moreover, it is not just that John knows or uses Mark and Luke; he devours and digests them: "In its general structure the outline of the Fourth Gospel is simple and clear, and reproduces that of Mark *as modified by Luke.*"[10] It is not surprising, then, that in commenting on the appropriation of Mark 6:14—9:50 by the fourth evangelist, Bacon can assert that he has used "every available shred of Mark in his own way; nor has he even added, except from Luke."[11]

Bacon was later to soften this position somewhat, granting that the fourth evangelist had sources other than the Synoptic Gospels, although the importance of direct Pauline influence seems to have receded perceptibly. But Bacon could still regard a Johannine narrative whose relation to the Synoptics was not obvious as having been derived from Mark, and perhaps from the other Synoptics or Q. For example, the healing of the lame man in John 5:1–8 Bacon regards as John's recasting of Mark 2:1–12. By the same token, John presents what Bacon describes as "a complete recasting of Mark's account of the call of the first disciples and the beginning of [the] miracles."[12] "Recasting" is a favorite word of Bacon for it aptly describes what in his view the fourth evangelist has done with the Markan, or synoptic, narrative. Thus John 1:19–51, Jesus' encounter with the Baptist and the adherence of the first disciples, is so clearly a rewriting of the Markan accounts "as to leave no question in any critical mind."[13] Similarly, the story of Jesus' dialogue with his brothers followed by the clandestine departure for Jerusalem is said by Bacon to be derived from Mark's mention of Jesus' unbelieving brothers (Mark 3:20–21, 31–35) and the secrecy of Jesus' departure from Galilee (Mark 9:30) for Jerusalem.[14]

---

[9] Benjamin W. Bacon, *The Fourth Gospel in Research and Debate* (New York: Moffatt, Yard & Co., 1910), 368.

[10] Ibid.

[11] Ibid., 381.

[12] Benjamin W. Bacon, *The Gospel of the Hellenists,* ed. Carl H. Kraeling (New York: Henry Holt, 1933), 156.

[13] Ibid., 188.

[14] Ibid., 198.

Not only is the narrative content—that is, the pericopes—of Mark taken up by the fourth evangelist but also the basic structure of his Gospel. In *The Gospel of the Hellenists* (1933), Bacon does not repeat his earlier statement (above) that John's outline is clearly that of Mark as modified by Luke. Nevertheless the structure of John, even as it left the evangelist's hands, reflects the synoptic, that is, Markan, outline.[15] The prologue (John 1:1–18) is, of course, entirely distinctive. There is then a pre-Galilean ministry (1:19—4:42), which begins with a "complete recasting" of the call and the beginning of the miracles.[16] Originally this concluded with 2:11, but it has been augmented by the later redactor, who inserted 2:12—3:21, 31–36, in part out of the material bequeathed to him by the evangelist.[17] Also the placing of the present chapter 5 before chapter 6 belongs to the total redactional design that led to this insertion.[18] Prior to that rearrangement, a brief pre-Galilean ministry (without synoptic parallels) was followed by a somewhat longer continuous Galilean ministry (4:43–54; 6:1–71), preceded by the scene of the woman at the well in Samaria (4:1–41). John deliberately substitutes the latter for Mark 7:24–37, the Syrophoenician woman, as he simultaneously works in themes derived from other synoptic and Pauline sources.[19] With 5:1 following upon chapter 6, the post-Galilean ministry of the original Gospel begins. It spans a year and substitutes a series of festal visits (chaps. 5; 7—12) of Jesus to Jerusalem for "the indefinite wanderings which the synoptic gospels assigns to this period." Interestingly enough, Bacon thinks the redactor moved 5:1–47 to its present position because he saw its fundamental thematic agreement with Mark 2:1–12, 23–28; 3:1–6;[20] Jesus and his Jewish opponents are locked in conflict. Thus he sandwiched it into the Galilean ministry where it makes better sense thematically than geographically. After the final festal journey to Passover (11:56—12:50), there follows the passion and resurrection narrative (13:1—20:31). The appendix, chapter 21, is the composition of the redactor. Bacon notes that according to his reconstruction, the original form of the Gospel, prior to redaction, was closer to the Synoptics in outline. The pre-Galilean ministry was shorter than in the present edition and the Galilean ministry longer. The post-Galilean ministry was John's original contribution, although even it contained many allusions and references to the Synoptics.

---

[15] Ibid., 139.

[16] Ibid., 156.

[17] Ibid., 169–71, 248–51. John 3:22–30 belonged to the earlier stratum that the redactor has reworked.

[18] Ibid., 187–89.

[19] Ibid., 413; cf. 177–82.

[20] Ibid., 188.

Not just the narrative portions of John are viewed by Bacon as in some significant sense derivative from the Synoptics but also the discourses. Thus Nicodemus of John 3 is more than the Naq Dimon Ben Gorion of rabbinic tradition. He is also the rich inquirer of Mark 10:17–22 and in part the scribe "not far from the kingdom of God" of Mark 12:28–34. Like Gamaliel of Acts 5:34, he stands up in the Sanhedrin on behalf of giving the accused a fair hearing.[21] More important, the debate of Jesus with his Jewish opponents that follows the healing narrative in John 5 is a development of motifs found in Mark 2:1—3:6;[22] against the background of Mark 2:23—3:6, the authority of Jesus as Son of man is contrasted with that of Moses.[23] Interestingly enough, aside from John 13, which parallels the synoptic traditions about the Last Supper, Bacon does not view the farewell discourses and high-priestly prayer of Jesus as having been derived directly from the Synoptics. By common consent, John 14–17 is the most distinctly Johannine part of the Fourth Gospel, and Bacon seems to acknowledge this fact.

In assessing Bacon's work, one might ask whether he actually proved more than he assumed. He assumed, because it was a given of the Gospel criticism of his day, that John knew and to some extent used Mark and the other Synoptics. Bacon believed that John's use, and disuse, of Mark or the Synoptics could be understood as a function of his distinctive purpose and perspective. Yet because John's knowledge of them was assumed, points of similarity were chalked up to it, points of difference that could reasonably be accounted for (i.e., Jesus' carrying his own cross) were laid to the evangelist's purpose, but other differences were ignored. One can only say that, in Bacon's approach, methodological controls, or criteria, by which to determine whether John must have used Mark or the Synoptics in distinction from whether he might have are lacking.

It does not follow that Bacon's viewpoint was necessarily wrong. He obviously found the hypothesis of John's knowledge and use of the Synoptics, especially Mark, an adequate and satisfactory basis for exegesis. He did not, therefore, give intensive or systematic consideration to the possibility that John drew upon a relatively independent strain of oral tradition or upon written sources of an analogous sort. There was, in fact, no reason to launch or pursue such an investigation as long as he found it satisfactory to regard John's narrative and structure as derivative from the Synoptics, while his

---

[21] Ibid., 413.
[22] Ibid., 187–91.
[23] Ibid., 407.

discourses were basically the composition of the evangelist, albeit under synoptic influence. Bacon had not seriously considered the possibility that it might be easier to explain the similarities of John to the Synoptics on the view that John was independent of them than to explain the differences on the assumption that the fourth evangelist knew and used them.

## HANS WINDISCH

If Bacon represents the consensus of scholarship in the early twentieth century, Hans Windisch marks the first major breakaway in a new direction.[24] Others had dissented from the prevailing common opinion, but Windisch was able to state a case for an alternative viewpoint in such a way that subsequent investigation could ill afford to ignore it. Unfortunately, however, this significant book has never been translated; I shall therefore summarize Windisch's argument in some detail.

Windisch's opening chapter on the historical development of the problem is a most useful *Forschungsbericht*, particularly for critical work antedating the twentieth century.[25] First, he describes the formation of what he calls the supplementation theory (*Ergänzungstheorie*) in the ancient church. As we have already noticed, the church fathers set forth the theory that John wrote with knowledge of the other Gospels, affirmed them, and intended only to supplement them, and this resolution of the problem became standard in traditional exegesis and interpretation of the Fourth Gospel. Then the rise of biblical criticism saw the appearance of three rival theories: the independence theory (*Unabhängigkeitstheorie*), the interpretation theory (*Interpretationstheorie*), and the displacement hypothesis (*Verdrängshypothese*). Windisch does not present himself as the first proponent of the displacement hypothesis; he knows well that he has had precursors. Rather, he determines to show the inadequacy of other positions and to argue fully the contention that John wrote a gospel intended to displace the others. Because throughout most of Christian history the supplementation theory has represented first church and then critical orthodoxy, Windisch concentrates his heaviest fire upon it.

Already before the end of the eighteenth century the inadequacy of the supplementation theory had been pointed out by Lessing and Herder. By the first half of the nineteenth century, Bretschneider and Wegscheider argued for

---

[24] Windisch, *Johannes und die Synoptiker.*
[25] Ibid., 1–40. For other surveys of scholarship, see chap. 1, n. 8.

the independence of the Fourth Gospel from the Synoptics, and in their van came no less a theologian than Schleiermacher. Windisch regards advocates of independence as correct insofar as they fully reject the idea, which he also deems insupportable, that John intended to supplement the Synoptic Gospels. In fundamentally challenging the traditional and conventional solution of the problem, early proponents of the independence theory were unwittingly clearing the ground for the displacement theory. In the meantime some critical scholars, aware of the difficulties of the supplementation theory, espoused the view that John intended to offer an interpretation or reinterpretation of the Synoptic Gospels or material. This position found support particularly among followers of the Tübingen school, for whom John seemed the culminating synthesis of New Testament thought.[26] Windisch names P. Corssen (1896) as the first to have inferred from the inadequacy of the various supplementation theories that John actually wished to displace the other Gospels with a more adequate one of his own. But it was left to F. Overbeck (1911) and E. Schwartz (1908) to set forth a case for the displacement theory. Although some well-known scholars (Wendland, Bousset, Heitmüller, and Edward Meyer) espoused the displacement theory, it was not much discussed. Although not widely accepted, it was also not systematically opposed or refuted, while the supplementation theory continued to command widespread allegiance. Thus Windisch thinks it imperative to examine the whole question in a thorough-going way, since it is a matter of considerable consequence for the interpretation of the Fourth Gospel.[27]

The first step in Windisch's work is a thorough airing of the problem of the literary relationship with a view to determining whether John knew the Synoptics.[28] Since the Gospel of John says nothing explicitly of its relationship to these, or any other writings, its relationship to the Synoptics must be inferred from the texts, whether by showing intentional allusions or purposeful omissions. At the same time, the question of John's use of the Synoptics cannot be considered apart from certain general historical considerations.[29] Is it not

---

[26] Ibid., 22, 179.

[27] Ibid., 28–34. English-speaking readers will be interested in the fact that Windisch took cognizance of literature outside the German sphere of influence. He was evidently interested in finding any presentation or suggestion of the displacement theory in English or American scholarship (pp. 27–28). This he was unable to find, although he notes that if his impression that it had not yet appeared is subject to correction, he will be only too glad to be apprised.

[28] Ibid., 42–54, for Windisch's treatment of this question.

[29] In Windisch's view, John was composed around A.D. 100 in Syria or Asia Minor by a second-generation Christian who sought to clothe the gospel in the form of an Oriental, Hellenistic message of redemption. Although the possibility that John contains a Palestinian tradition associated with the son of Zebedee or with an ancient Jerusalem apostle is not excluded, exegesis can scarcely take for granted the historical character and purpose of the Fourth Gospel. (Ibid., 41.)

likely that John would have been in a position to know other Gospels? Windisch rightly regards it as virtually certain that at the end of the first century (the point at which the Fourth Gospel was presumably written) there was no threefold gospel canon in all or most churches. Rather, the ancient and original situation, in which each major church had one gospel, prevailed. John may not have known more than one of our Synoptic Gospels, but on these terms it is prima facie probable that he knew at least one. (Possibly he would have known two; conceivably he knew all three.) Thus a general historical consideration is marshaled on the side of John's having known at least one of the other canonical Gospels. Yet Windisch is wary of too quickly drawing conclusions. That John has so little of the synoptic material and, where he does have parallel pericopes, departs so frequently from the synoptic narrative suggests the possibility that the evangelist got his synoptic-like material from another, related tradition. Windisch himself had once thought this was the case.[30] Yet the number and nature of contacts between John and the Synoptics finally convinced him of the probability of John's acquaintance with all three Synoptic Gospels.

John's knowledge of Mark is a certainty. "There are no synoptic narratives in John which do not show traces of Mark."[31] The synoptic narratives include such episodes as the appearance of John the Baptist at the beginning of the Gospel, the feeding of a multitude and Jesus' walking on the sea, as well as numerous incidents associated with the passion of Jesus. Within these stories there are some exact verbal agreements between Mark and John. Windisch readily concedes that the number of Markan stories in John is relatively small. Although Mark is not ignored, his material is pushed into the background in favor of other kinds of tradition, not to mention the free compositions of the evangelist. Nevertheless one can also trace the influence of Mark in non-Markan Johannine pericopes, as, for example, in the word of Jesus to the healed man in John 5:8–9 (cf. Mark 2:11): "Arise, take up your bed, and walk." Some words of Jesus found in the Fourth Gospel, perhaps in distinctive Johannine dress, appear also in Mark. Thus the word about saving one's life and losing it in Mark 8:35 may be reflected in John 12:25, and the word about a prophet being without honor (Mark 6:43) is found in John 4:44. Some of these logia could also have been known to John from Matthew,

---

[30] See Hans Windisch, "Die Dauer der öffentlichen Wirksamkeit Jesu nach den vier Evangelisten," *ZNW* 12 (1911): 141–75, esp. 174–75.

[31] Windisch, *Johannes und die Synoptiker*, 46. That the healing of the ruler's son (John 4:46–54) is found only in Luke and Matthew is apparently not considered by Windisch. Otherwise, the statement is generally true.

Luke, or even Q, yet the evidence seems to confirm that John knew and used Mark. Windisch is careful not to claim as certain more dependence on Mark than the evidence allows. He argues, however, that after the relationship between John and Mark has been established on the basis of clearly parallel pericopes, one may go farther to uncover (i.e., to establish as probable) influences or polemical connections that were not at first so obvious (the procedure followed also by Bacon).

In addition to the Markan connection, Windisch finds allusions to, or contacts with, Matthew and Luke in passages not paralleled in Mark. For example, only in Luke and John does the Baptist explicitly deny that he is the Christ (John 1:20/Luke 3:15), and only in Matthew and John is Zechariah 9:9 cited in connection with Jesus' entry into Jerusalem (John 12:15/Matt. 21:5). The number of points of contact between John and Matthew and/or Luke only (i.e., which are not also contacts with Mark) are, however, smaller than those that seem to be primarily with Mark.

In summary, Windisch claims:

> John must have known a small number of Galilean, as well as a number of Jerusalem stories (the latter principally related to the Passion Narrative) in a text form which we now read in Mark (Matthew, Luke); possibly he may have known and considered these same stories as they are found in Matthew and Luke as well. He seems also to have taken into account some stories which are distinctive of Luke. Finally, he must have used a collection of Jesus' words, as Matthew and Luke took them up into their Gospels. The thesis that John knew and occasionally used our Mark, which had already been in circulation two or three decades when he wrote, is most probable. Although one may doubt that John also knew, used, and presupposed, Matthew and Luke, it is nevertheless probable . . . that he was also acquainted with both these Gospels.[32]

In working out his thesis, Windisch will presuppose that John knew all three. Yet in doing so, he recognizes how little regard John had for these other Gospels, whether as historical sources or religious tracts. The relatively few allusions, scattered at random through the Fourth Gospel, suggest that the evangelist referred to the other Gospels only from memory without looking up and copying down the passages he had in mind.

Having satisfied himself that John knew the Synoptics, especially Mark, Windisch proceeds to examine in great detail theories of supplementation. In

---

[32] Ibid., 52. Windisch does not exclude the possibility that the Gospel of John employed earlier sources or was subjected to redaction. He is, however, interested in the present text of the Gospel and showing that it manifests the intention of displacing the Synoptics. If all the synoptic material could be assigned to later redaction, Windisch's thesis would be affected, but it is too deeply embedded in the Gospel to be disposed of so easily. (Ibid., 54–58.)

doing so, he believes that he is also putting interpretation theories (even critical interpretation theories) to the test, since they actually share similar foundations or presuppositions.[33] Windisch's criticism of supplementation theories begins with his own distillation of five considerations generally advanced in their favor,[34] which I have restated (in italics) at appropriate points in what follows.

1. *John did not intend to write a complete account but only a series of scenes, between which the knowledgeable reader is supposed to insert or supply the synoptic reports.* To the contrary, Windisch argues that the structure of the Fourth Gospel does not at all support the view that John intended the reader to supply synoptic materials at appropriate places.[35] For example, that the Galilean ministry described in the Synoptics is to be interpolated into the Johannine account by the reader is nowhere suggested. John's notices about Galilean activity (2:11) may be understood within the framework of the Fourth Gospel, and there is no actual hint that one is to supply something from the Synoptics at this point. Although an intentional connection with the Synoptics seems more probable for 3:24 ("for John had not yet been cast into prison"), it too can be understood within the Johannine framework. In 5:35 Jesus looks back on the Baptist's work ("He *was* . . . ," etc.) as if it were by then completed. Apparently it was, at that point; but at 3:24 in the narrative it is still going on, and that fact is therefore noted. There is, however, no indication of exactly when the arrest of the Baptist occurred, as one would expect if the reader were to know where to insert the beginning of the synoptic Galilean ministry. If one takes the view that the purpose of 3:24 is to reconcile John with the Synoptics, then the passage is most easily understood as a redactional gloss inserted for that purpose. In that case it would accomplish this as an afterthought, so to speak, and not as part of a carefully conceived plan to mesh the Johannine account with the synoptic.

Perhaps more important as a test case of the supplementation theory is whether John intended the reader to presuppose and supply the institution of the Lord's Supper and for that reason could omit it from his account.[36] At the time Windisch wrote, Catholic exegetes particularly agreed that John presupposed this cultic act on the part of Jesus, but they were unable to agree on where in the Johannine account it was to be inserted. Unlike some exegetes, Windisch is unable to see in the mere mention of a supper in 13:2 an indication that the institution of the Lord's Supper is to be understood as having taken

---

[33] Ibid., 97.
[34] Ibid., 59.
[35] Ibid., 60–70.
[36] Ibid., 70–79.

place at that point. In that case John would then purport to narrate only what took place after and beside this acknowledged central act. But there is no indication in the Johannine text that John assumes, or expects the reader to supply, the institution of the Lord's Supper at this point. Had he wished his readers to presuppose or supply this event, it is difficult to imagine why John would have failed to give them some clear indication of his intention. Rather than arguing that John assumed the institution and expected his readers to supply it, Windisch thinks we should recognize that the evangelist has deliberately ignored it in this context while substituting the foot washing for it. At the last meal Jesus institutes the washing of the disciples' feet instead of the Eucharist! This act, whose goal is the same ethical-cultic community as is represented in the Lord's Supper, is then reinforced by the "new commandment" to love one another (13:34–35) and the allegory of the vine (15:1ff.). Several liturgical formulae stemming from, or concepts associated with, the Eucharist are then incorporated into the story of the miraculous feeding and the ensuing discourse in John 6. The solution of the problem of John's omission of the synoptic eucharistic accounts is not, therefore, to be sought in some harmonizing theory, but rather in the recognition that John did not accept as valid the institution of the Lord's Supper at the Last Supper. In all probability the Johannine version of the Lord's Supper looks back instead to the miraculous feeding at an earlier Passover, where Jesus allowed the Galilean populace to participate. Quite possibly he took this position in order to reject an all too pagan sacramental understanding of the rite (i.e., the identification of the elements in some magical way with the body and blood of Christ). In any event, John's text must be understood with reference to itself and to the evangelist's purpose rather than in an alleged, but unclear, relationship to the synoptic accounts, which he deliberately ignores.

Windisch understands the Johannine passion to be complete in itself and not in need of supplementation from the Synoptics.[37] No conspicuous lacunae are to be filled from the Synoptics. There are, however, two instances in which the Johannine account may seem to presuppose the synoptic.

First, John's mention of the appearance of Jesus before Caiaphas (18:24, 28), as well as the hearing before Pilate, seems to indicate or presuppose that the Sanhedrin condemned Jesus, as reported in the synoptic account. Windisch proposes, however, that John does not assume knowledge of the Synoptics but intentionally omits the scene in which Jesus is tried before Caiaphas so as to portray Jesus as condemned by Pilate alone, although at the insistence

---

[37] Ibid., 79–86.

of the leaders of the Jews. Moreover, the Jews' offense at Jesus' messianic confession could no longer constitute any sort of high point in the narrative, since in John Jesus had long since made messianic claims evoking the same kind of Jewish outrage that is expressed by the high priest at the Sanhedrin trial. "The Synoptic scene of the trial before Caiaphas was therefore superfluous."[38] If Pilate also seems to presuppose the condemnation of the Jewish authorities, that is at most a bit of awkwardness (*Ungeschicklichkeit*) in his account.

Second, the Johannine treatment of the Barabbas scene (18:38–40) could also be taken to suggest that John intended his readers to hold his account over against the synoptic. John does not introduce Barabbas at all, either directly or through the words of Pilate. Instead, in 18:39 Pilate begins by referring to the custom of releasing a prisoner at the Passover. It is the crowd who first mention Barabbas as if he is already known. Yet the Johannine report is quite sufficient in itself. John gives an adequate if brief account of who Barabbas is in 18:40b. Windisch might have added that when in Mark 15:1 Jesus is taken to Pilate, there is no explanation of who Pilate is.

What has been said of the passion narrative is equally true of the reports of resurrection appearances. That is, there is no indication that John makes omissions which he understands the reader will supply from the synoptic account. Windisch sums up his findings to this point: "The Fourth Gospel is no collection of paralipomena; it is not intended to supplement the older accounts or be supplemented by them; it is rather understandable on its own terms, complete in itself, sufficient, and gives a picture of Jesus intended to push to one side all previous attempts."[39]

2. *Where John's reports are parallel to the synoptic, it is clear that his goal is not completeness (Vollständigkeit). Rather, he intends to supplement, to shed new light upon, or in small ways to correct them.* Against this second pillar of the supplementation theory, Windisch argues that the character of the synoptic-like pericopes in John, like the total shape and structure of the Fourth Gospel, scarcely admits the view that the fourth evangelist's purpose was to supplement the Synoptics. (Having argued that John does not intend to be supplemented from the Synoptics, Windisch now maintains the obverse: that John does not intend to supplement the Synoptics.)[40] If the Fourth Gospel is intended to be supplemented by the Synoptics and to supplement them, why should it contain

---

[38] Ibid., 82.
[39] Ibid., 87. One could scarcely imagine a stronger statement of the Fourth Gospel's independence, in the sense of self-sufficiency, than is found on pp. 87–88.
[40] Ibid., 89–98.

narratives that are parallel to the Synoptics at all? Advocates of the supplementation theory have maintained that John wishes sometimes delicately to correct the parallel pericopes in the Synoptics, sometimes to supplement them, but in other respects only to show them to be trustworthy, particularly insofar as they confirm his own account. In order to refute this view Windisch goes straight through the pericopes and passages that are parallel in John and the Synoptics looking for indications that John reported only sketchily, or not at all, what he could assume readers would know on the basis of the Synoptics. As in the case of the total framework, Windisch finds in this investigation no compelling indication that John assumes the Synoptics in his own narration. In all significant respects, his narratives stand on their own. Thus the fourth evangelist's account of the Baptist as well as the narrative of the calling of disciples may be read as complete and independent reports that do not require the synoptic accounts to be understood. Again, John did not have in mind readers with the Synoptics open before them as he wrote up his account of the temple cleansing and put it near the beginning of the Gospel. Had he had them in mind, it would be difficult to account for his failure to supply any clarifying explanation of what he was doing. "Not one of the synoptic parallels in John is put together in such a way that the appropriate synoptic pericope must be adduced and compared with it in order to illumine and supplement it."[41] The fourth evangelist offers no helpful or comforting word at any point to the reader of other Gospels who might be perplexed and discomforted by the way his own narrative differs from it. Implicitly he offers the reader a choice between the old wine and the new. When he takes up material from the Synoptics, he does so not because he has parallel tradition with which to correct or supplement it. The further implication might then be that when he left synoptic material alone he approved it, which is emphatically not the case. Much of what he found in the Synoptics he simply could not use. Rather, he took up what could best serve his distinct literary and theological purpose, altered it as he saw fit, and left the rest aside.

3. *Occasionally, the fourth evangelist gives a subtle allusion to something in the Synoptics, which indicates that he presupposes that the reader is familiar with that richer tradition represented by them.* The alleged allusions to the Synoptics in the Fourth Gospel that lie outside the parallel pericopes are examined by Windisch with a view to ascertaining whether they really require the Synoptics in order to be understood.[42] The confirmation of the existence of such allusions

---

[41] Ibid., 96.
[42] Ibid., 99–105.

would not, however, necessarily change the view of the Fourth Gospel that Windisch is developing. (That is, such allusions could exist even if John intended to displace the other Gospels.) For example, John's statements about Jesus' birthplace, paternity, and lineage (1:45; 6:42; 7:41–42) actually do not afford support for the view that John presupposes the Synoptics and builds upon them. These uncorrected statements that Joseph was the father of Jesus and that Jesus was born in Galilee (rather than Bethlehem)—and by implication was not of Davidic lineage—would have left readers who were familiar with the Matthean and Lukan birth accounts uncomfortable and confused. John does nothing editorially to allay that discomfort and confusion, as he should have if he had intended to affirm, augment, or interpret the synoptic accounts. In the case of the Baptist's activity and references to the Twelve, John does presuppose a certain familiarity on the part of his readers. Yet it is difficult to be sure that he presupposes our specific synoptic accounts. For example, his mentioning the Twelve does not demand for its intelligibility the synoptic account of their appointment. (Windisch might have observed that Paul also knew of the existence of the Twelve.) Even the references to Mary, Martha, and Bethany (John 11:1–2), which clearly seem to be references to another and older tradition, do not have to be understood in relation to the specific synoptic accounts in which these women appear (Luke 10:38–42; cf. Mark 14:3–9 = Matt. 26:6–13). Although John speaks of signs of Jesus other than the ones he recounts (2:23; 3:2; 12:37; 20:30–31), there is no proof that by these he is referring to the miracles recorded in the Synoptic Gospels. Moreover, his concluding remarks (20:30–31; cf. 21:24–25) clearly indicate that he regards the signs recounted as quite sufficient for his purpose without supplementation from another source. If he presumed and intended to supplement the other Gospels, he would have given more explicit indication of this in the colophon.[43] Again Windisch concludes that there is no unambiguous evidence that John intends to refer to other writings that he presupposes, much less the Synoptic Gospels, for a proper understanding of his work. John is autonomous and self-sufficient. "Another strong underpinning of the supplementation theory has crumbled."[44]

4. *Where John omits or does not mention events, it is because they have already been adequately reported in the Synoptics.* According to the supplementation theories, synoptic materials are omitted from John because they can be presupposed. It is not surprising that Windisch strongly dissents.[45] Rather, most

---

[43] Ibid., 104–5, 121–24.
[44] Ibid., 105.
[45] Ibid., 106–20.

of what is found in the other Gospels John ignored as superfluous or unsuitable for his purposes. He used synoptic material that conformed, or could be conformed, to his own distinctive goal of proving the divine origin and mission of Christ. But certain pericopes he revised considerably before incorporating them into this Gospel, for example, the baptism, the cleansing of the temple, the confession of Peter, and the arrest. Other incidents, such as the temptation, Gethsemane, and the cry of dereliction, he omitted because they did not conform to his purpose and Christology. Much was thus omitted because it was of no use to him or detrimental to his purpose. Clearly he felt it unnecessary to recount more miracles just because the stories were available to him. As to the tradition of Jesus' teaching, John might well have said about it what he did about the signs in 20:30–31. Yet it cannot be assumed that John presupposes his readers' acquaintanceship with, for example, the Sermon on the Mount or the tradition contained in it. His "new commandment" (13:34–35) displaces not only the Old Testament, but the older traditions of Jesus' sayings and does not require the latter to be understood (as is evident also from the First Epistle).

5. *John's unique selection of material, like his supplementation, is part and parcel of the particular* Tendenz *of his Gospel: "He wants to strengthen the believers of his time in the struggle against Judaism and against Gnosticism and to set in a proper light the manifestation of the divine glory and God's sending of Christ to earth, which in the older gospels was not given sufficiently clear treatment." Thus John's purpose, rather than any antipathy toward the Synoptics, explains why he has omitted so much of their material in favor of this own.* That John's selection of the material incorporated into his Gospel reflects his purpose and *Tendenz* Windisch would readily acknowledge. Indeed, he intended to strengthen readers in the struggle against Judaism and Gnosticism and to emphasize adequately the manifestation of the divine glory in Jesus. But that such a purpose is compatible with the traditional view that John affirmed the value of the other Gospels Windisch emphatically denies. Indeed, precisely because of his distinct purposes John rejects the other Gospels as inadequate and undesirable.

Windisch's understanding of John's purpose vis-à-vis the Synoptics is a matter of nuance, but for Windisch the proper nuance is so clear as to leave little room for doubt. For the fourth evangelist the choice cannot be both/and; it must instead be either/or. This becomes particularly clear in his interpretation of the colophons of the Gospel (20:30–31; 21:25). Windisch emphasizes strongly that the point of both, especially the earlier, is the sufficiency of the Fourth Gospel. If the Gospel has been written so that the reader may believe and have life, what else is needed? (The "many other signs" of 20:30 is taken to refer to Jesus' entire ministry, not just to resurrection appearances.)

That "many other books" are referred to (21:25), but not commended, is said to be telling. The implication is not that these other books are commended but that they are superfluous! Whether the colophons represent such an "absolute disavowal" of other gospels the reader will have to decide. In any event, I must demur from his claim that "the closing statements present the last and perhaps the strongest arguments that can be adduced against the supplementation hypothesis, as well as the interpretation hypothesis, and in favor of the displacement theory."[46] Yet perhaps inadvertently Windisch is correct in the sense that his statement calls attention to the uncertain foundation of his position. If the colophons are the strongest evidence for the displacement theory, it is much less certain than Windisch thinks.

Finally, Windisch anticipates that objections may be raised: (1) John nowhere cites, criticizes, or expressly rejects the Synoptics; (2) John could not have rejected all the contents of the Synoptics (since he draws upon them) but only some stories and sayings; (3) the fourth evangelist could not have hoped to overturn the Synoptics and displace them in church usage as late as A.D. 100; and (4) John has found a place in canon alongside other Gospels and could scarcely have claimed more.[47]

Windisch grants the truth of objection 1, but he believes that John's rejection of the other Gospels, while indirect, is sharp and clear enough throughout his Gospel in that he so pointedly ignores the others. Perhaps one can be satisfied with the mediating position that John only wished to reinterpret the gospel tradition so as to set aside difficulties and misunderstandings (so Werner and Jülicher). But, given Windisch's interpretation of the Gospel's two closing statements, the displacement theory is more compelling. Objection 2 (that John accepts some synoptic material by *using* it) is also not without foundation in fact, but Windisch calls attention to the much greater amount of synoptic material that the fourth evangelist omitted and therefore evidently regarded as irrelevant, if not actually vexatious and offensive. Obviously he felt himself unable to issue a new recension of the older Gospels but felt obliged to compose a radically new one. As to John's hope of success in objection 3, Windisch grants the seriousness of this objection but points out that there was no threefold, or synoptic, canon when John wrote. Moreover, the existence of several Gospels constituted a theological problem for the early church, and the preference for one Gospel only had primitive precedent as well as subsequent support (Marcion, the *Diatessaron*). The effort to impose one rather

---

[46] Ibid., 124. Windisch deals with the colophons on pp. 121–24.
[47] Ibid., 128.

different Gospel upon the church would not be unexampled in later times (again Marcion as well as Tatian). If John did not in fact succeed in displacing the other Gospels with his own, as in objection 4, that is scarcely surprising and no grounds for denying that he tried. One must not underestimate the ability of the early Christians to overlook discrepancies for the greater good of reconciling and holding on to books widely regarded as authoritative. (In this connection, however, one remembers the so-called *Alogoi*, who rejected the Fourth Gospel, perhaps because they found it impossible to reconcile with the Synoptics.) As far as Windisch is concerned, this much is certain:

> John did not intend to write a supplement to the other Gospels. Nor did he have as his secondary aim that his Gospel should be read alongside others, for nowhere is there reference to other writings and nowhere does he suggest that his Gospel can be understood only in light of the others. John intended to write an autonomous and self-sufficient book in the fullest sense of the word, and he fully ignored all other writings which were known to him, including (in all probability) the Synoptic Gospels.[48]

He intended to displace all other Gospels.

With all theories of supplementation Windisch also rejects modern interpretation theories. John no more intended to interpret older documents and the traditions they embody than he meant to supplement them. Obviously, if Windisch is right in his view of John's attitude toward his predecessors, any interpretation theory—and the positive view of the Synoptics which it must presuppose—will seem a vain effort to rescue in part a traditional way of viewing John over against the Synoptics.

In the penultimate chapter, Windisch presents a psychologically plausible explanation of the fourth evangelist's intention of displacing the other Gospels.[49] It is not necessary to imagine that he was arrogant or presumptuous. Perhaps it goes without saying that Windisch rejects the possibility that the evangelist could arrogate such importance to his purpose and to himself because he was an eyewitness. The picture of Jesus that John presents is clearly not that of an eyewitness, who would scarcely have put forward such a presentation or rejected so much (authentic) Jesus tradition. The basis of John's independence and purpose was, rather, his conviction about the rightness of his distinctive theological understanding of the kerygma and his confidence in the inspiration of the Spirit. The truth of the gospel required, in John's view, a radically different Gospel.

---

[48] Ibid., 134.
[49] Ibid., 135–50.

Moreover, John's intention to displace other documents or traditions is not unprecedented in the history of Israel and early Christianity.[50] It appears as far back as the literary history of the Pentateuch and continues in the work of the Chronicler. Within early Christianity, John's attitude toward the Synoptics is really little different from Paul's view of the Judaizers or even the original apostles. Both John and Paul put the exalted Lord and the Spirit ahead of any quasi-historical tradition. Among the Gospels it is clearly the case that Luke intended to supplant his predecessors (Luke 1:1–3), while Matthew very nearly succeeded in supplanting Mark and driving it into oblivion.[51] The later, noncanonical evangelists apparently intended to displace the canonical Gospels with their writings. In the second century there were attempts to preserve the one-gospel principle, directed now against the canonical books. For a long time Tatian's composite gospel, the *Diatessaron*, displaced the canonical four where it was adopted. Marcion's attempt to institute a one-gospel canon with his expurgated version of the Gospel of Luke was an explicit rejection of the fourfold canon. Clearly, then, John's effort to produce a gospel that would take the place of the others is psychologically conceivable and supported by prior and subsequent historical analogies.

The evangelist's motivation was entirely theological. Although influenced by Gnosticism, he wished to oppose a purely gnostic interpretation of the gospel. He fought also against Judaism and a Judaizing interpretation while seeking to advance his own distinctive theology, his particular interpretation of the Christian kerygma. To serve these purposes John found the Synoptics, Gospels of which he knew, inadequate and sought therefore to displace them with his own. Therefore, according to Windisch, the Gospel of John is not really a synthesis marking the culmination of a process of development in New Testament thought. Rather, by reason of the author's purpose in writing as well as its explicit content, the Fourth Gospel is very much a polemical book.

## REACTION TO WINDISCH

One can scarcely speak of a reaction to Windisch's work in the English-speaking world, where it was noted but its thesis not extensively discussed.

---

[50] Ibid., 151–80. This chapter (10) is entitled "Related Literary Processes in the Old Testament, in Judaism, and in Early Christianity."

[51] Ibid., 164. Also Vincent Taylor, *The Gospel According to St. Mark: The Greek Text with Introduction, Notes, and Indexes*, 2d ed. (London: Macmillan & Co., 1966), 9, points out, "In the fifth century Victor of Antioch says that he had not been able to find the work of an earlier commentator [on Mark], and the next of whom we know is the Venerable Bede three centuries later." Apparently Matthew and Luke very nearly succeeded.

To what extent it was actually read in England and America is a good question. A decade and a half later Robert M. Grant expressed agreement with Windisch, saying that the research of Gardner-Smith bore out his thesis that John intended not merely to supplement but to supplant the other Gospels.[52] As we shall see, however, Gardner-Smith, who apparently did not know Windisch, was led to a rather different conclusion. Ernest C. Colwell in *John Defends the Gospel* (1935) advanced a thesis broadly similar to Windisch's, that John wrote to correct the major inadequacies of the other Gospels, which he found misleading.[53] Although Colwell knows and cites Windisch, he works out his own thesis quite differently, and apparently not under Windisch's influence. On the Continent, Windisch's work was, of course, widely reviewed, and within a decade a full-scale dissertation devoted to its refutation was published. (In 1939, however, Bruce M. Metzger, then a Th. M. candidate at Princeton Theological Seminary, presented a thesis, "John and the Synoptic Gospels," in which he discussed and debated Windisch's thesis, which he rejected in favor of the independence theory!)

Even within a year of the publication of Windisch's book, Friedrich Büchsel responded in a review article, and by no means altogether negatively.[54] He fully agreed that John intended to write an entirely independent gospel, but without regard to the other Gospels. The fourth evangelist is more independent than Windisch thinks. That is, the evangelist simply goes his own way. There is nothing in John's statement of purpose or elsewhere to indicate that he wrote with the intention of suppressing the Synoptic Gospels. Büchsel thinks that one can only conjecture that John knew any of the Synoptics, although in fact he believes it likely that John knew at least Mark. John wrote, however, in order to give his eyewitness, historical picture of Jesus. Albeit, admits Büchsel, "historical" can only be used in a highly specialized sense of the Fourth Gospel's portrayal of him.

Windisch lost no time in replying to Büchsel. Within the year, he published a fifty-page article on the *Absolutheit* of the Gospel of John, in which he undertook a point-by-point response and rejection of Büchsel's arguments.[55] Because Büchsel had argued that John, while fully independent of the Synoptics, did not intend to displace or suppress them, Windisch focused upon the crucial question of the intention of the author as it can be deduced from

---

[52] Robert M. Grant, "The Fourth Gospel and the Church," *HTR* 35 (1942): 95.

[53] Ernest C. Colwell, *John Defends the Gospel* (Chicago: Willet, Clark & Co., 1936).

[54] Friedrich Büchsel, "Johannes und die Synoptiker," *Zeitschrift für systematische Theologie* 4 (1926): 240–65.

[55] Hans Windisch, "Die Absolutheit des Johannesevangeliums," *Zeitschrift für systematische Theologie* 5 (1927): 3–54.

the text and reiterated strongly his view that it was John's conscious and principal purpose to displace the other, Synoptic Gospels in the usage of the church. His Archimedean point continues to be that, unlike Matthew, Luke, and even Tatian, John did not appropriate the traditions made available to him by his predecessors but for the most part rejected them. Because John ignored his predecessors he disavowed them and, one can infer, wished to supplant them, for he nowhere gives any indication of how his Gospel may be used in a supplementary way.

Against Büchsel, Windisch cannot agree that the Fourth Gospel was intended to present a superior or more authoritative historical witness, however that may be defined. Although John doubtless employed traditional narratives—but in the public ministry mainly narratives not found in the Synoptics—the framework into which he put them and the words of Jesus that interpret them are mainly his own creation, albeit under the inspiration of the Spirit and in the service of his understanding of the gospel message and the needs of the churches. Taken together, John's use of a largely different tradition and his authoritative, creative freedom in reworking it speak on the side of his having consciously intended to displace the other Gospels. Windisch reiterates a number of his specific arguments. Thus, for example, John's omission of the Eucharist at the Last Supper and of the trial before the Sanhedrin really does not square with the view that he acknowledged or accepted them. Rather, in intending to supplant the other Gospels, John represents the older tradition of a one-gospel canon honored by Marcion and Tatian.

Interestingly enough, Windisch also notes the view of Martin Dibelius, communicated by letter, that the Gospel of John was never intended for the church generally but for circles of early, "mystical" Christians. Therefore John had no illusions that his constituency and readership was, or would become, the predominant form of Christianity in the foreseeable future. Against Dibelius, Windisch holds there is no clear indication that John contemplates two types or levels of Christian faith, a common and a mystical. But if he did, his purpose would then be very similar to Marcion's, and Dibelius's position not far from Windisch's. Dibelius's demurral is significant, for the view that John is the Gospel of a distinct type or circle of Christianity has since become widely held, if not in the form that Dibelius proposed. For Windisch, however, it is important not only that John knew the other canonical Gospels but that he intended to *compete* with one or all of them for the position of *the* canonical Gospel in the usage of the church. Windisch rightly sees Dibelius's proposal as a threat to his own thesis in that it represents a different picture of the anticipated readership and intended function of the Gospel of John vis-à-vis the other Gospels in the general church setting toward the end of the first century.

In this connection it is worth observing that Walter Bauer had already suggested that the fourth evangelist found the earlier Gospels and their traditions inadequate for the message he sought to convey.[56] But Bauer felt that the very question of whether John knew and used the Synoptics was anachronistic, inasmuch as it is put from the standpoint of the established four-gospel canon, which of course did not exist when John wrote. After Windisch's work appeared, Bauer voiced qualified approval of his general thesis, but with the proviso that John intended to displace not merely the Synoptic Gospels, but the whole gospel tradition that had preceded him.[57] Thus both Bauer and Dibelius, for different reasons, demur from accepting Windisch's view that John's departure from the Synoptics must reflect his hostility toward them specifically.

Of considerable interest also is Rudolf Bultmann's review of Windisch.[58] Bultmann, who had already begun the work that would lead to the publication of his own great commentary more than a decade later, could not agree that the evidence warrants the view that John wrote specifically to displace the synoptic accounts. On the other hand, Windisch's argument that John went his own way in composing his gospel is certainly correct. It is not meant to be read as a supplement of anything or as requiring supplementation but is an independent work. Bultmann's fundamental question to Windisch, however, is whether he has too easily accepted the commonly held view that John knew the Synoptic Gospels.[59] Obviously John could not have written his gospel to displace the Synoptics if he had not known them! Although not denying that John knew a rich tradition, which contained much material related to the Synoptics, and that he suppressed or altered some traditions known from the Synoptics (e.g., Gethsemane), Bultmann rejects the view that John was driven primarily by a polemical aim. John is not so negative toward the other traditions alive in the church as Windisch thinks. Rather, his basic thrust was positive, to present his own understanding or interpretation of the gospel.[60]

---

[56] Walter Bauer, *Das Johannesevangelium*, Handbuch zum Neuen Testament 6 (Tübingen: J. C. B. Mohr [Paul Siebeck], 1925), 238–39.

[57] Walter Bauer, "Johannesevangelium und Johannesbriefe," *ThR* 1 (1929): 135–60, esp. 138–40.

[58] Rudolf Bultmann, *TLZ* 52 (1927): 197–200.

[59] Ibid., 198.

[60] Bultmann (ibid., 199) also rejects Windisch's contention that John intended to set aside such sayings tradition as is found in the Sermon on the Mount and Jesus' commandment to love one's enemies by the new, love commandment. That commandment does not reject Jesus' teaching as reported in the Synoptics but comprehends it. (It is noteworthy that Bultmann's commentary does not presuppose John's knowledge of the Synoptics, although the redactor is said to have added material from that source.)

Nearly a decade after the publication of Windisch's *Johannes und die Synoptiker*, Timotheus Sigge, a Roman Catholic scholar, put forward a thoroughgoing criticism of his work in a dissertation presented to the Catholic faculty of the University of Münster.[61] Although Sigge agrees with Windisch that John knew the Synoptics, he undertakes a step-by-step refutation of the view that John intended to displace them with his own gospel, independent as it may seem. Probably the author's intention of defending church tradition by presenting what he regarded as a critical version of the supplementation theory accounts for the predictability and uniformity of Sigge's rejection of Windisch's position and insights. As Windisch observed in his not unkind review, the fundamental weakness of Sigge's dissertation was his a priori and complete acceptance of the traditional supplementation theory, for which he offers a critical apology and defense. Characteristically, Sigge argues that whatever in John *may* be understood as supplementation was intended to be supplementary.[62]

Typical of Sigge's perspective is his acceptance of the historicity of John's placing the cleansing of the temple at the beginning of the ministry rather than at the end, and especially his contention that John made this change from the Synoptics for the sake of historical accuracy.[63] The same may be said for his resolution of the problem posed by John's assertion (19:17) that Jesus carried his own cross and the Synoptics' statement that it was borne by Simon of Cyrene (Mark 15:21 par.): Jesus carried it partway and was then relieved by Simon.[64] As a historical conjecture, this cannot be dismissed as impossible— it first occurred to Tatian—but there is nothing in the Johannine account to suggest or justify this harmonization. The method involved is not atypical of Sigge, who more than once attempts to resolve a contradiction or problem among parallel or competing texts by reference to the presumed historical basis. Moreover, he oftentimes reconstructs these facts on the basis of a harmonization of the Johannine and synoptic reports, giving priority to the Johannine, in such a way as to remove the difficulty or make John appear to

---

[61] Timotheus Sigge, *Das Johannesevangelium und die Synoptiker: Eine Untersuchung seiner Selbständigkeit und der gegenseitigen Beziehungen*, Neutestamentliche Abhandlungen 16, 2/3 (Münster: Aschendorff, 1935).

[62] For example, with reference to the Easter stories and against Windisch, Sigge indicates (*Das Johannesevangelium und die Synoptiker*, 209) that he must ask "ob sich die johanneischen Ostergeschichten mit den synoptischen vereinigen lassen, ob *irgendwie* die Annahme einer positiven Berücksichtigung der älteren Berichte begründet werden kann." Then (ibid., 213): "Fragen wir nach der Tendenz gegenüber den Synoptikern, die im Gesamtbericht des Johannes herrscht, so kann man sagen, dass in allgemeinen eine *Harmonisierung* der Erzählungen *möglich* ist" (italics mine).

[63] Ibid., 139–49.

[64] Ibid., 205–6.

be correcting the Synoptics. But the harmonization is not usually suggested by anything explicit in the Johannine text, and it generally presupposes an interest in historical reporting and chronology on the part of the fourth evangelist that is hard to square with the content and character of his gospel. Although Sigge's book looks like nothing so much as a rearguard action on behalf of the supplementation position, it nevertheless stands as a valuable compendium of the kinds of arguments and evidence that can be adduced in support of the traditional view.[65]

Exactly a decade after the appearance of Windisch's book, the American scholar Ernest C. Colwell argued that the Gospel of John was intended to correct the misapprehensions about Jesus that would have arisen from the Synoptics. In his provocative *John Defends the Gospel*, Colwell mentions Windisch's work in passing,[66] but in effect he moves beyond Windisch by attempting to show very specific—as opposed to more general theological—reasons for John's rejection of the Synoptics. According to Colwell, the Synoptics present Jesus as a magician (demon exorcisms), a baptist (follower of John), a Jew, a mere human being, a friend of sinners, and a crucified criminal. Thus they contribute to the popular view that Christianity is a form of superstition or a revolutionary movement. Accordingly, the fourth evangelist systematically eliminates, among other things, such typical synoptic features as the demon exorcisms, the Jewish characteristics of Jesus (who is now clearly of another order than John the Baptist), apocalyptic eschatology, and scenes in which Jesus appears to fraternize with or condone unsavory people. A member of the Chicago school, Colwell sets his explanation in the context of the relevant social world or social history. John is motivated to revise the synoptic portrait by a desire to appeal to a constituency of higher education and social standing.[67] Colwell's procedure is quite clearcut: "Since we still possess the books that served John as framework [i.e., the Synoptic Gospels], the task of determining the distinctive purpose of John is relatively simple. The changes he made by way of omission, addition and transformation should give us the clue as to his dominant distinctive purpose."[68] This method and

---

[65] In his review of Sigge, Windisch rightly observes that his conservative presuppositions determine his results. Cf. *Theologische Studien und Kritiken* 106 (1934–35): 409–10. More positive evaluations are given by A. E. Brooke, *JTS* 36 (1935): 308–9, who, however, has apparently not read Windisch's work, and Friedrich Büchsel, *TLZ* 60 (1935): 401–2. For a criticism similar to our own, see the review of Martin Dibelius, *Deutsche Literaturzeitung* 58 (1937): 1811–14.

[66] Colwell does not define the purpose of his own study in relation to Windisch, although he knows and cites his book (*John Defends the Gospel*, 7).

[67] Yet for precisely this insight Colwell acknowledges indebtedness to Windisch (*John Defends the Gospel*, 57; cf. Windisch, *Johannes und die Synoptiker*, 112–13).

[68] Colwell, *John Defends the Gospel*. Colwell's concession, in a review of Gardner-Smith (*JBL* 58 [1939]: 290), that John probably used other sources as well as the Synoptics somewhat weakens the force of his own interpretive method.

its results are as attractive as they are simple. We have here the fundamental principle of redaction criticism, although at this juncture there was not a name for it. Whether the method and its assumptions do justice to the complexities of the Gospel is another matter.

As we have noted, Windisch's view of John's reasons for wanting to displace the Synoptics, as distinguished from Colwell's, have to do with the general christological inadequacy and are not defined so specifically in terms of objectionable features in the synoptic accounts. Therefore much of what he says about the character and completeness of the Fourth Gospel would stand, even if his displacement hypothesis were refuted. The validity of Colwell's entire book is, however, much more closely tied to the view that John's text intended to correct the Synoptics at specific points where they are misleading. In other words, Colwell's thesis is clearcut, specific, and simple, but his book would have much less validity if the reasons that he adduces for John's rejection of the Synoptics' point of view proved to be invalid. Windisch, on the other hand, arrives at many valid, or at least viable, insights about the Fourth Gospel that really do not depend upon his central thesis that it was written to displace the Synoptics.

## PERCIVAL GARDNER-SMITH

Basing his arguments largely on the inadequacies of the supplementation theory, Windisch definitively set forth the case for John's having written in order to displace the Synoptic Gospels. Sigge responded with a tireless effort to revise and rehabilitate that traditional view. Perhaps sufficient to shore up its bulwarks before its anxious supporters, it was not well calculated to win a significant number of new adherents.[69] Colwell, on the other hand, took Windisch's position to a kind of logical conclusion, attempting to specify why John took exception to the Synoptics and how he set about to correct their inadequacies. All three accepted the traditional view that John knew and used the Synoptic Gospels.

It remained for Percival Gardner-Smith of Cambridge University to open the next round in the discussion of John and the Synoptics by suggesting that a great deal can be said for the view that John knew none of the Synoptic Gospels. Gardner-Smith took full cognizance of the dominant position that

---

[69] Büchsel's review, *TLZ* 60 (1935): 401–2, was, however, moderately favorable, and Colwell spoke favorably of Sigge's work in his review of Gardner-Smith, *JBL* 58 (1939): 290.

John knew and wrote in the light of the Synoptics, as this view was represented among scholars in the English-speaking world at the time (1938).[70] He makes no mention, however, of the books of Windisch, Sigge, and Colwell. One must assume that he was unfamiliar with them. Nevertheless his viewpoint, if correct, would set aside supplementation (or interpretation) theories on the one hand and displacement theories on the other.

Gardner-Smith's *Saint John and the Synoptic Gospels* is a disarmingly simple and brief book. With the air of understatement and diffidence so typical of the Cambridge don, he begins by conceding that his whole undertaking may be a case of labor misspent. Scholars both ancient and modern have spoken with rare unanimity in favor of John's knowledge of the Fourth Gospel. On the side of this orthodox view Gardner-Smith cites W. F. Howard, Benjamin W. Bacon, and B. H. Streeter, among other modern scholars, as well as the famous quotation from Clement of Alexandria (Eusebius, *Ecclesiastical History* 6.14.7): "John divinely moved by the Holy Spirit, wrote a spiritual Gospel on observing that the things obvious to the senses had been set forth in the earlier Gospels."[71] Although Gardner-Smith seems to know of no opposing view, Windisch points out that a minority of scholars, particularly in the late eighteenth and the nineteenth century in Germany, had already favored John's independence of the Synoptics. Windisch briefly discusses the representatives of this position, which he himself had earlier entertained and abandoned.[72] If Gardner-Smith knows of previous proponents of the independence theory, however, he gives no hint of it. In any event, he accurately represents the preponderance of critical opinion in his day, not only in Great Britain but also in Germany and America, as he portrays himself as a voice about to cry in the scholarly wilderness.

It is worth observing that the recession of the independence theory on the Continent, where it had been first propounded, during the first third of this century (and at the time Gardner-Smith wrote) was quite possibly related to its association with conservative opinion, particularly the view that the Fourth

---

[70] Gardner-Smith, *Saint John and the Synoptic Gospels*, vii–ix.

[71] Ibid., vii (presumably Gardner-Smith's translation).

[72] Windisch, *Johannes und die Synoptiker*, 9–20; see above n. 30. Interestingly enough, Gardner-Smith had not yet developed his position on John's independence when he published *The Narratives of the Resurrection: A Critical Study* (London: Methuen, 1926); cf. pp. 50–60, 97, for his tentative acceptance of the prevailing view—with the qualification that John may have known the synoptic tradition rather than those gospels. In the same year, however, Gardner-Smith published the articles in which he espoused the independence of the *Gospel of Peter* vis-à-vis the canonical Gospels: "The Gospel of Peter" and "The Date of the Gospel of Peter," *JTS* 27 (1925–26): 255–71, 401–7. Thus the movement of his thought in the direction of the independence theory is clear. It would be a fine irony if both Windisch and Gardner-Smith had reversed their respective positions, but with Gardner-Smith this is not quite the case.

Gospel is the work of John, the son of Zebedee, or some other apostolic eyewitness. With the establishment of the two-document hypothesis as the solution of the synoptic problem went certain views or predispositions about the character of the Gospels and the trajectory along which they were to be located. Thus Mark was regarded as the oldest and most primitive gospel, very likely also the most valuable historically. Matthew and Luke were viewed as developments on the basis of Mark (and Q, perhaps M and L also). John seemed yet a further stage of development, another step removed, but still not unrelated to the other three. If the Gospel of John's literary relationship to Matthew was difficult to establish, certainly his dependence upon Mark and Luke was clear. Thus, to regard John as an independent gospel was to become associated with incongenial conservative views of its origin, while at the same time rejecting this logical scheme of historical development.

In this situation Gardner-Smith's work makes a new start in the consideration of Johannine origins and sources. With little apparent intention of proving the primitive or historical character of John—his conclusions do not move as far in this direction as some of his successors and followers would like—Gardner-Smith takes a fresh look at the problem of John and the Synoptics. He puts forward two fundamental, but often overlooked, considerations that have engendered in him the conviction that the critical case for the traditional view is not convincing. In the first place, with the rise of *Formgeschichte*, scholarship has become increasingly aware that the church of the first century was largely and initially dependent on oral tradition rather than written sources for its knowledge of Jesus. This insight has distinct relevance to the problem of John and the Synoptics. Second, the discussion of their relationship has curiously fixated upon the points of agreement and has tended "to ignore the much greater and surely no less significant differences which require to be explained."[73] On this second point Gardner-Smith asks a simple but telling question: Is it easier "to account for the similarities between St. John and the Synoptists without a theory of literary dependence, or to explain the discrepancies if such a theory has been accepted?"[74] With the confidence of a man in possession of an idea whose time has come, he responds that it is easier to explain the similarities without recourse to literary dependency.

Rather than focus primarily upon the similarities or agreements between John and the Synoptics, Gardner-Smith proposes to look at both. He goes

---

[73] Gardner-Smith, *Saint John and the Synoptic Gospels*, x–xi. The quotation is from p. xi.

[74] Ibid., x. In another book published the same year, Gardner-Smith had already suggested an answer. Cf. his *The Christ of the Gospels: A Study of the Gospel Records in the Light of Critical Research* (Cambridge: Heffer & Sons, 1938), 58.

systematically, if somewhat briefly, through the entire Gospel, in effect asking his question of the parallel and relevant texts. Where there are clear similarities or verbal agreements Gardner-Smith weighs the possibility of common oral tradition against the usual explanation of literary dependence. If the charge were made that Gardner-Smith all too willingly accepts the possibility of explaining similarities by recourse to a hypothetical common oral tradition, he would doubtless reply that earlier scholars had all too willingly ascribed any agreement, apparent relationship, or suggestion thereof to literary dependence.

For example, Gardner-Smith rejects as quite gratuitous the assumption that the fourth evangelist's statements about John the Baptist (even in 1:19–34) must have their source in the Synoptic Gospels. "John was writing for Christians and every Christian in the first century must have heard of the Baptist."[75] In considering John's account of the healing of the official's son (4:46–54), Gardner-Smith grants that it has parallels in Matthew (8:5–13) and Luke (7:1–10). How is the obvious relationship to be explained? "We must conclude either that John has treated the synoptic narrative with something like contempt, or that the tradition which he worked into his Gospel did not reach him in the same form as that which appears in either Matthew or Luke." As far as Gardner-Smith is concerned, the choice is not difficult: the tradition reached him in a different form.[76] In these and many other instances, John's alterations or contradictions are found to be "really pointless," not the kinds of changes one would expect of an author of John's skill and purpose, but the kind of variation one could expect to have occurred in underlying, probably oral, tradition.[77] Time and again Gardner-Smith challenges the generally held view that the curious combination of wide divergencies and curious agreements between John and the Synoptics is best understood as the result of a literary process. To think of it in that way says more about the habits of modern scholars than about the nature of the actual evidence. Even the relatively few verbatim agreements (in comparison to those found among the Synoptics) often occur at about the point one would expect in orally transmitted material. For example, the word of Jesus, "Arise, take up your bed, and walk," found in John 5:8 and, in a different narrative context, in Mark 2:9, does not require literary dependence of Mark upon John for its explanation. It is the kind of word of Jesus that would easily impose itself upon the memory.

---

[75] Ibid., 9.
[76] Ibid., 23.
[77] Ibid., e.g., 7, 16, 23–24, 48, 57–58, 64.

Turning to the relationships of the Gospels of John and Mark specifically,[78] Gardner-Smith observes that John's dependence on Mark has generally been based on two considerations: (1) agreement in the general scheme and order and (2) a small number of verbal agreements, often in unimportant words or phrases such as the one noted above. In his judgment the structural similarities are few enough and can be explained as a derivation from the early kerygma itself rather than the result of literary dependence. (Is the influence of C. H. Dodd here already at work?) The similarity is of a very general sort, beginning with the activity of John, followed by a period of ministry of teaching and healing which evokes (Jewish) opposition, and concluding with events leading up to the crucifixion in Jerusalem. As to the verbal agreements, Gardner-Smith has contended all along that they are few enough. They do not outweigh in number or importance the many instances in which John for no apparent reason differs in details or wording from his synoptic counterparts. On this point Gardner-Smith is able to quote Streeter against the latter's own position: "A standing difficulty of New Testament scholarship has always been to explain why the author of the Fourth Gospel goes out of his way, as it were, to differ from the Synoptists on points having no theological significance."[79] Just such seemingly pointless differences, which make difficulties for the theory of literary dependence, are easily accounted for on the basis of parallel streams of oral tradition.

At the end of his book, Gardner-Smith broaches the possibility that the oral tradition upon which the Gospel is based may have had ancient or primitive roots. It follows, therefore, that it may prove to be a valuable source for the life of Jesus, or at least for traditions current in the church between A.D. 50 and 100. Gardner-Smith very carefully qualifies this claim, however:

> Not that critics are likely to accept the Johannine account as historical in the narrower sense of the term; the influence of interpretation is too obvious for that; but where the Fourth Gospel differs from the Synoptics it may henceforth be wise to treat its testimony with rather more respect than it has lately received, and perhaps in not a few cases it may prove to be right.[80]

While the independence theory may have attracted adherents because of an appeal to conservative instincts, there is little reason to think that Gardner-Smith himself put forward his proposal in order to advance certain conservative or apologetic interests. As we have seen, the classic churchly or traditional view is actually that John wrote last, with full knowledge of the other Gospels.

---

[78] Ibid., 88–97.
[79] Ibid., 91, quoting Streeter, *The Four Gospels*, 417.
[80] Ibid., 97.

An interesting and significant feature of Gardner-Smith's book is that he confines himself to the text of the Fourth Gospel and especially to the (mostly narrative) pericopes that are parallel to the Synoptics. He does not attempt to canvass the situation from the other side. That is, he does not begin with the Synoptics in order to ask how much of that material is paralleled in any shape or form in the Gospel of John. Thus, when he speaks of divergencies of John from the Synoptic Gospels, he refers mainly, if not entirely, to divergencies within pericopes that are parallel or offer distinct similarities. There are, of course, a very large number of pericopes, sayings, and parables in the Synoptics, particularly in the pre-passion material, that have no parallels whatever in John. The obverse is also the case. That is, most of the material in the Fourth Gospel has no obvious synoptic parallel. These areas of divergence are not the subject of Gardner-Smith's study, although he is, of course, aware of them.

Presumably Gardner-Smith's case would not be weakened by a consideration of the large amount of material in the Synoptics that has no counterpart at all in John, and vice versa. On the other hand, the view that John knew the Synoptics does not require that he should have retailed their content, but the nature of the putative omissions needs to be considered and the reasons for them explained if the case for John's use of the Synoptics is to be established. By the same token, it is clear enough, or at least on the face of it probable, that the nonsynoptic materials in John (i.e., materials without synoptic parallel) are not best understood as midrash upon, or derived from, the synoptic accounts. On the other side of the ledger, one might ask of Gardner-Smith whether oral tradition suffices to explain the verbatim agreements and other parallels between John, and especially Mark, that occur, for example, rather frequently in the initial Baptist narrative and at a number of points in the passion particularly. Do these agreements not comport better with the use of other written sources (if they do not imply a direct relationship to the Synoptics) than with oral tradition?

Obviously Gardner-Smith's version of the independence theory undercuts the essential presupposition of the view of Windisch, for, as Bultmann observed, John could not have intended to displace what he did not know. Yet in some important respects Windisch and Gardner-Smith are not so far apart. Both emphasize the independence of John over against the Synoptics. To use Gardner-Smith's own formulation, both emphasize the wide-ranging divergencies and differences rather than the similarities and agreements. Both, in effect, agree that supplementation and even interpretation theories do not adequately account for the nature and extent of John's differences from the

Synoptic Gospels. Thus Gardner-Smith represents what from Windisch's perspective might have been the only viable option to the position that John wrote to displace the Synoptics, namely, that he wrote without knowledge of them. But Windisch, having earlier embraced John's independence, at length found the evidence of his use of the Synoptics—and his repudiation of them—overwhelming.

# 3

# The Formation
# of a Consensus

## THE IMPACT OF GARDNER-SMITH

The impact of Percival Gardner-Smith's *Saint John and the Synoptic Gospels* was felt almost immediately in the English-speaking world.[1] In 1945 Erwin R. Goodenough published a major article, "John a Primitive Gospel,"[2] which was devoted in large part to arguing and refining the case for John's independence of the Synoptics. (Obviously an early date for John is unlikely if independence from the Synoptics cannot be established.) Goodenough took note of Gardner-Smith, affirming his work and indicating his fundamental agreement.

In his own article, Goodenough points out that of the nineteen items or events listed by Ernest C. Colwell in *John Defends the Gospel* as points of agreement between John and Mark, thirteen occur in the events of the passion week where, it is generally agreed, Mark used a special source that John may have shared. Three of the six remaining items fall in John 6, where they may point to a source common to Mark and John, rather than John's dependence

---

[1] Ernest C. Colwell reviewed Gardner-Smith in *JBL* 58 (1939): 289–90 and rendered a negative judgment, saying that the author had not come to terms with the evidence for John's use of the Synoptics assembled by Windisch and Sigge. R. H. Lightfoot's review in *JTS* 41 (1940): 70–72 was, however, more favorable. Although he expressed reservations, Lightfoot obviously found Gardner-Smith's work stimulating. Pierre Benoit, *RB* 48 (1939): 457–59, finds the book "court mais très suggestive" and agrees that John is fundamentally independent of the Synoptic Gospels. Nevertheless the problem is more complex than Gardner-Smith imagines, because the Gospel of John grew over a fairly long period of time and was subject to successive redactions. Benoit's proposals prefigure the work of his colleague-to-be in the Ecole Biblique, M.-E. Boismard (see below).

[2] Erwin R. Goodenough, "John a Primitive Gospel," *JBL* 64 (1945): 145–82.

on our Mark.[3] Apart from these two blocks of material, what Colwell has dubbed the Markan framework in John disappears. Rather, "the notorious contrast between Jn and the Synoptics is precisely that Mt and Lk are in a Markan framework of which Jn shows no trace, except in that it begins with John the Baptist, and ends, naturally, with the crucifixion and resurrection."[4] Goodenough concludes, with Gardner-Smith, that such a minimal sense of order may well have been derived from oral tradition.

For reasons that seem obvious to parties on both sides of the issue, the discussion about John and the Synoptics becomes at bottom a discussion about John and Mark. This is in part because Mark is taken to be the oldest of the Synoptic Gospels and the chief narrative source of Matthew and Luke. Therefore, if John knew any of the Synoptics, he must have known Mark. Moreover, the verbatim agreements with Mark are more striking, the distinctive Matthean and Lukan material is not well represented in John, and the kerygmatic character and theological profile of John seems more closely paralleled in Mark than in the other Synoptic Gospels.

Goodenough proceeds to evaluate the argument for John's dependence on Mark that is based on verbal agreements or similarities in parallel passages: the anointing at Bethany (John 12:1–8; cf. Mark 14:3–9; Luke 7:36–49); the healing by the pool of Bethzatha (John 5:2–9; cf. Mark 2:1–12); the feeding of a multitude followed by the walking on the sea (John 6:1–21; cf. Mark 6:30–52, etc.); certain events at the Lord's Supper (John 13; cf. Mark 14); Peter's denials of Jesus (John 18:15–18, 25–27; cf. Mark 14:53–54, 66–72); and the mocking of Jesus (John 19:2–5; cf. Mark 15:16–20).[5] Typical of Goodenough's assessment of the significance of these agreements is his judgment about the anointing story: "That the author of Jn wrote this story with Mk and Lk before him, and took one phrase from one, another from the other, is of all reconstructions the most artificial. The phenomena of agreement and disagreements in the stories are those of oral transmission, not of documentary evidence at all."[6] In Goodenough's judgment, the evidence for John's dependence on Mark consists only of passing phrases except in the case of three pericopes: the anointing, the feeding and walking on the sea, and the mocking of Jesus. For these three accounts, and for the passion generally, Mark and John probably possessed "a common (or similar) written

[3] Ibid., 150–51.
[4] Ibid., 151.
[5] Ibid., 152–60.
[6] Ibid.; 153.

source." But, thinks Goodenough, "other similarities between the two Gospels are adequately accounted for by oral tradition."[7]

On individual points of agreement or disagreement Goodenough has characteristically sharp opinions. John's form of the commissioning of the disciples (20:21–23) is more primitive than anything in Matthew, and John scarcely gives evidence of knowing the Matthean form of the tradition (whether in Matthew 16 or 28).[8] John 7:41–43 does not indicate John's knowledge of the Matthean infancy narratives but presents the Jewish objections to Jesus' Messiahship to which those narratives are a response. (Presumably John would then represent an earlier stage of the Christian apologetic tradition.)[9] John's silence on the institution of the Eucharist at the Last Supper is explained by his ignorance of it, although he is not ignorant of the rite itself, as John 6 certainly shows. His eucharistic tradition, based on traditional Jewish ideas of a messianic meal, finds a parallel in the *Didache's* eucharistic liturgy, in which there is also no mention of a Last Supper setting for the institution.[10]

Goodenough then agrees in spades with Gardner-Smith, and in a significant sense also with Windisch, when he writes: "No more irrelevant description of its character was ever forced upon a document than the current [and, one might add, ancient] conception that Jn was written to correct or supplement the Synoptics."[11]

Goodenough's views were immediately countered by R. P. Casey, who argued that the comparison of extant documents where obvious similarities exist in order to establish literary relationships is a more profitable enterprise than the kind of exercise in hypothetical oral and written sources that Goodenough had conducted.[12] By way of rejoinder, Goodenough stuck to his basic thesis, saying that to refuse to countenance oral tradition and the possibility of no longer extant written sources is to ignore reality.[13] Like Gardner-Smith, Goodenough invoked the discipline and results of form criticism in support of his claims about the necessity of taking seriously the existence of oral tradition. The premises and perspectives of Casey and Goodenough would characterize the discussion for the decades to come.

As we shall see, the impact and influence of Gardner-Smith's slim volume continued and grew in the English-speaking world, although it was not widely

---

[7] Ibid., 160.
[8] Ibid., 169.
[9] Ibid., 171.
[10] Ibid., 173–76.
[11] Ibid., 169.
[12] R. P. Casey, "Professor Goodenough and the Fourth Gospel," *JBL* 64 (1945): 535–42.
[13] Erwin R. Goodenough, "A Reply," *JBL* 64 (1945): 543–44.

known on the Continent and apparently not known at all in Germany for some time after World War II. The direct and immediate effect of Gardner-Smith's work on Anglo-Saxon scholarship is well documented by Josef Blinzler, who in his review of scholarship on the question of John and the Synoptics also reports that the book was scarcely obtainable at all in Europe until well after World War II.[14]

Yet the view that John was little influenced by the Synoptic Gospels, if he knew them at all, was meanwhile gaining strength and adherents there also. In his commentary on the Fourth Gospel, which has had an enormous influence on the Continent, Rudolf Bultmann saw very little if any direct synoptic influence on the Gospel of John.[15] In Bultmann's view, the Gospel is constituted out of a number of sources or literary layers as well as the material that was composed by the evangelist himself.[16] Except at the final, redactional stage, the influence of the Synoptics is principally the influence of synoptic-like tradition that is mediated through the evangelist's sources. Because denial of John's use of the Synoptic Gospels was not an important item on Bultmann's agenda, that his exegesis of the Fourth Gospel did not presuppose them is all the more impressive.

Bent Noack was one of the first European scholars to show acquaintance and fundamental agreement with Gardner-Smith, although his thesis and work are substantially independent.[17] Appropriately, the first thoroughgoing attempt to trace the roots of the Fourth Gospel to oral tradition was to come from a Scandinavian scholar. As in the case of Bultmann, Noack's primary purpose was not to show John's independence of the Synoptics. Rather, he intended to demonstrate that the Johannine material had an oral history of transmission prior to its incorporation into the present Gospel. In Noack's

---

[14] Blinzler, *Johannes und die Synoptiker,* 19–20. (Gardner-Smith was, however, favorably reviewed by Benoit; see n. 1 above.)

[15] Rudolf Bultmann, *Das Evangelium des Johannes,* Kritisch-exegetischer Kommentar über das Neue Testament, 2d section, 10th ed. (Göttingen: Vandenhoeck & Ruprecht, 1941), a volume that was repeatedly reprinted and in 1957 and 1966 was supplemented by *Ergänzungshefte.* Subsequently it appeared in English translation under the title The *Gospel of John: A Commentary,* trans. George R. Beasley-Murray, et al. (Philadelphia: Westminster Press, 1971).

[16] For a full description of Bultmann's source theory, see D. Moody Smith, "The Sources of the Gospel of John: An Assessment of the Present State of the Problem," *NTS* 10 (1963–64): 336–51, or idem, *The Composition and Order of the Fourth Gospel: Bultmann's Literary Theory,* Yale Publications in Religion 10 (New Haven and London: Yale University Press, 1965). Also see below, pp. 65–66.

[17] Bent Noack, *Zur johanneischen Tradition: Beiträge zur Kritik an der literarkritischen Analyse des vierten Evangeliums* (Copenhagen: Rosenkilde og Bagger, 1954), esp. 89–109 (on sayings), 109–25 (on narratives), where Noack deals with Johannine-synoptic relations.

view, therefore, the Gospel is not based on written sources at all, much less on the Synoptic Gospels.[18]

In the course of arguing this thesis, Noack deals first with synoptic logia, words of Jesus with more or less obvious synoptic parallels (e.g., John 1:27; cf. Mark 1; 7; Matt. 3:11; Luke 3:16. John 6:42; cf. Matt. 13:55 par. John 5:8; cf. Mark 2:11. John 4:44; cf. Matt. 13:57; Mark 6:4; Luke 4:24. John 15:20; cf. Luke 6:40; Matt. 10:24, as well as John 13:16). In such parallel logia, which commentators and exegetes have generally taken to be well established, there are mainly similarities of content rather than significant verbal agreements, and Noack does not find sufficient agreement to justify the common assumption that John was in any instance dependent upon the Synoptic Gospels.

The narratives that Noack treats are principally those that are obviously parallel to synoptic accounts (i.e., John 2:14–16; 4:46–53; 6:1–13; 6:16–21; 12:1–8; 12:12–16; 13:21–30; 13:36–38; as well as the passion narrative proper). He finds in them a characteristic Johannine style, which can be explained neither as an expansion or alteration of the Synoptics nor as the result of the evangelist's use of another written source. Rather, it is best accounted for here, as in the logia, on the premise that the evangelist was writing down material that he had received through the mediation of his church, where it resided in the form of oral tradition. The same is true of John's Old Testament citations.[19] Although Noack's style of analysis and argumentation were obviously different from Gardner-Smith's, his conclusions both about John's disuse of the Synoptics and about the Fourth Gospel's basis in oral tradition were remarkably similar.

It is worth noting at this juncture that already seven years before the publication of Noack's work, the Swiss scholar Philippe-Henri Menoud published a report on the state of Johannine scholarship in which he briefly reviewed the question of John and the Synoptics, citing the works of Windisch, Sigge, and Gardner-Smith.[20] He himself concluded that the Fourth Gospel probably represents a formulation of the tradition more or less contemporary with and parallel to, but independent of, the synoptic. This position was actually developed in the same author's earlier (1930), unpublished Th.D. dissertation at Union Theological Seminary (New York) entitled "The Fourth

---

[18] Bultmann rejected Noack's general thesis but agreed on John's independence of the Synoptics. Cf. *TLZ* 80 (1955): 521–26, esp. 521, 524.

[19] Ibid., 88–89.

[20] Philippe-Henri Menoud, *L'Evangile de Jean d'après les recherches récentes,* Cahiers théologiques de l'actualité protestante 3 (Neuchâtel: Delachaux and Niestlé, 1947), 27–29.

Gospel and the Gospel Tradition." That work, which is almost unknown, I found intriguing and in many ways foreshadowing the arguments of Gardner-Smith and C. H. Dodd. Unfortunately the young scholar, doubtless struggling to express himself in English, did not have adequate help in composing or proofreading the dissertation, so that a number of infelicities and errors appear, at least in the copy that I read. Moreover, the dissertation becomes rather thin toward the end. Yet it is nevertheless in concept, and to a considerable extent in execution, a remarkable achievement, particularly when viewed against the background of scholarly opinion more than a half century ago.

Apparently the first German scholar to take account of Gardner-Smith's, as well as Noack's, work on the relationship of John to the synoptic tradition was Ernst Haenchen. In a *Forschungsbericht* published in 1956, Haenchen proposed that the fourth evangelist probably used as his source a miracle gospel no longer extant, a sort of crude form of the Gospel of Mark, which placed heavy emphasis on the miraculous manifestation of the divine glory, rather than the Synoptic Gospels as we know them.[21] Several years later in an article entitled "Johanneische Probleme,"[22] Haenchen undertook to examine in greater detail the theses of Gardner-Smith and Noack: (1) that John is independent of the Synoptics and (2) that the Fourth Gospel represents the initial fixation of an oral tradition whose historical worth may be much greater than had heretofore been imagined. Haenchen notes incidentally that the independence of John from the Synoptics had been defended prior to the works of Gardner-Smith and Noack. In order to evaluate their positions, Haenchen proposes to examine very closely narrative pericopes that John and the Synoptics share. Thus, he chooses the healing of the official's son (John 4:46–54); the feeding and walking on the sea (6:1–21); the cleansing of the temple (2:14–22); and the healing by the pool (5:1–14). (The healing of the man by the pool of Bethzatha, 5:1–14, has no exact parallel in the Synoptics, but it is a story with affinities with the material of those gospels.) In each case, Haenchen finds a complex source situation rather than simple dependence of John on one or more of the Synoptics. For example, he finds not three but six versions of the healing of the ruler's son. (Matthew 8:5–13; Luke 7:1–10 and John 4:46–54 make three, and there are then three different

---

[21] Ernst Haenchen, "Aus der Literatur zum Johannesevangelium 1929–1956," *ThR* 23 (1955): 295–335, esp. 303. Haenchen also suggests the evangelist may have drawn his material from the evangelical tradition as he heard it in the worship of his congregation. (In the bibliography of this article, Haenchen indicates that he knows Gardner-Smith's book only secondhand.)

[22] Ernst Haenchen, "Johanneische Probleme," *ZTK* 56 (1959): 19–54. Republished in Haenchen's collected essays, *Gott und Mensch: Gesammelte Aufsätze* (Tübingen: J. C. B. Mohr [Paul Siebeck], 1965), 78–113, according to which we cite him here.

*Vorlagen,* or sources underlying each.[23]) The Johannine source differs from that of Matthew and Luke in that in it the central point is not human faith but Jesus' miracle. Comparison shows that the Johannine version is not dependent on either of the Synoptics. Such an interest in the miraculous is typical of the Johannine source. Within the Johannine account one can separate a traditional *Vorlage* from the evangelist's annotations (e.g., 4:48–49) and may therefore infer that the tradition was already fixed in written form.

Haenchen's investigation partly supports and partly calls into question the views of Gardner-Smith and Noack.[24] On the one hand, he finds that contacts with the Synoptics, even in the parallel accounts, are at a minimum. Longer verbal agreements, such as one might expect in cases of literary dependence, are lacking. There is no compelling reason for thinking that John drew upon the Synoptic Gospels or that he composed his gospel freely, by poetic license, on the basis of them. John evidently did not use the Synoptic Gospels but a tradition related to them. Probably at the time John wrote, near the end of the first century, no single church possessed all three Synoptic Gospels. Rather, each church had its own, solitary gospel. Possibly John did not even know the Synoptics, and to that extent Gardner-Smith and Noack may be correct.

On the other hand, Haenchen cannot agree that John's Gospel is the first literary fixation of a previously oral tradition. To Haenchen, the tradition gives clear indication of having reached a more advanced stage of development relative to the Synoptics. For this reason and because he can separate tradition from redaction in each case, Haenchen thinks the narratives had already been written down. Again he suggests they were derived from the primitive gospel current in John's own congregation, which naturally became the basis of his work.[25] Although not one of the Synoptic Gospels, it bore some relation to the narratives of that tradition. Haenchen does not define this primitive gospel more closely and leaves open the possibility that John had access to other traditions, whether written or oral. In a later essay on the Johannine passion, Haenchen does not attempt to advance or develop the source theory that he suggested.[26] Rather, he is content to leave open the question of whether John's source was known to the evangelist in written or oral form.[27] Haenchen's

---

[23] Haenchen, *Gott und Mensch,* 82–90.

[24] Ibid., 109–13.

[25] Ibid., 112–13.

[26] Ernst Haenchen, "Historie und Geschichte in den johanneischen Passionsberichten," in his *Die Bibel und wir: Gesammelte Aufsätze* (Tübingen: J. C. B. Mohr [Paul Siebeck], 1968), 2:182–207.

[27] Ibid., 192 n. 25: "Der Evangelist schreibt nicht (umarbeitend) eine Quelle aus, sondern erzählt eine ihm—vielleicht nur vom Hören bekannte—Geschichte neu auf seine Weise."

position as set forth in his commentary will be discussed later on in this chapter.

Finally, it should be noted that before Gardner-Smith's work had its major impact, similar views had been expressed in English-speaking scholarship. Even before Gardner-Smith published, a now little-known British scholar, Percy G. S. Hopwood, attributed to the Beloved Disciple (not John the son of Zebedee) "a semi-independent corpus of gospel tradition which took its own way and grew alongside the more authoritative Synoptic account."[28] In 1940, writing with cognizance of Gardner-Smith, an American, H. E. Dana, took a position similar to his.[29] More than a decade or so later, another British scholar, H. E. Edwards, espoused John's independence of the Synoptics but without reference to Gardner-Smith's work. Edwards characterized as "disastrous" the assumption that John wrote last and in the light of the other three. Moreover, he scathingly dismissed the supplementation theory.

> Its upholders can account for all the Evangelist has to say in three ways. If the author of our Gospel says what they say, he is quoting them; if he says what is out of harmony with their accounts, he is correcting them; if he tells us anything that is not found in their pages, he is supplementing them. In fact, this theory will account, not only for all that the Fourth Evangelist has written; it would account equally well for anything he *might have* written.[30]

In a doctoral dissertation presented at Southern Baptist Theological Seminary in 1955, Edwin Dargan Johnston defended the independence of the Gospel of John from the Synoptics. Johnston, writing now nearly two decades after Gardner-Smith's *Saint John and the Synoptic Gospels*, demonstrates an awareness of the scholarly literature, including Hans Windisch as well as Gardner-Smith.[31] Essentially, his position is like that of Gardner-Smith. He concentrates, however, on several Johannine episodes paralleled in the Synoptics, in order to show their independence: the feeding of the five thousand, the anointing of Jesus, and the cleansing of the temple.

Like Dana and Edwards, Johnston was motivated by historical interests. That is, he wanted to show that the Johannine narratives have an independent

---

[28] Percy G. S. Hopwood, *The Religious Experience of the Primitive Church: The Period Prior to the Influence of Paul* (New York: Charles Scribner's Sons, 1937), 21.

[29] H. E. Dana, *The Ephesian Tradition: An Oral Setting of the Fourth Gospel* (Kansas City, Kansas: Kansas City Seminary Press, 1940).

[30] H. E. Edwards, *The Disciple Who Wrote These Things: A New Inquiry Into the Origins and Historical Value of the Gospel According to St. John* (London: J. Clarke, 1953), 111.

[31] Edwin Dargan Johnston, "A Re-examination of the Relation of the Fourth Gospel to the Synoptics" (Th.D. diss., Southern Baptist Theological Seminary, 1955). Johnston published a part of his research in much-abbreviated form: "The Johannine Version of the Feeding of the Five Thousand—An Independent Tradition?" *NTS* 8 (1961–62): 151–54.

traditional basis and might therefore be historically valuable. A few years later a better-known British scholar with similar interests also espoused John's independence of the Synoptics. A. J. B. Higgins's brief book on the historicity of the Gospel of John takes its lead from Gardner-Smith. Higgins writes that he has "long been convinced of the Fourth Gospel's independence of our other written Gospels, as argued by Gardner-Smith."[32] Although their work is motivated by historical interests that may be theologically grounded, it should not be simply dismissed for that reason. Believing or hoping something is true does not necessarily mean that it is not!

## C. H. DODD

When in his first major work on the Fourth Gospel, C. H. Dodd announced that he had been impressed by Gardner-Smith's arguments in favor of John's independence of the Synoptics,[33] he gave a clear indication of the way the winds of scholarship were blowing. If Gardner-Smith had done nothing more than convince Professor Dodd, his Cambridge colleague, of the rightness of his cause, he would have by that achievement alone enormously advanced the influence and reception of his own viewpoint. During the middle decades of the twentieth century, there was no more dominant and influential figure among English-speaking New Testament scholars than Dodd.

Therefore, when a decade after *The Interpretation of the Fourth Gospel* Dodd published *Historical Tradition in the Fourth Gospel*,[34] its basic theme came as no surprise. Dodd there fills out the program he had suggested at the end of the earlier book. This second work provides an exhaustive comparison and analysis of the material in John that is parallel, or even more remotely related, to the Synoptic Gospels. Moreover, at every point a thorough case is made exegetically for the oral character and transmission of the Johannine material in its pregospel form and thus for its possibly primitive nature and historical value. (Interestingly enough, there is no mention of the earlier work of Noack or of Haenchen.) Once again Dodd singles out Gardner-Smith's work, which

---

[32] A. J. B. Higgins, *The Historicity of the Fourth Gospel* (London, Lutterworth Press, 1960), 12–13.

[33] C. H. Dodd, *The Interpretation of the Fourth Gospel* (Cambridge: Cambridge University Press, 1953), 449.

[34] C. H. Dodd, *Historical Tradition in the Fourth Gospel* (Cambridge: Cambridge University Press, 1963).

he says crystallized the doubts of many, himself included, about the long-held dogma of John's dependence on the Synoptic Gospels.

The primary question that dominates Dodd's entire investigation is whether one can actually identify a strain of tradition lying behind (and within) the Fourth Gospel that is both distinctive of it and independent of the other known strains of tradition.[35] This question then leads immediately to the problem of the relationship of John to the Synoptic Gospels, since for so long so many scholars have assumed that John depended on the Synoptics. But in view of recent research, especially form criticism, which has emphasized the existence and importance of oral tradition in the early church, the kinds and extent of similarities between John and the Synoptics are scarcely sufficient to establish a literary relationship or dependence. In other words, in the aftermath of the development of form and tradition criticism, it can no longer be assumed that early Christian tradition traveled *von Schreibtisch zu Schreibtisch*.[36] Therefore, while Dodd does not set out to show that John did not use the Synoptics, he regards the assumption that he did as now questionable and to be tested at every point. He states his method and perspective quite clearly:

> In comparing, therefore, a given passage in the Fourth Gospel with a parallel passage in the other gospels, we have to inquire whether there are coincidences of language or content going beyond what might be reasonably expected in works having behind them the general tradition of the early Church, and next whether any marked differences might be accounted for (supposing he were copying the Synoptics) by known mannerisms of the evangelist, or his known doctrinal tendencies. If not, then there is a *prima facie* case for treating the passage as independent of the Synoptics, and we have to ask whether it has characteristics, in form or substance, or possible indications of a *Sitz im Leben*, which would associate it with traditional material so far as this is known to us.[37]

The importance of the impact upon Dodd of form criticism together with its investment in the history of tradition is well worth observing. Yet it would be wrong to characterize Dodd as a passive recipient of the method of form and tradition history. He was very much one of its early practitioners outside

---

[35] Ibid., 8–9. According to Donald A. Carson, "Historical Tradition in the Fourth Gospel: After Dodd, What?" in *Gospel Perspectives*, vol. 2: *Studies of History and Tradition in the Four Gospels*, ed. R. T. France and David Wenham (Sheffield: JSOT Press, 1981), 85: "Dodd approaches the question of historical tradition by examining the fourth gospel's relation to the Synoptics. Essentially *HTFG* is a detailed (one might almost say, microscopic) examination of that relationship." In pursuit of the historical tradition (and motivated by the historical question) "the vast majority of the book is given over to the minute defence of John's literary independence from the synoptic gospels" (p. 89). Carson's assessment is entirely correct.

[36] The phrase is Ernst Haenchen's, in a letter to me dated November 5, 1969.

[37] Dodd, *Historical Tradition in the Fourth Gospel*, 9.

continental Europe, as *The Apostolic Preaching and Its Developments* (1935) attests. In *Historical Tradition in the Fourth Gospel*, form criticism functions not so much as a set method but as a perspective and attitude. True, in his chapter on stories of healing, Dodd is able to show formal similarities between the Johannine and the synoptic stories, which imply a similar origin, function, and mode of transmission.[38] For the most part, however, formal (in the sense of structural) analogies between individual items of tradition are not sought. Rather, the impact of form criticism is felt in matters of perspective, the modes of interrogating a text, and the appreciation of its likely ambience.

In brief but important discussions of the chronology and structure of the Gospels, Dodd notes that in these respects both the Synoptics and the Fourth Gospel are largely determined by nonchronological factors.[39] Here again the influence of form (and redaction) criticism is evident. The relevance of this matter is, of course, that the Synoptics, fundamentally Mark, can no longer be regarded as normative historically, or in any other way, as far as the course of Jesus' ministry is concerned. John and the Synoptics stand on an equal footing. Always respectful of ancient tradition, Dodd then turns to the question of authorship, which he rightly concludes is insolvable.[40] Moreover, given the right perspective and appreciation of the character of the material, this question is no longer crucial. (On the matter of authorship, Dodd's use of the analogy of Plato and Socrates is illuminating: no one doubts that Plato was a disciple of Socrates, but scholars agree that his dialogues do not represent the *ipsissima verba* of the teacher!)

The bulk of this sizable volume is not devoted to method or perspective, however, but to an extensive and painstaking examination of the texts of the Gospel, which Dodd approaches in an order very much influenced by form-critical perspective. Thus he begins with that part of the Gospel where the parallels to the Synoptics are most frequent and the influence and weight of tradition would be strongest, namely, the passion narrative.[41] In treating the passion, Dodd considers seriatim: (1) the introductory portion of the passion, which in the common plan underlies all the Gospels including the Last Supper, (2) the Old Testament testimonies, (3) Jesus' taking leave of his disciples, (4) the arrest, (5) the trial, (6) the execution, and (7) the reunion (resurrection appearances). Items 3 to 7 form the basic plan of the passion narrative common

---

[38] Ibid., 174–95.
[39] Ibid., 9–10.
[40] Ibid., 10–17.
[41] Ibid., 21–151.

to each Gospel (and possibly to tradition), except that in Mark the appearance of the risen Christ is, of course, lacking.

Typical of Dodd's approach is his treatment of the Old Testament testimonies.[42] (He finds eight such testimonies in John 18–19.) In the passion, John shares no Old Testament testimonies with Matthew or Luke that are not found also in Mark. Of Mark's seventeen testimonies, John has only four (John 13:18, quoting Ps. 40:10LXX; John 19:24, quoting Ps. 21:19LXX; John 19:28–29, quoting Ps. 68:22LXX; and John 19:1, 3, quoting Isa. 50:6), and of these only two could be plausibly supposed to have come from Mark (John 19:24 and 19:28–29). John's use of the Old Testament hardly seems to be derived from Mark, much less from the other Synoptics. Moreover, John's testimonies from the Old Testament are not obviously shaped by the evangelist's theological interests. Yet they are, on the whole, farther from the LXX text than Mark's. Both these characteristics bespeak their traditional character. True, they are drawn from the same parts of the Old Testament as those found in the Synoptics (Psalms of the righteous sufferer, suffering servant passages of Second Isaiah, and Zechariah's references to a martyred leader). They therefore provide the same kind of theological key to the meaning of Jesus' death. But this view of Christ's death was in all probability primitive and widespread, and one may fairly argue that John derived it from pre-canonical tradition rather than from the other Gospels.[43]

Dodd goes through the Johannine passion narrative in detail, asking how its noteworthy features are best understood with respect to origin as well as purpose. Time and again he finds John's divergencies from Mark or the other Synoptics very difficult to explain as the fourth evangelist's deliberate alternations of a synoptic source. Just because such differences in detail are frequently trivial, Dodd has great difficulty viewing them as the result of either careful copying or purposeful alternation. Thus, for example, the presence of a Roman cohort at Jesus' arrest (18:3), which answers to no clear Johannine theological interest (for John is interested in showing the culpability of the Jews), is probably derived from the nonsynoptic source or tradition upon which the evangelist drew.[44] By the same token, the Johannine account of the Jewish trial, the hearing before Annas, is bereft of theological interest. On the other hand, the Markan account of Jesus' trial before the Sanhedrin has profound theological interests that seem to square with those of the fourth

---

[42] Ibid., 31–49.

[43] Cf. the earlier work of C. H. Dodd, *According to the Scriptures: The Sub-Structure of New Testament Theology* (London: Nisbet, 1952).

[44] Ibid., 73–74.

evangelist.[45] Are we to believe that the evangelist omitted or suppressed the Markan account in order to describe the relatively insignificant hearing before Annas?

In contrast to the Jewish trial, the Roman trial before Pontius Pilate is recognizably the same event in John as in the Synoptics. Although the Johannine motifs are plentiful and clearly discernible, Dodd nevertheless remains unconvinced that John's source is Mark, or any of the Synoptics, and finds that the points of contact between them are relatively rare.[46] Yet there are verbal agreements as well as a certain similarity in order, so that here John's dependence on the Synoptics can be plausibly argued. The most striking aspect of the Johannine scene, which comes to expression mainly in phrases that are apparently the composition of the evangelist, is, however, its political dimension. Jesus makes very clear to Pilate the non-political nature of his activity (and by implication of the community of his followers). But in his doing so, the suspicion or allegation that Jesus and his earliest followers posed some sort of political threat is allowed to surface. Precisely these political overtones have been suppressed in the Synoptics, especially in Matthew and Mark, but John brings them into the open in order to show Jesus innocent. Such verisimilitude, such an evocation of the actual situation of the time of Jesus, would scarcely have been invented by the fourth evangelist at the end of the first century.[47] Certainly it is not derived from the Synoptics. In all likelihood it reflects a tradition—albeit now cast in the evangelist's prose— that is primitive, that is, antedating A.D. 70.

In his account of the execution of Jesus, John again omits Markan details— for example, the darkness at noon, the rending of the temple veil, the centurion's acclamation of Jesus as the Son of God—of which the evangelist could have made good use had he had Mark's Gospel, or the Synoptics generally, before him.[48] Not only do these details heighten the tension of the drama but they represent Johannine theological themes: darkness and light; Jesus and the temple as places of revelation; Jesus as Son of God. Dodd finds it easier to believe that John did not have Mark than that he deliberately, or carelessly, omitted such details.

The Johannine account of the resurrection is in principle similar in its relationship to the Synoptics. There are affinities, although perhaps not so many as in the passion proper. Yet it is difficult to understand the Johannine

---

[45] Ibid., 92.
[46] Ibid., 88–120, esp. 120.
[47] Ibid., 114–15.
[48] Ibid., 129–30.

accounts as simply derivative from the synoptic, despite certain special connections between John and Luke particularly. Here as in the passion narrative Dodd finds that the evidence that suggests literary dependence of John upon the Synoptics is insufficient to prove it against reasonable grounds for doubt. Rather, its cumulative weight is on the side of John's having relied upon a different, if related, strain of tradition.[49] It is perhaps worth remarking parenthetically that Dodd's construal of the evidence remains contingent upon the validity of the assumption that John was not limited to the other Gospels, that he could, and likely did, have other sources, whether oral or written. At the same time, the textual relationships, or lack thereof, enhance the plausibility of such a hypothesis.

In a section entitled "The Ministry," Dodd treats what he calls the prelude to the passion (the triumphal entry, the cleansing of the temple, the anointing of Jesus at Bethany), healing stories, the feeding and related material, the miracle of the wine, the raising of Lazarus, and, finally, transitional passages and topographical notices. Obviously he is dealing mostly with narrative or narrative-related material. It is perhaps not surprising that Dodd finds that such narratives, even when they have clear synoptic parallels, differ unaccountably from their counterparts. Thus, for example, he has great difficulty understanding why the fourth evangelist, if he had Mark before him, would have changed Jesus' word about his anointing for burial from the clear statement we find in Mark 14:8 to the rather perplexing one that now stands in John 12:7. The difficulty disappears, however, if one supposes that John is relying upon some tradition or source other than Mark.[50] To take another instance, if John's rendition of the feeding miracle (John 6:1–14) is to be derived from synoptic accounts, one must believe that John drew items or details from the stories of both Mark 6 and 8 as well as Matthew (John 6:3 = Matt. 15:29). But such a process of conflation is very hard to understand or explain, not only in principle but in relation to specific texts.[51] Even in the accounts of the activity of John the Baptist, where similarities to the synoptic accounts are relatively plentiful, Dodd feels they do not require literary dependence for their explanation. Moreover, he finds in the Johannine account some distinctive features that do not seem to be attributable to any of that Gospel's well-established theological interests (e.g., the motif of the hidden Messiah in 1:26–27).[52] To the degree that such traditional motifs can be

---

[49] Ibid., 150–51.
[50] Ibid., 167–69.
[51] Ibid., 205–16.
[52] Ibid., 266–69.

established, the idea of a separate tradition is strengthened and the necessity of Johannine dependence on the Synoptics correspondingly weakened. Indeed, synoptic-like features in this Gospel, if they do not obviously betray knowledge of the Synoptic Gospels themselves (and they generally do not), tend to strengthen the case for an independent strand of tradition behind John. Where in formally parallel stories John and the Synoptics clearly go their separate ways and, in fact, tell different stories (e.g., the narratives of the calling of the disciples), literary dependence is difficult to establish. If John knew the Synoptics, such instances pose a serious question as to how he regarded them.

Finally, Dodd canvasses the sayings of the Fourth Gospel in search of synoptic parallels and other possible indications of John's use of tradition.[53] Clearly the Johannine discourse style is rather different from the synoptic and bears a marked formal resemblance to the Hermetic dialogues, as different as the context of the two may be.[54] In fact, with respect to style at least the Johannine dialogues owe little or nothing to the specifically Christian tradition. Nevertheless there are sayings common to the Synoptics also (e.g., John 13:16 and Matt. 10:24–25; John 12:25 and Mark 8:35 par., etc.) As a rule, these synoptic-like sayings do not seem to have been drawn by John directly from the Synoptic Gospels. The parable is but weakly represented in the Gospel of John, although one finds a few "parable forms," as Dodd calls them (e.g., John 12:24; 16:21; etc.). There are also brief dialogues, somewhat more like the synoptic in style (e.g., John 6:67–70; 4:31–34), and instances in which synoptic themes are set forth or treated in John (e.g., signs in John 2:18; 4:48; 6:30; cf. Mark 8:11–12; Matt. 12:38–39). One finds evidence of common context or origin, but there is little reason to posit a literary relationship.

Clearly Dodd can be only more or less certain that a specific Johannine saying or pericope is independent of the synoptic. Yet he is quite unambiguous in his judgment that in the majority of cases, whether narrative or discourse, direct literary relationship between John and the Synoptics is unlikely. Since the preponderance of evidence is seen to lie on the side of independence, Dodd is inclined to doubt that John drew upon the Synoptics in the much smaller number of individual cases in which such dependence seems to be a stronger possibility. If John had known the Synoptics, one would expect more widespread or extensive traces of such direct literary dependence. The fewer the specific cases suggesting such dependence, the easier it becomes to explain

---

[53] Ibid., 313–420.
[54] Ibid., 321.

those that exist without suggesting that John knew our Synoptics. If he knew them, it is not clear why he did not follow them more closely, more frequently, and at greater length. In some such sense, then, Dodd believes that the evidence against John's knowledge and use of the Synoptics is cumulative. Therefore Dodd is willing to claim a high degree of probability for the conclusion that the Fourth Gospel is based on "an ancient tradition independent of other gospels."[55] While it is impossible to prove that John was not familiar with the Synoptics (and Acts), so that he subconsciously could incorporate aspects of them into his gospel as he wrote, Dodd does not believe the evidence actually suggests this. Furthermore, it is no longer possible to date John so late or the Synoptics so early that the former's knowledge of the latter is on the face of it highly probable.

That John had all the Synoptics before him and composed a mosaic from them is a hypothesis that Dodd believes the evidence simply will not bear. Possibly John knew them all so well, and by implication had known them so long, that reminiscences of them influenced him subconsciously. Such a hypothesis cannot be disproved, but it seems unlikely. Moreover, it requires us to believe something inherently unlikely, namely, that there was some one Christian center at or before the end of the first century "where, in the short time since their publication, all three Synoptic Gospels had attained, together, such a position that it would be natural for a writer to use all three as equipollent sources, and still more unlikely that they had held this position long enough for him to have soaked himself in them so thoroughly."[56] To sketch such a scenario is, obviously, to underscore its improbability.

One sees in Dodd the obverse of the perspective and method of scholars such as Bacon and Windisch. Whereas they established what they regarded as clear instances of John's dependence upon the Synoptics and moved out from there to show his use of them in less obvious places, Dodd doubts the necessity of positing dependence in the relatively fewer places where resemblances are closest, because elsewhere and for the most part divergencies are preponderant. Otherwise, Dodd's arguments constitute a sort of pincers movement against the older view that John drew heavily and directly upon the Synoptic Gospels. On the one side, Dodd finds in the material—especially the narratives but also the sayings—forms, indications of time and place, linguistic peculiarities, details, and other data that suggest the presence of traditional material. On the other, in just such places in the Gospel where evidence of

---

[55] Ibid., 423.
[56] Ibid., 424.

tradition is found, indication of dependence upon the Synoptics seems minimal, even where John and the Synoptics have parallel accounts. There are, of course, some verbal and other agreements between John and the Synoptics, but only such as one would expect to find in relatively independent streams of oral tradition with a common point of origin and some contact in transmission. Thus for Dodd the case for a Johannine oral tradition and the case against John's use of the Synoptic Gospels go hand in hand.

Dodd does not exclude the possibility of some written recension of parts of this Johannine tradition having appeared between the oral stage and our present Gospel. But his interest is solely in the establishment of the existence of that independent, early oral stage.[57] Thus he concludes that "behind the Fourth Gospel there lies an ancient tradition independent of other gospels, and meriting serious consideration as a contribution to our knowledge of the historical facts concerning Jesus Christ."[58]

Dodd's work, a considerable accomplishment in its own right, served to magnify the impact of Gardner-Smith's small book, especially in the English-speaking world. Possibly Dodd's book has been more heavily reviewed than any other in the field of Johannine studies.[59] These reviews are mostly positive, if not laudatory, and even reverential. Yet one can discern, amid the paeans of well-merited praise, a significant dissonance of critical opinion. Allen Wikgren, who entitles his review article "A Contribution to the New Quest,"[60]

---

[57] Ibid., 424.

[58] Ibid., 423. Contrast Barrett, *The Gospel According to St. John,* 2d ed., viii: "I do not believe that John intended to supply us with historically verifiable information regarding the life and teaching of Jesus, and that historical traditions of great worth can be disentangled from his interpretive comments." Perhaps not coincidentally, Barrett continues to believe that John knew and used the Synoptic Gospels. Carson, "Historical Tradition," 86, points out how Dodd makes seemingly contradictory evidence work for him: "What Dodd argues is that where the Fourth Gospel is close to the Synoptics, it constitutes powerful *independent* evidence for a common dependence upon pre-canonical (and presumably oral) tradition; and where the Fourth Gospel stands at some distance removed from the synoptics, it very often shows signs of passing on solid tradition, inasmuch as that tradition is rarely tangled up with Johannine themes and therefore to be distrusted."

[59] Edward Malatesta, *St. John's Gospel 1920–1965: A Cumulative and Classified Bibliography of Books and Periodical Literature on the Fourth Gospel,* Analecta Biblica 32 (Rome: Pontifical Biblical Institute, 1967), 45, lists twenty-nine reviews as against twenty-eight for Dodd's *The Interpretation of the Fourth Gospel* and a similar number for Barrett's commentary. Astounding is the fact that Malatestals list goes down through 1965 only and thus does not include a number of reviews: e.g., Ernst Haenchen, *TLZ* 93 (1968): 346–48; M. Simon, *JTS* 18 (1967): 189–92. The list of reviewers is also impressive. Aside from Haenchen and Simon, it includes, among others, Robert M. Grant, Archibald M. Hunter, G. Strecker, Amos N. Wilder, Reginald H. Fuller, Norman Perrin, F. W. Beare, and Raymond E. Brown. Carson, "Historical Tradition," 89–94, analyzes and classifies reviews of Dodd's work.

[60] Allen Wikgren, "A Contribution to the New Quest," *Interpretation* 20 (1966): 234–38.

evidently perceives Dodd's contribution as lying in the area of historical research on Jesus' ministry. He specifically rejects Dodd's view that John is independent of the Synoptics but does not say why he finds it unconvincing. Some other reviewers largely ignored this aspect of Dodd's work in order to concentrate on his form and tradition-critical analysis,[61] historical implications of his thesis,[62] or other, broader issues of interpretation.[63] Among those reviewers who single out the issue of John's relationship to the Synoptics for special comment, Ernst Haenchen and Raymond E. Brown are of particular interest. Haenchen notes that Dodd has devoted an extraordinary amount of space to the attempt to prove John's independence of the Synoptics and pronounces this proof significantly successful.[64] Similarly, Brown agrees with Dodd's finding that John is independent: "Thus Dodd comes to the almost inescapable conclusion that there is a considerable nucleus of historical tradition in the Fourth Gospel, independent of a similar body of historical tradition in the Synoptic Gospels."[65] Probably the opinions of Haenchen and Brown were broadly representative of critical reaction to this aspect of Dodd's work, while Wikgren's, if not an aberration, was at best a minority report.

If Dodd's work did not put an end to the discussion of the relation of John to the Synoptics, it nevertheless marked the culmination of a period in which there had been increasing skepticism about the older orthodox (and orthodox critical) position that John wrote with the other Gospels in view. That some scholars remained, and remain, unconvinced of John's independence goes without saying.[66] Yet Dodd's book had sufficient impact, even among those who remained unpersuaded, to cause a temporary moratorium in the discussion and to allow an interlude and a valuable perspective from which to assess matters. There is now, however, ample indication that this interlude has come to an end.

---

[61] G. Strecker, *Gnomon* 36 (1964): 773–78, who is quite critical of Dodd at many points.

[62] F. W. Beare, *NTS* 10 (1963–64): 517–22, warned that conservative readers would take more encouragement from Dodd than his book, or the Fourth Gospel, warrants.

[63] Amos N. Wilder, *JBL* 83 (1964): 303–6.

[64] Haenchen, *TLZ* 93 (1968): 346–48, esp. 347: "Dabei verwendet er ausserordentlich viel Raum für den Nachweis, dass Johannes nicht von den synoptischen Evangelien abhängig ist. Man wird es als ein besonderes Verdienst des Buches betrachten dürfen, dass dieser Nachweis wirklich gelungen ist."

[65] Raymond E. Brown, *Theological Studies* 25 (1964): 431.

[66] Cf. Blinzler, *Johannes und die Synoptiker,* 33–49. Blinzler objects to earlier statements of mine regarding an emerging consensus of opinion on John's independence of the Synoptic Gospels (pp. 31–33), citing a number of scholars who at that time (1965) still adhered to the view that John stands in some direct relationship of dependence to one or more of the Synoptics.

## AFTER DODD

The magisterial book of C. H. Dodd, then, affords a convenient benchmark, indeed a watershed, in the history of the discussion of this problem. With Dodd the question of the relationship of John and the Synoptics seemed to have been resolved in favor of John's independence. The quarter of a century between Gardner-Smith and Dodd saw the development of an increasing consensus[67] that by the end of the 1960s was quite striking and found expression in several major commentaries published at that time or shortly thereafter. It would be inaccurate and unfair to the commentators to suggest that they were persuaded or influenced solely by Dodd or Gardner-Smith. Nevertheless, the latter were major molders of critical opinion, particularly in the English-speaking world. At the same time, commentaries are at once the barometers and eventually shapers of that opinion. We shall now look briefly at major and representative commentaries and then at introductions and other works.

*Commentaries*

The commentaries of R. H. Lightfoot and C. K. Barrett published in the 1950s illustrate the fact that the consensus of which we speak had not yet emerged. Barrett's commentary was to go through a revised edition twenty or more years after publication and to be translated into German for the famous Meyer (Kritisch-exegetischer Kommentar) series.[68] Barrett has become the standard commentary on the Greek text in the English-speaking world. Like so many others before him, Barrett is impressed with the parallel sequences of events in John and Mark, particularly in the middle portion of the Gospel and in the passion narrative, as well as the verbatim agreements in wording at several

---

[67] I referred to this consensus in 1964. See D. Moody Smith, *Johannine Christianity: Essays on Its Setting, Sources, and Theology* (Columbia, S.C.: University of South Carolina Press, 1984), 57–58. The article in question, "The Sources of the Gospel of John: An Assessment of the Present State of the Problem," is reprinted from *NTS* 10 (1963–64): 336–51. The year following, Blinzler, *Johannes und die Synoptiker*, 31–33, challenged my assessment, denying such a consensus. Then Frans Neirynck, in his "John and the Synoptics," in *L'Evangile de Jean: Sources, rédaction, théologie*, ed. M. de Jonge, BETL 44 (Louvain: Louvain University Press, 1977), 73, agreed with me about the consensus, but with Blinzler about John's use of the Synoptics.

[68] Barrett, *The Gospel According to St. John*, 34–45; 2d ed., 42–54; cf. Barrett's "John and the Synoptic Gospels," *Expository Times* 85 (1974): 228–33. The German translation of Barrett's commentary has appeared under the title *Das Evangelium nach Johannes*, trans. Hans Bald, ed. Karl Matthiae, Kritisch-exegetischer Kommentar über das Neue Testament, Sonderband (Göttingen: Vandenhoeck & Ruprecht, 1990).

points. In the 1978 revision of his commentary, Barrett reiterates his position that John knew at least Mark and Luke.

In affirming John's knowledge of the Synoptics, Barrett was joined by another well-known British commentator, R. H. Lightfoot.[69] Lightfoot emphasizes the intrinsic improbability of John's having been ignorant of the Synoptics at the time he wrote and urges that his gospel may best be viewed as a deepening and theological clarification, that is, an interpretation, of the others. In this he agrees with Barrett, who writes: "John does not so much import foreign matter into the gospel as bring out what was already inadequately expressed in the earlier tradition."[70] Both take up a theme that was fundamental to the earlier commentary of Hoskyns. John is the interpreter of the Synoptic Gospels or, at least, the traditions set forth therein. Hoskyns obviously found congenial the view that John knew and presupposed the Synoptics. Yet in his finely nuanced discussions he seems to leave open the possibility that the evangelist may have known the synoptic traditions in some form other than those gospels which have been canonized.[71] In any event, John is interpreting a given synoptic-like tradition.

In more recent English-language commentaries, the picture has, however, changed. Raymond E. Brown, whose commmentary is most widely used on this side of the Atlantic, comes down emphatically on the side of John's independence of the Synoptics. Brown states his position succinctly: "If one cannot accept the hypothesis of a careless or capricious evangelist who gratuitously changed, added, and subtracted details, then one is forced to agree with Dodd that the evangelist drew the material for his stories from an independent tradition, similar to but not the same as the traditions represented in the Synoptic Gospels."[72] For Brown, as for Gardner-Smith and Dodd, John's many unaccountable differences from the Synoptics outweigh his agreements and similarities with them, since, if he knew the Synoptics, his manner of dealing with them is, strictly speaking, incomprehensible. In Great Britain,

---

[69] R. H. Lightfoot, *St. John's Gospel: A Commentary,* ed. C. F. Evans (Oxford: Clarendon Press, 1956), 26–42. Lightfoot considers, but respectfully rejects, the independence theory as put forward by Gardner-Smith.

[70] Barrett, *The Gospel According to St. John,* 2d ed., 53.

[71] Edwyn C. Hoskyns, *The Fourth Gospel,* ed. F. N. Davey, 2d ed. (London: Faber & Faber, 1947), 58–85, esp. 59–60, 68–69, 70–73, 77, 82. Hoskyns died in 1937, the year before Gardner-Smith published.

[72] Raymond E. Brown, *The Gospel According to John (i–xii),* Anchor Bible 29 (Garden City, N.Y.: Doubleday & Co., 1966), lxv. Cf. Brown's earlier essay, "Incidents That Are Units in the Synoptic Gospels But Dispersed in St. John," *CBQ* 23 (1961): 143–60.

Barnabas Lindars adopts a similar position in his New Century Bible Commentary.[73] Also J. N. Sanders's posthumously published commentary takes a negative view of the fourth evangelist's use of the Synoptics.[74] Moreover, the Australian scholar Leon Morris, in what is in many respects a conservatively oriented commentary on the Fourth Gospel, maintains that "while there is some relationship between the tradition embodied in the Synoptists and that in John there is no valid reason . . . for maintaining that the connection is written. It is much more likely to be oral."[75]

Probably the two most important German-language commentaries to appear since World War II are Rudolf Bultmann's famous work, which although completed in 1941 has had its impact during the period we are considering, and Rudolf Schnackenburg's massive three-volume commentary. Both are now available in English translation.[76] Neither is predicated upon John's use, or even knowledge, of the Synoptic Gospels. The same may be said of Haenchen's more recent commentary, which, although published posthumously on the basis of early drafts and subsequently translated into English, gives no indication that the author was contemplating altering the position he had earlier set forth.[77]

Bultmann does not announce his view at the outset, inasmuch as he has no introduction at all but simply begins with his analysis of the text. Nevertheless a very clear and coherent pattern emerges from his exegesis. John is not based on the Synoptics, nor did the evangelist use the Synoptics as sources; perhaps he did not know the Synoptics. The discourse material is

---

[73] Barnabas Lindars, *The Gospel of John*, New Century Bible Commentary (Grand Rapids: Wm. B. Eerdmans Publishing Co., 1972), 25–28. See also Lindars's monograph, *Behind the Fourth Gospel*, Studies in Creative Criticism 3 (London: SPCK, 1971), in which John's independence of the Synoptics is more or less a working hypothesis; as well as his "John and the Synoptics: A Test Case," *NTS* 27 (1981): 287–94.

[74] J. N. Sanders, *A Commentary on the Gospel According to St. John*, ed. B. A. Mastin, Harper's New Testament Commentaries (New York: Harper & Row, 1968), 8–12.

[75] Leon Morris, *The Gospel According to John: The English Text with Introduction, Exposition and Notes*, New International Commentary on the New Testament (Grand Rapids: Wm. B. Eerdmans Publishing Co., 1971), 49–52. Earlier, Morris had published a lengthy article defending the independence of the Fourth Gospel, "The Relationship of the Fourth Gospel to the Synoptics," in *Studies in the Fourth Gospel* (Grand Rapids: Wm. B. Eerdmans Publishing Co., 1969), 15–63. Probably Morris will now be superseded as the leading conservative commentator by Donald A. Carson, *The Gospel According to John* (Grand Rapids: Wm. B. Eerdmans Publishing Co., 1991), who thinks John likely knew other Gospels. His work came into my hands too late to be included in the discussion.

[76] Bultmann, *The Gospel of John*; and Rudolf Schnackenburg, *The Gospel According to St. John*, trans. Kevin Smyth et al., 3 vols. (New York: Crossroad, 1968–82).

[77] Ernst Haenchen's work appeared in English translation in two volumes entitled *John 1* and *John 2*, ed. Ulrich Busse and Robert W. Funk, trans. Robert W. Funk, Hermeneia (Philadelphia: Fortress Press, 1984).

obviously different and, insofar as it is not the composition of the evangelist himself, was drawn from a revelation-discourse source. In the narratives the closest contacts with the Synoptics or synoptic tradition appear. These are to be accounted for in various ways. As far as the passion account is concerned, John drew upon a source parallel with, but not identical to or derivative from, the Synoptics. Similar or parallel miracle stories in the account of the public ministry were drawn from the signs source that the evangelist employed. Certain narratives were derived from other sources or tradition similar and parallel to the synoptic accounts, for example, the anointing of Jesus and the cleansing of the temple. Finally, some of the verbatim agreements with the Synoptics (e.g., 1:22–23, 27, 32; parts of 26, 31, and 33) are the product of the ecclesiastical redaction, which was intended, among other things, to bring the gospel into closer accord with them.[78] Thus when Bultmann announced in a 1955 review that he accepted Noack's position on John's independence of the Synoptics, the die had been cast years before. We have already observed that as early as his review of Windisch in 1927, Bultmann expressed doubt that John knew the Synoptics.[79] Obviously his intense exegetical labor on the Fourth Gospel did not convince him that the hypothesis of dependence on the Synoptics was necessary or fruitful for exegesis.

Schnackenburg devotes a section of his commentary's introduction to the question of the relation of John to the Synoptics and arrives at very similar conclusions.[80]

> A direct literary dependence of John on the Synoptics is improbable. . . . The Johannine tradition is on the whole independent, and even where it deals with matters found in the Synoptics, it does not seem to pass any judgment on them. . . . [The evangelist] supposes his reader's knowledge of several matters which are known to us from the synoptic tradition, as for instance, the baptism of Jesus. . . . But such information need not be derived from the synoptic Gospels.[81]

Schnackenburg's position is doubtless derived from his exegesis. Like Bultmann, but without attempting the same precision of definition, Schnackenburg believes that the evangelist drew upon a signs source for his miracle stories and that he also used a passion source rather than the Synoptic Gospels. But

---

[78] For a detailed account of Bultmann's source theory, see D. Moody Smith, *Composition and Order of the Fourth Gospel*.

[79] For Bultmann's review of Noack, see *TLZ* 80 (1955): 521–26; on Windisch: *TLZ* 52 (1927): 197–200.

[80] Schnackenburg, *The Gospel According to St. John*, 1:26–43.

[81] Ibid., 41–42.

Schnackenburg is willing to allow the relationship of this passion account to the signs source to remain undefined.

For many years Haenchen had taken the position that John's Gospel was not based principally on the Synoptics but neither was it the initial fixation of an independent oral tradition of great historical worth (Dodd). Rather, the evangelist seems to have drawn upon a primitive gospel of nonsynoptic type.[82] Haenchen maintained this position for over two decades without attempting to define closely the content of this gospel. So in the edited form of his commentary, Haenchen basically sticks with his early position: that John knew any or all of the Synoptics is anything but certain; and Gardner-Smith is cited as having shown that the Johannine narrative is basically independent of the synoptic.[83] "He did not intend to supplement them, to improve them, or to replace them," writes Haenchen of John's relation to the Synoptics.[84]

In the commentary, Haenchen distinguishes three basic literary strata: the traditions employed by the evangelist, the voice of the evangelist himself, and a later redaction.[85] At the same time, he is acutely conscious of the difficulty of making precise source-critical judgments. The traditional source is, however, sometimes characterized as a miracle gospel, which the evangelist found in his own church or community.[86] Yet it also contained a passion narrative and linked Jesus' miracle-working ministry to the passion (cf. 11:45–57)[87]; presumably the source contained a narrative of the resurrection as well.[88]

It is significant, and obviously not merely coincidental, that confidence in the existence of hypothetical sources behind the Gospel of John goes hand in hand with the view that these sources were not the Synoptic Gospels as we know them. Schnackenburg, and especially Bultmann and Haenchen, find in the course of exegesis that John's sources and traditions, which were real enough, were not identical with the Synoptic Gospels. There are clear points of contact with the Synoptics, but they occur in the midst of such far-reaching differences and contradictions that to explain them as the consequence of John's direct dependence upon the Synoptics raises more problems for exegesis than it solves. More likely the Fourth Evangelist drew upon other sources.

The number of commentaries appearing seems now to increase by geometric proportion. For the most part, they are not full-scale, scholarly treatments

---

[82] Haenchen first set forth this view in "Johanneische Probleme." See above, pp. 50–51.
[83] Haenchen, *John 1*, 75; and *John 2*, 69.
[84] Haenchen, *John 1*, 238.
[85] Haenchen, *John 1*, 257, 260.
[86] Ibid., 283; cf. *John 2*, 71–72.
[87] Haenchen, *John 2*, 76–81.
[88] Ibid., 213–17.

that thoroughly explore such questions as John's relationship to the Synoptics. It would obviously be impossible to give an inventory of them all.

Of many recent English-language commentaries, perhaps the weightiest is that of George R. Beasley-Murray in the Word Biblical Commentary series. Although the author modestly presents his own work as a commentary at a lower level than those of Bultmann, Barrett, and others, it is really a first-line critical commentary of more than five hundred pages based on the Greek text. Beasley-Murray refers to Robert Kysar's statement in (1975) about "the near demise of the proposition that the Fourth Evangelist was dependent upon one or more of the synoptic gospels," and after briefly describing the consensus that existed at that time, points out that it is now under attack and can no longer be assumed. In conclusion, he cites my own Society for New Testament Studies paper on the subject and agrees with the position that whether or not John knew the Synoptics, the Gospel is essentially independent of them and has its own distinct agenda. This does not mean that the Synoptics can be ignored in the exegesis of John, particularly where their contents run parallel, but it does mean that there is "no warrant for treating any divergence from the Synoptics as *prima facie* a deliberate and intentional departure." Although Beasley-Murray is appropriately wary, given the present state of scholarship, his position does not differ fundamentally from that of the commentators who did not find dependence on the Synoptics a necessary hypothesis for the exegesis of John.[89]

Several recent popular, or less technical, commentaries by well-established scholars should also be mentioned. Siegfried Schulz, who earlier published a couple of monographs on the Fourth Gospel, has written the current commentary in the nontechnical but important German series Das Neue Testament Deutsch.[90] Where John and Mark (or the other Synoptics) run parallel, Schulz takes the position that John is not dependent on the Synoptics but uses distinct, if related, tradition. The same may be said of Jürgen Becker's two-volume commentary which appeared in 1979 and 1981.[91] George MacRae, in his brief

---

[89] George R. Beasley-Murray, *John*, Word Biblical Commentary 36 (Waco, Tex.: Word Books, 1987), xxxvi–xxxvii. The quotation from Robert Kysar is from his *The Fourth Evangelist and His Gospel*, 55. My position is found in "John and the Synoptics: Some Dimensions of the Problem," published first in *NTS* 26 (1980): 425–44, and re-presented in *Johannine Christianity*, 145–72, esp. 171–72.

[90] Siegfried Schulz, *Das Evangelium nach Johannes übersetzt und erklärt*, Das Neue Testament Deutsch 4 (Göttingen: Vandenhoeck & Ruprecht, 1972).

[91] Jürgen Becker, *Das Evangelium nach Johannes*, Ökumenischer Taschenbuchkommentar zum Neuen Testament 4, 2 vols. (Gütersloher Verlagshaus Gerd Mohn, 1979–81), 2:36–38. Already in 1970 Becker had defended the *semeia*-source theory in his article "Wunder und Christologie: Zum literarkritischen und christologischen Problem der Wunder im Johannesevangelium," *NTS*

commentary for lay people, does not deal with the question except to acknowledge that John knew much of what is contained in the Synoptics and may have known one or more of those Gospels.[92] While John's knowledge of the Synoptics is thus not excluded, very little in the commentary itself is predicated on that supposition.

Subsequently, in another commentary intended primarily for use within the church, Robert Kysar, who has carefully followed the course of scholarly discussion on this and other issues, judiciously affirms the consensus of which we have spoken. While Kysar acknowledges that John's use of the Synoptic Gospels is now once again widely advocated, he nevertheless indicates that he will not presuppose a directly literary relationship but only knowledge of similar or related traditions. In fact, Kysar believes that the evangelist knew and employed a signs source, a passion source, and some sort of source for Jesus' sayings.[93] In J. Ramsey Michaels's relatively more conservative Good News Commentary on the Gospel of John,[94] which appeared just a couple of years before Kysar's, the difficulty of the problem of John and the Synoptics is readily acknowledged. Yet Michaels concludes that the evangelist "for the most part . . . seems to have written independently of the others . . . ," and he goes on to say that the fourth evangelist obviously drew upon the same or similar traditions. We are seeing a certain reluctance or wariness about embracing the Gardner-Smith consensus, but finally not a break with it.

To the best of my knowledge, in the past three decades there has been no major new commentary in English, French, or German in which the fourth evangelist's knowledge of the Synoptics has been presupposed. Presumably the same could be said of most of the the many nontechnical commentaries that have appeared in the same period. At first glance, the major exception would seem to be the weighty commentary of M.-E. Boismard and A. Lamouille,[95] according to which the evangelist first composed his gospel on the basis of other traditional sources and later revised it in the light of the Synoptics.

---

16 (1969–70): 130–48. In Becker's subsequent *Forschungsbericht*, "Aus der Literatur zum Johannesevangelium (1978–1980)," 279–301, 305–47, his position on the basic independence of John from the Synoptics becomes clear. See esp. pp. 289–94 on John and the Synoptics; pp. 294–301 on the *semeia* source; and pp. 305–12 on the Johannine community and the relationship of its development to the source problem.

[92] George MacRae, *Invitation to John: A Commentary on the Gospel of John with Complete Text from the Jerusalem Bible* (Garden City, N.Y.: Doubleday & Co., Image Books, 1978), 19.

[93] Robert Kysar, *John*, Augsburg Commentary on the New Testament (Minneapolis: Augsburg Publishing House, 1986), 12.

[94] J. Ramsey Michaels, *John*, Good News Commentary (Hagerstown, Md.: Harper & Row, 1984), xxv.

[95] M.-E. Boismard and A. Lamouille, *L'Evangile de Jean: Commentaire*, vol. 3 of *Synopse des quatres Evangiles en français* (Paris: Editions du Cerf, 1977). See below, chap. 6.

But this theory is, in effect, a complex development of the positions of Bultmann and Brown, both of whom believed the published (canonical) version of the Gospel of John betrays knowledge of the other Gospels in the final stage of its composition only. Moreover, we have been dealing with commentaries that seek to explain the text as a whole. The Boismard-Lamouille volume is both more and less than that, in that the authors are primarily interested in developing a literary theory to explain the Gospel's composition and origin, and the commentary is largely a device through which they do so.

It has now been a decade and a half since Kysar wrote of "the near demise of the proposition that the fourth evangelist was dependent on one or more of the synoptic gospels."[96] Kysar himself later writes that although ten years previously one could speak with some confidence of a tendency to deny John's dependence on the Synoptics and of a consensus on their independent use of a common tradition, "this tendency toward consensus has been abruptly halted, and the issue . . . is once again a hotly debated question."[97] Nevertheless, as we have seen, in his own more recent commentary Kysar continues to prefer that consensus.

The trend among commentators to deny that John knew or depended upon the Synoptics is significant, but one should not overplay it. On the one hand, it becomes clear that knowledge of the Synoptics directly is a hypothesis unnecessary for the satisfactory explanation of the sense of the Gospel. On the other, it is also true that no one attempts to explain John without reference to the Synoptics. Obviously there is an identity of subject matter, Jesus, and a considerable overlap in the presentation of him. There is a difficulty, however, in the application of the redaction-critical method, if John's knowledge of the Synoptics is invoked. Once Matthew's or Luke's knowledge and use of Mark is acknowledged and made a working hypothesis for exegesis, one can rather easily see how the later authors have understood, appropriated, or at some place suppressed the work of the earlier. If, however, one adopts the working hypothesis that John knew the Synoptic Gospels, or even Mark alone, the principles by which he decided to appropriate or delete their specific narratives, as distinguished from the content of tradition they embody, are not at all obvious. In fact, his appropriation, or lack of appropriation, of the Synoptics is in large part impossible to fathom. While one may object to the positing of otherwise unknown sources of the Gospel of John, it is not the case that any hypothetical element is removed by assuming John's use of the Synoptics. On

---

[96] Kysar, *The Fourth Evangelist and His Gospel*, 55.
[97] Kysar, "The Gospel of John in Current Research," 316.

the contrary, explanations of John's use or disuse of the Synoptics, or the assumption of the evangelist's knowledge of them, are themselves quite hypothetical, and the number of possible interpretations of such use or disuse seems almost infinite.

## Works Dealing with Johannine Narratives and Other Relevant Scholarship

The search for John's narrative sources has led to conclusions similar to those of the commentaries. In important monographs separated by almost two decades, Robert T. Fortna has analyzed the Johannine narratives with a view to identifying the source material the evangelist used and understanding his method in using it. In the first, *The Gospel of Signs,* Fortna took his start from Bultmann's work and revised and refined the latter's arguments, relying more heavily on contextual clues (traces of redactional activity) and less on stylistic and particularly theological differentia.[98] In the second book, *The Fourth Gospel and Its Predecessor,* Fortna developed his method and results by focusing on the evangelist's use of his source in developing his distinctive theological perspective.[99] This is not the place for a detailed summary and review of Fortna's work, but his conclusions are worth noting. By means of intense exegetical scrutiny, Fortna reconstructs a series of narratives, including a passion (and resurrection) narrative, that exhibit general and generic similarities to the synoptic narratives, but do not seem to have been derived from them. It is important to notice that Fortna did not set out to demonstrate John's independence from the Synoptic Gospels. Arguably, he was influenced by the emerging consensus on this point, but his own methodology and work were not governed by that consensus. At most, they could be construed as confirmation of it. Even if one is not convinced by the more hypothetical aspect of Fortna's thesis, namely, that the source material he identified had already been assembled into a Gospel of Signs—a primitive gospel narrative held to be authoritative by the evangelist, a narrative that Fortna essays to reconstruct—

---

[98] Robert Tomson Fortna, *The Gospel of Signs: A Reconstruction of the Narrative Source Underlying the Fourth Gospel,* SNTSMS 11 (Cambridge: Cambridge University Press, 1970). Originally a dissertation with J. Louis Martyn, Fortna's work was completed before the publication of the first edition of Martyn's own book (see n. 100 below) in 1968 but was published a couple of years later.

[99] Robert Tomson Fortna, *The Fourth Gospel and Its Predecessor: From Narrative Source to Present Gospel* (Philadelphia: Fortress Press, 1988).

the seriousness and objectivity of his exegetical work cannot be ignored. The inherent plausibility of some such primitive gospel narrative does not depend on all the details of Fortna's reconstruction.

J. Louis Martyn, in his important work, *History and Theology in the Fourth Gospel,* cautiously correlated Fortna's Gospel of Signs with his own view of the Jewish, synagogal milieu and origin of the Fourth Gospel. According to Martyn, something like the Gospel of Signs was the gospel or missionary tract of followers of Jesus within the synagogue. Because of their success, hostility against them arose, and they were ultimately expelled. The traces of that struggle and expulsion from synagogues can be clearly seen in the present text of the Gospel of John (9:22; 12:42; 16:2). Moreover, Martyn also thinks it highly unlikely that the fourth evangelist had at his disposal one or more of the Synoptic Gospels.[100]

W. Nicol, in another attempt to characterize the signs source, recognizes the problem Fortna encounters in trying to delineate it so precisely.[101] Nevertheless he agrees in principle that John used an independent miracle tradition and that in all probability it came into his hands in written form. Like Fortna, Nicol places the source against the background of Jewish expectations and theology. Jesus is not presented as a Hellenistic *theios anēr* (divine man). Subsequently, Urban C. Von Wahlde has set about on a similar task and has offered yet another reconstruction of the Gospel of Signs based on criteria different from Fortna's or Nicol's.[102] Von Wahlde's primitive gospel is not, however, confined to narrative, but includes significant discourse material, in which Jesus' miracles are called signs (rather than works) and his enemies are called Pharisees (rather than Jews).

In fact, since Bultmann, most studies of the Johannine signs have found the Johannine miracle traditions to be independent of the Synoptic Gospels.

---

[100] J. Louis Martyn, *History and Theology in the Fourth Gospel,* rev. ed. (Nashville: Abingdon Press, 1979), 12, 24, 64–65, 164–68, on the relationship of Martyn's thesis to Fortna's work; on Martyn's view that John did not use the Synoptics, see pp. 20–21. As noted above (n. 98), Fortna was Martyn's doctoral student and presumably worked out his dissertation proposal in conversation with him. Martyn clearly regards Fortna's work as profitable and probably correct, while not tying his own thesis to any single source reconstruction.

In Excursus E of the revised (1979) edition of his work (pp. 164–68), Martyn offers a succinct description of the origins of the signs-source hypothesis and assesses its probability as a preface to a bibliography of works in which the question of this source is debated. He concludes (p. 166): "And while it would be highly presumptuous to predict the outcome of the debates, I must say that the Signs Source theory itself seems to enjoy a considerable degree of probability, especially as it has been developed in the extraordinarily careful analysis of Robert T. Fortna."

[101] W. Nicol, *The Sēmeia in the Fourth Gospel: Tradition and Redaction,* NovtSup 32 (Leiden: E. J. Brill, 1972), 5, n.1.

[102] Urban C. Von Wahlde, *The Earliest Version of John's Gospel: Recovering the Gospel of Signs* (Wilmington, Del.: Michael Glazier, 1989).

This is as true of Wilhelm Wilkens's attempt to trace the *Entstehungsgeschichte* of the Fourth Gospel as an internal development in which the evangelist writes and rewrites his own sources as it is of Wolfgang J. Bittner's recent study of the theological significance of the signs in the Gospel of John.[103] In other words, even exegetes who reject the signs source hypothesis are not inclined to derive the Johannine miracles from the synoptic.

Such source theories as those of Wilkens, Fortna, Nicol, and Von Wahlde obviously minimize, if they do not in principle exclude, John's knowledge of the Synoptic Gospels. We cannot consider all the monographic or journal literature that in one way or another touches upon the problem; our purpose is to examine works that focus directly and primarily upon it. Nevertheless several other scholars, who are representative of the scope and range of work that is implicated in the problem of John and the Synoptics deserve to be noted, in part because they are so different in their purpose and conclusions.

Günter Reim's study of the Old Testament background of the Gospel of John[104] is devoted to a wide spectrum of relevant matters but particularly to the Old Testament quotations and their sources. After examining each Old Testament quotation closely, Reim concludes that in no case did John derive such a quotation from the Synoptic Gospels.[105] The fact that John employs some of the same, as well as closely related, scriptural quotations that are used by other gospel and New Testament authors, means only that they have drawn on a common or similar tradition. The lack of clear evidence for John's

---

[103] Wilhelm Wilkens's Basel dissertation, *Die Entstehungsgeschichte des vierten Evangeliums* (Zollikon: Evangelischer Verlag, 1958), was followed more than a decade later by the same author's *Zeichen und Werke: Ein Beitrag zur Theologie des vierten Evangeliums in Erzählungs- und Redestoff*, ATANT 55 (Zurich: Zwingli Verlag, 1969), in which Wilkens maintains his earlier view of the development of the Fourth Gospel and elaborates on the signs, particularly as they relate to the discourses and passion in the evangelist's theology. In a strictly formal sense, Wilkens's position is not unlike Fortna's.

The recent work of Wolfgang J. Bittner, *Jesu Zeichen im Johannesevangelium: Die Messias-Erkenntis im Johannesevangelium vor ihrem jüdischen Hintergrund*, WUNT 26 (Tübingen: J. C. B. Mohr [Paul Siebeck], 1987), is devoted to the theological significance of signs in the Fourth Gospel, not to the source problem. Nevertheless he rejects all signs-source proposals (pp. 2–14). On the other hand, Bittner understands the Johannine miracle tradition to have had its life and origin from within the Johannine school, not to have been merely derivative from the Synoptics (pp. 205–08).

[104] Günter Reim, *Studien zum alttestamentlichen Hintergrund des Johannesevangeliums*, SNTSMS 22 (Cambridge: Cambridge University Press, 1974).

[105] Ibid., p. 92. In this respect Reim's conclusions differ significantly from those of his predecessor, Edwin D. Freed, *Old Testament Quotations in the Gospel of John*, NovtSup 11 (Leiden: E. J. Brill, 1965), still a very useful book for its presentation of the textual evidence from LXX, MT, and Targum. Barnabas Lindars, in his review of Reim (*JTS* [1975]: 165–67), speaks of the latter's work as having superseded Freed's. Earlier, Charles Goodwin, "How Did John Treat His Sources?" *JBL* 73 (1954): 61–75, had argued that John's loose quotation of the Scriptures was paralleled by his loose use of the Synoptic Gospels (esp. pp. 74–75).

use of the Synoptics for this purpose evidently leads Reim to offer proposals about the sources and composition history of the Fourth Gospel. In his view, John drew not upon the Synoptics but upon a signs source for miracle tradition, and also upon what Reim describes as a Fourth Synoptic Gospel, from which he obtained his passion tradition as well as some other synoptic-like material. It cannot be said that Reim devotes the same attention to this question that he does to the Old Testament quotations.[106] Nevertheless the impression that he has derived from that research is of some significance, and his own proposals bear a certain similarity to those of other scholars, such as Fortna and Haenchen.

Entirely different from Reim's work and opposed to his source-critical conclusions is the magnum opus of John A. T. Robinson, *The Priority of John*.[107] Robinson does not end, but begins, with the conclusion of Gardner-Smith, Dodd, and others that the Gospel of John is independent of the Synoptics. This position is not surprising in view of his title and his earlier work *Redating the New Testament*.[108] In the more recent book, Robinson is not concerned to show that John is prior to, in the sense of the source of, the other Gospels. Rather, the priority of John means the Fourth Gospel's independence of the others, and Robinson argues that John's witness, even and particularly his historial witness, should not be taken to be secondary to the Synoptics or judged in the light of them. The arguments for John's independence have been made by Gardner-Smith, and the evidence presented exhaustively by Dodd, so that Robinson can, for example, simply ask why John, had he known Mark, omitted such events as the rending of the temple veil, the centurion's confession of Jesus as Son of God, or the darkness at noon at Jesus' crucifixion.[109] John's ignorance of the Synoptics is the most obvious explanation. Robinson seems more interested in calling Fortna's source-criticism into question than in beating such a dead horse, although, of course, he and Fortna agree that the narratives of the Gospel of John were not derived from the Synoptic Gospels. That Robinson was interested in making a case for John as an independent theological and historical witness is plain enough; he is quite explicit about this. His argument is also clearly driven by his perception of

---

[106] For Reim's discussion of the "Fourth Synoptic Gospel" and the composition history of the Fourth Gospel, see his *Studien*, 209ff. and 233–45.

[107] John A. T. Robinson, *The Priority of John*, ed. J. F. Coakley (London: SCM Press, 1985). The book waited two years for publication in the United States (Oak Park, Ill.: Meyer-Stone Books, 1987).

[108] John A. T. Robinson, *Redating the New Testament* (Philadelphia: Westminster Press, 1976), 254–311, on the dating of the Gospel of John.

[109] Cf. Robinson, *The Priority of John*, 10–13, on the independence of John.

the fragility of common views or assumptions regarding the secondary character of the Gospel of John. Therefore it is all the more noteworthy that he regards John's independence as one of the relatively few established results of criticism. Of course, John's independence supports, or is the necessary ground or corollary of, Robinson's work. (On the other hand, one cannot accuse Robinson of defending early church traditions, according to which the Fourth Gospel was later than the others and, in a significant sense, presumed them.) It is at least equally possible—and fairer—to suppose that Robinson's position developed on the basis of his having become convinced of John's independence of the Synoptics.

Because Robinson's work is widely regarded as extreme or eccentric, his testimony is not likely to carry much weight in many quarters. His view on the relationship of John to the Synoptics was, of course, much closer to the mainstream of scholarship than his own distinctive position. Certainly the mainstream of Johannine scholarship contains a variety of tributaries and eddies; there is scarcely unanimity.[110] Nevertheless there has been a wide consensus on such things as the likelihood that the Gospel of John represents a distinct form of early Christianity arising out of a Johannine circle or community and that this community possessed traditions about Jesus independent

---

[110] A couple of other works that deal with, or turn upon, our question deserve mention. In his monograph on the literary origin and sources of the Gospel of John, Howard Teeple devotes a chapter to the question of John and the Synoptics: *The Literary Origin of the Gospel of John* (Evanston, Ill.: Religion and Ethics Institute, 1974), 59–83. His concluding statement (p. 82) has proven correct: "The variety of opinion on the relation of John to the Synoptics indicates that this problem is not yet solved." Teeple's discussion of this issue is mainly a *Forschungsbericht*, in which the opinions of many scholars are mentioned and evaluated. Unfortunately it is marred by two recurrent features: (1) brevity, which makes accurate summation difficult, if not impossible; and (2) the author's consistent tendency to attribute the opinions of those who espouse the independence of the Fourth Gospel to their conservative bias. Thus the view that John draws upon a tradition (often described as oral) independent of the Synoptics is allegedly motivated by a desire to preserve its historicity. How then are the conservative Zahn and the church fathers found among those who acknowledge John's use of the Synoptics while Morton Smith and Erwin R. Goodenough, scarcely "conservatives," are among those who insist on the importance of oral tradition and John's independence of the Synoptics? His apparent animus against those who espouse John's independence notwithstanding, Teeple's own literary theory ascribes little by way of dependence to the Synoptic Gospels. His S (narrative) source looks more than anything else like Fortna's *Gospel of Signs*.

Sydney Temple's effort to extract an earlier core gospel, consisting of both narrative and discourse, from the Gospel of John was, perhaps not surprisingly, predicated on the assumption of the Gospel's independence of the Synoptics. See *The Core of the Fourth Gospel* (London and Oxford: A. R. Mowbray & Co., 1975). He quotes to good effect Archibald M. Hunter's judgment that on the question of their relationship, Gardner-Smith has become the new critical orthodoxy (see below, p. 139). Temple is quite clear in his intention to find an original, historically valuable, gospel-like narrative at the basis of the Gospel of John, thus fulfilling Teeple's worst fears—in this case justifiable! See the temperate but negative reviews by Barnabas Lindars: of Teeple, *JTS* 26 (1975): 167; of Temple, *JTS* (1976): 456–58.

of, if not unrelated to, the synoptic. Such consensus embraces scholars as different and distinctive in outlook as Ernst Käsemann, Oscar Cullmann, and Georg Richter.

In his much discussed work *The Testament of Jesus,* Käsemann is little concerned with questions of source and redaction. He does, however, assume that the Gospel of John is representative of a type of early Christian community that was charismatic, or Spirit-inspired, and opposed to the emerging early catholic orthodoxy of the end of the first century. (In a quite real sense John was swimming against the stream.) Nevertheless, in writing an account of Jesus' earthly ministry John could not dispense with traditions, and we should not be surprised to find that he made use of them.

> More astonishing is the fact that John, living at the end of the first century and situated, it would seem, not too far from Palestine, possibly in Syria, in all probability does not know the Synoptics themselves, but rather a tradition whose purer and more original form is preserved in the Synoptics, and which is known to him in a version which has to some extent run wild.[111]

Both components of the scholarly consensus of which we have spoken are represented here: John is representative of a distinctive Christian community and employs in his gospel that community's Jesus traditions.

Oscar Cullmann, scarcely Käsemann's ally in either exegesis or theology, nevertheless espouses a general viewpoint that is remarkably similar in a couple of important respects. Toward the latter part of a career that already covered almost a half century, Cullmann wrote in *The Johannine Circle* what he conceived of as his introduction to commentary or, as he put it, "prelude to exegesis." The title already reveals Cullmann's basic assessment of Johannine origins; the Gospel arose out of a distinctive Christian community. As to John's use or disuse of the Synoptic Gospels or synoptic tradition, Cullmann is brief and to the point:

> As the Gospel of John has a number of features in common with the synoptic gospels, and especially with Luke, the first question is whether the author knew them or at least made use of one or the other of them. To begin with, however, it must be stressed that nowhere, not even in the passion narrative, is the literary affinity so close that a *literary* relationship *has to* be supposed comparable to that which exists between the individual synoptic gospels themselves.[112]

---

[111] Ernst Käsemann, *The Testament of Jesus: A Study of the Gospel of John in the Light of Chapter 17,* trans. Gerhard Krodel (Philadelphia: Fortress Press, 1968), 36.

[112] Oscar Cullmann, *The Johannine Circle,* trans. John Bowden (Philadelphia: Westminster Press, 1976), 5.

After noting a couple of instances in which John seems to presuppose knowledge of the Synoptics (1:40; 3:24), Cullmann concludes that "in each case it is sufficient to assume that the author knew the *tradition* underlying the synoptic gospels, without necessarily referring to the *documents* themselves."[113] In the same context Cullmann goes on to cite the work of such scholars as Gardner-Smith, Dodd, and Fortna.

Not so well known in the English-speaking world, because his work has never been translated, Georg Richter is nevertheless representative of the prevailing continental opinion at the end of the third quarter of the twentieth century. A post-Vatican II Catholic exegete, Richter was more closely attuned to Protestant exegesis than the earlier Rudolf Schnackenburg or Raymond E. Brown. Like Käsemann and Cullmann, he devoted relatively little attention to the question of John's use of the Synoptics, perhaps because he regarded it as settled. To begin with, Richter viewed our present Gospel as the product of more than one hand, indeed, as the fruition of a theological discussion and debate that had gone on within what Cullmann would have called the Johannine circle:

> Since, furthermore, each of these authors did not write from an academic ivory tower (*vom grünen Tisch aus*) but out of the concrete situation of a community (or a group of communities) and is to be viewed as its representative, one can recognize in the process of the literary development of the Gospel of John—or more broadly viewed in the literary levels of the Gospel and Epistles of John— also a significant portion of the church history and theological history of the Johannine communities.[114]

The bottom layer of the development that Richter envisions was a *Grundschrift*—Richter hesitates to call it a gospel because it seems to lack Jesus' teaching—independent of the Synoptics. This document was the product of a Jewish-Christian community that had been expelled from the synagogue (9:22; 12:42) and in this document sought to define itself over against its adversaries:

---

[113] Ibid., 6.

[114] Georg Richter, "Präsentische und futuristische Eschatologie im 4. Evangelium," *Studien zum Johannesevangelium*, ed. Josef Hainz (Regensburg: Friedrich Pustet, 1977), 354. (Translation mine.) Richter died, tragically, in 1975 at the age of fifty-six. This book is a posthumous collection of his articles, which had appeared between 1962 and 1976. The essay on present and future eschatology was published in 1975 in *Gegenwart und kommendes Reich: Schülergabe Anton Vögtle zum 65. Geburtstag*, ed. Peter Fiedler and Dieter Zeller (Stuttgart: Katholisches Bibelwerk, 1975), 117–52. There is a useful, extensive summary of this article by A. J. Mattill, Jr., "Johannine Communities Behind the Fourth Gospel: George Richter's Analysis," *Theological Studies 38* (1977): 294–315.

The author of this document had from the Christian tradition available to him sought out the material most suitable to his purpose and interpreted it afresh in the sense of his intention. This tradition was that of his community, and despite many similarities to the synoptic was identical neither with the Synoptic Gospels nor with the tradition used by the synoptic authors.[115]

Again we see both components of a consensus: a Johannine community and a gospel tradition distinctive of it. Actually, the two go together and are fundamental to Richter's perspective. The impression that the Fourth Gospel is a community product suggests that it is based upon a distinctive and relatively independent tradition. It is not surprising then that the recently renewed espousal of John's dependence upon the Synoptic Gospels has been accompanied by a recession of interest in, if not the denial of, a Johannine community.

The Bultmannian tradition of John's independence of the Synoptics, formulated quite independently of Anglo-Saxon scholarship, has in a sense been carried forward by Haenchen and Käsemann, although their grasp of the theology and literary history of the Fourth Gospel is not dependent on Bultmann's work. Perhaps James M. Robinson's 1968 essay "The Johannine Trajectory" extends the position of Bultmann in ways most compatible with his perspective on a number of fronts, not just with respect to the question of John and the Synoptics.[116] Robinson wants to see John and the Synoptics as representing, or moving along, two separate trajectories as the result of common forces or impulses in the development of early Christianity. While Robinson devotes most of the essay to defending the signs-source hypothesis and early Gnosticism as ingredient to any proper understanding of the origin and character of the Fourth Gospel, John's independence of the Synoptics is a fundamental tenet or corollary of his position. If the Gospel of John were simply a development of, or Midrash on, the Synoptics, the nerve of Robinson's approach would be cut. The independence of John is ingredient to the notion of a Johannine trajectory.

---

[115]Richter, "Präsentische und futuristische Eschatologie im 4. Evangelium," 355. On the original Johannine community's exclusion from the synagogue, see also pp. 401–4. Curiously, Richter seems to mention Martyn's *History and Theology in the Fourth Gospel* only in connection with Fortna's source hypothesis or in a rather critical way.

[116] James M. Robinson, "The Johannine Trajectory," in *Trajectories Through Early Christianity,* James M. Robinson, with Helmut Koester (Philadelphia: Fortress Press, 1971), 232–68; see esp. pp. 234–35, 266–68, on the question of John and the Synoptics. Cf. also Robinson's "On the Gattung of Mark (and John)," in *Jesus and Man's Hope* (Pittsburgh Theological Seminary 1970), 1:99–129. On the question of the *Gattung* "gospel," which Robinson raises in an acute way, see now the article of Johannes Beutler, "Literarische Gattungen im Johannesevangelium: Ein Forschungsbericht 1919–1980," in *Aufstieg und Niedergang der römischen Welt,* ed. H. Temporini and W. Hasse (Berlin: Walter de Gruyter), II.25.3 (1985), 2506–68.

*Introductions*

As a rule, introductions move in the wake of research published in monographs, periodicals, and even commentaries, and appropriately so. We have already noted that at the beginning of this century introductions reflected the critical consensus of the time that John knew and used the Synoptics. Do introductions indicate that there is now a new critical consensus, or has such a consensus already come and gone? To discuss the treatment of John and the Synoptics in all introductions and introductory books, even those of the past couple of decades, would require the extension of this survey beyond all practical limits. Nevertheless it will be useful to see where the issue now stands in representative works.

In the English-speaking world, the most influential introduction to appear after Moffatt but before the translation of W. G. Kümmel was A. H. McNeile's *An Introduction to the Study of the New Testament,* revised by C. S. C. Williams in 1953.[117] In that revised edition, Gardner-Smith's work, as well as Windisch's, is taken into account, but the balance struck between independence and the older view of John's cognizance of the Synoptics tilts in favor of the latter: "But it would be surprising that none of the synoptic gospels should have been known to a writer in Ephesus, or still more in Antioch, at a date at least twenty years after the publication of the earliest of them; and of course the earlier they were dated the more surprising it becomes."[118] Given Williams's assumptions about date and place of origin, his conclusion is not surprising. About a decade later, Robert M. Grant leaves open the question of John's knowledge of the Synoptics and possible use of them as sources but is apparently inclined to regard John as independent, inasmuch as he dates the Gospel soon after A.D. 70.[119] Similarly, Willi Marxsen without really discussing the question assumes John's independence of the Synoptics.[120] But about a decade later Norman Perrin in his introduction remains unconvinced of John's independence of Mark particularly.[121] Moreover, Kümmel's *Introduction,* considered a standard work in both the German- and English-speaking worlds,

---

[117] A. H. McNeile, *An Introduction to the Study of the New Testament* (Oxford: Clarendon Press, 1927). On John and the Synoptics the revised edition by C. S. C. Williams (Oxford: Clarendon Press, 1953) expands upon the 1927 original, largely by way of dealing with Gardner-Smith's book, which had appeared subsequently.

[118] Ibid., 269–70.

[119] Robert M. Grant, *A Historical Introduction to the New Testament* (New York: Harper & Row, 1963), 154–55, 159–60.

[120] Willi Marxsen, *Introduction to the New Testament: An Approach to Its Problems,* trans. G. Buswell (Philadelphia: Fortress Press, 1968 [from the 3d, 1964, German ed.]), 251–60.

[121] Norman Perrin, *The New Testament, An Introduction: Proclamation and Parenesis, Myth and History,* rev. ed. Dennis C. Duling (New York: Harcourt Brace Jovanovich, 1982), 334. The revised edition by Duling nuances the question a bit more but maintains Perrin's position (of 1974). Both Perrin and Duling allow for the evangelist's use of a signs source as well as Mark. On Perrin's argument that John used Mark's passion narrative, see below, pp. 113–14.

stands by the older view that the fourth evangelist certainly knew Mark and very likely knew Luke as well. Kümmel weighs the evidence of agreement and dissimilarity and emphasizes the parallel sequences of scenes (or brief historical notes) in John and Mark as well as the several instances of verbatim agreement. Moreover, the presence of some of the same persons (Mary, Martha, Lazarus, Annas), similarities in numerous details, and particularly common features of the anointing stories convince Kümmel that the fourth evangelist knew Luke. In any case, knowledge of the Synoptics as a genre must be presupposed for the composition of John to be intelligible.[122] Thus it can scarcely be said that modern critical introductions published since World War II have embraced the view that John is independent of the Synoptics. On the contrary, two weightier introductions by Protestant scholars, McNeile and Kümmel, are both inclined in the opposite direction, McNeile somewhat cautiously and Kümmel more emphatically.

Among introductions by Catholic scholars, the earlier editions of Alfred Wikenhauser's work were judiciously neutral on the question of John's use of the Synoptics, although the author notes that most exegetes assume that the fourth evangelist knew Mark and probably Matthew or Luke as well.[123] The later edition which was thoroughly reworked by Josef Schmid takes an even more finely nuanced position. Schmid is cognizant of the work of Gardner-Smith, Dodd, Noack, Bultmann, Haenchen, and others, without coming down decisively on their side. On the one hand, he shows a very good grasp of the reasons for thinking that John is independent of the Synoptics. On the other, he concedes that John must have at least been aware of the synoptic tradition, although he may not have had it in the form in which we find it in the Gospels.[124] In the massive introduction edited by A. Robert and A. Feuillet, John's independence of the Synoptics is described as the view of Bultmann and Gardner-Smith. Most scholars, it is said, disagree with them, and one at first has the impression that Feuillet (who writes this section of the book) numbers himself among them. Yet he goes on to suggest that "what John knows, or supposes that his readers will know, is perhaps the great living

---

[122] Werner George Kümmel, *Introduction to the New Testament*, rev. ed. trans. Howard Clark Kee (Nashville: Abingdon Press, 1975), 201–4. In the most recent German edition, revised in 1978 and reissued with an extensive bibliographical apppendix in 1983, Kümmel's position remains unchanged: *Einleitung in das Neue Testament*, 19th ed. (Heidelberg: Quelle & Meyer, 1983), 167–70.

[123] Alfred Wikenhauser, *New Testament Introduction*, trans. Joseph Cunningham (New York: Herder & Herder, 1958 [German, 1956]), 301.

[124] Alfred Wikenhauser and Josef Schmid, *Einleitung in das Neue Testament*, 6th, revised ed. (Freiburg: Herder, 1973), 317–21.

tradition rather than written works."[125] John draws upon a parallel and contemporary tradition, in certain respects earlier. Quite conceivably, the Johannine tradition has influenced, as well as having been influenced by, the synoptic. In particular, there was probably some Johannine influence upon Luke.

Among more recent introductions, Luke T. Johnson discusses the relationship between John and the Synoptics theologically, without explicitly deciding the question of literary dependency. He does, however, agree with the traditional view that John supplements the Synoptics, in the sense of offering a theological interpretation of their story of Jesus.[126] Raymond F. Collins's *Introduction to the New Testament*, which bears the Nihil Obstat and Imprimatur, is thoroughly abreast of the latest methods of criticism and interpretation. Indeed, it is a helpful classification and compendium of them. Because of Collins's method-oriented approach, the question of the relationship of John and the Synoptics does not receive extensive treatment. Nevertheless he can tersely summarize the present state of the problem:

> Since Gardner-Smith's *St. John and the Synoptic Gospels* appeared in 1938, there has been a growing consensus on John's independence of the Synoptics. Demurrers from the consensus have been raised by Frans Neirynck and a number of North American scholars whose redactional studies on Mark have led them to conclude that John knew and used Mark . . . [they] point to the passion narrative as a case in point.[127]

As we shall see, this remarkably brief statement is accurate in all its aspects.

Conservative Protestant opinion, as represented by the work of the British scholar Donald Guthrie, continues to support what Windisch described as the supplementation theory, as did Theodor Zahn nearly a century ago. The independence theory is said to be problematic for a number of reasons. For example, "It is extremely difficult . . . to see why John should omit all direct reference to the ordinances [sacraments] if he were ignorant of the other Gospels."[128] Moreover, if John is considered to be relatively late, it is hard to imagine a historical situation in which the Synoptics would not be known. Guthrie maintains that this difficulty has led scholars who advocate independence to propose an early date for John. Perhaps so, but Goodenough,

---

[125] A. Robert and A. Feuillet, *Introduction to the New Testament*, trans. P. W. Skehan et al. (New York: Desclée, 1965), 663.

[126] Luke T. Johnson, *The Writings of the New Testament: An Interpretation* (Philadelphia: Fortress Press, 1986), 474.

[127] Raymond F. Collins, *Introduction to the New Testament* (London: SCM Press, 1983), 146.

[128] Donald Guthrie, *New Testament Introduction*, 3d ed. (Downer's Grove, Ill.: Inter-Varsity Press, 1971), 298; cf. 287–300.

whom Guthrie cites as postulating an early date for John to *avoid* the problem of why he did not know the Synoptics, actually argues somewhat differently. That John did not know the Synoptics is a part of his overall argument that John was a primitive gospel. But the position that John is primitive was scarcely forced on him on account of his view of the independence of John. It would be more accurate to say that John's independence of the Synoptics opens the way for an earlier dating. A conservative American scholar, Everett F. Harrison, in his introduction acknowledges a movement of opinion in the direction of John's independence but also continues to prefer the view that John was written later than the Synoptics and with cognizance of them.[129] Is it the case that conservative opinion resists the view that John wrote in complete independence of the Synoptics and insists that the Fourth Gospel is relatively late?

The most recent full-scale scholarly introduction in the modern Protestant, continental tradition, published first in German and subsequently in English, comes down on the side of John's independence of the Synoptic Gospels.[130] Perhaps Helmut Koester's work marks the entry of the independence theory into standard introductions. Yet Koester does not base his view of John's independence so much on earlier scholarly demonstrations as on his own observations. John's Gospel is the product of a Syrian Christian tradition, independent of, but not completely isolated from, the tradition now found in the Synoptics.

For Koester, the evidence of John's relation to tradition found in the apocryphal gospels is of fundamental importance.[131] The account of the raising of the young man in Clement's *Secret Gospel of Mark* is obviously parallel to the raising of Lazarus in John 11. Yet the story is relatively free of Johannine redactional elements, indicating that the *Secret Gospel* did not receive it from John. It is a variant, not a derivative, form of the Johannine story. The Passion narrative of the *Gospel of Peter* contains features that can be traced back to a state in the development of the passion narrative and the story of the empty tomb that is older than that represented by the canonical Gospels.[132] It is interesting that the *Gospel of Peter* agrees with John, against the other gospels, that Jesus was crucified the day before the feast. John, Mark, and Peter bear

---

[129] Everett F. Harrison, *Introduction to the New Testament*, rev. ed. (Grand Rapids: Wm B. Eerdmans Publishing Co., 1971), 216–17.

[130] Helmut Koester, *History and Literature of Early Christianity*, vol. 2: *Introduction to the New Testament* (Philadelphia: Fortress Press, 1982), 178.

[131] Ibid., 49, 168, 183.

[132] Ibid., 163.

witness, independently, to a basic primitive passion narrative.[133] (Therefore, John does not have to rely on Mark for his passion account.) Egerton Papyrus 2 contains two incidents reminiscent of John: a controversy of Jesus with "the rulers of the people" (cf. John 5:39; 5:45; 9:29) and an attempted stoning and arrest of Jesus (cf. John 7:30; 10:31, 39).[134] Despite a certain Johannine coloring in the case of the controversy incident, some typically Johannine terms are missing. In the other instance we have a short report, which the author of John seems to have known. Koester finds it difficult to conceive of the author of Egerton Papyrus 2 having put his text together out of a number of Johannine (and synoptic) passages, as must have happened if that apocryphal fragment is viewed as derivative from the canonical Gospels. If anything, the opposite is the case. Finally, Koester concedes that some direct contact between John and the Synoptics may have occurred, but only at the final, redactional stage in the development of John's Gospel.[135] One recalls that assimilation to the Synoptics had been one of the aims and results of the editorial work of the ecclesiastical redaction proposed by Bultmann as of Brown's final edition. Ironically, the unequivocal espousal of the independence theory in a major introduction came just at the time when the consensus in favor of it was being sharply challenged in some quarters.

Obviously, we have not attempted to make a thorough survey of commentaries on John and introductions to the New Testament, much less other works that might be cited. Our sampling is, however, representative of the present state of the question. As we have observed, the vast majority of recent commentaries represent the consensus attained in the 1960s that John does not depend upon the Synoptic Gospels per se, although he at least knew traditions similar to those found in the Synoptics. Thus the kind of redaction-critical analysis of John's narrative represented by Benjamin W. Bacon's exegesis in the earlier part of this century or Frans Neirynck's today is relatively rare. The perspectives of Käsemann, Cullmann, or Richter are still more typical of the present state of affairs in Johannine exegesis. With respect to introductions, the situation is distinctly different. Kümmel's *Introduction*, widely regarded as the standard in English as well as in German, forthrightly asserts John's knowledge of at least Mark and Luke. Otherwise, opinions vary widely. The statement found in Howard Clark Kee's widely used textbook is typical of our present situation:

> Although it is clear that John did not depend directly on Mark for his major source and structure, as did Matthew and Luke, the general pattern of a Gospel

---

[133] Ibid., 163, 167.
[134] Ibid., 182.
[135] Ibid., 178.

and even the broad sweep of Mark's narrative seem to have had an important influence on John. But since with few exceptions, John's content is wholly independent of Mark, on what sources is it likely that John drew?[136]

Kee goes on to reject source theories generally, so that in principle there is no answer to his question, and the reader puzzles over the assertion that Mark has had an important influence on John when the Fourth Gospel's content is, with a few exceptions, largely independent of it. Thomas S. Kuhn, in *The Structure of Scientific Revolutions* (Chicago: University of Chicago Press, 1962), speaks of established scientific models or paradigms being taught in textbooks. If John's independence of the Synoptics (or, indeed, his dependence upon them) is a scientific paradigm, it has not been established in the sense that it is generally stated in standard textbooks. Nevertheless John's independence is the working premise of most commentaries. Certainly there has been a consensus that has dominated commentaries and exegesis. At length it began to turn up in introductions, just as it came under fire. Perhaps this last state of affairs is mirrored in the passage just cited, where Mark's influence upon John is affirmed in one statement but John's independence of Mark's content in the next!

---

[136] Howard Clark Kee, *Understanding the New Testament*, 4th ed. (Englewood Cliffs, N.J.: Prentice-Hall, 1983), 155. John Ashton, *Understanding the Fourth Gospel* (Oxford: Clarendon Press, 1991), takes a position similar to Kee's, on the one hand accepting John's knowledge of at least Mark (p. 81), but on the other making little of this in his presentation of the Gospel's development and thought.

# 4

## *John and Luke:*
## *A Parallel Consensus*

As we have observed, the problem of John and the Synoptics is often thought of principally in terms of John and Mark. Obviously Benjamin W. Bacon thought of it in this way. He and scholars such as Streeter, Barrett, and Kümmel are inclined to say that John certainly knew Mark, probably knew Luke, and possibly knew Matthew, although the last is much less certain.[1] The reasons for this order of probability are not far to seek. Most of John's agreements with Mark are also agreements with Matthew. Because Mark is generally regarded as the source of Matthew, and a couple of decades earlier, it seems reasonable to suppose that Mark is the source of their agreement. There are some subtle agreements or points of contact between John and Matthew only, but the points of agreement between Matthew and John in order of episodes or events and in verbatim wording are as a rule also points of agreement with Mark.

Possibly the fact that scholars are accustomed to finding in Mark the source of Matthew and of Luke inclines them to prefer Mark as the source of John. If Mark was so widely used as to influence two later Gospels, why not all three? Yet this tilting toward Mark squares well with the evidence as well as with the supposed historical situation. John may have used Matthew as well

---

[1] Thus Kümmel, *Introduction to the New Testament*, 204; Barrett, *The Gospel According to St. John*, 2d ed., 42–54, esp. 45–46; earlier, J. H. Bernard, *A Critical and Exegetical Commentary on the Gospel According to St. John*, International Critical Commentary (Edinburgh: T & T Clark, 1928), xciv–cxxi; and Streeter, *The Four Gospels*, 396. H. Holtzmann, "Das schriftstellerische Verhältniss des Johannes zu den Synoptikern," *Zeitschrift für wissenschaftliche Theologie* 12 (1869): 69–85, presented a great deal of evidence for what he considered John's literary dependence upon Luke.

as Mark, but the evidence is of smaller scope and more ambiguous. As far as the Gospel of Luke is concerned, there is a somewhat different state of affairs. Where the Gospels are parallel, longer verbatim agreements are fewer between John and Luke than between John and Mark, or Matthew for that matter. (Of course, by the same token the verbatim agreements between Luke and Mark are fewer than those between Matthew and Mark.) On the other hand, there are a number of other kinds of agreements or points of contact between John and Luke. These fuel the problem of the relationship between John and Luke specifically as a special field of study.

To characterize these agreements or points of contact generally or briefly is difficult, for they are of different sorts. As we have said, they are not for the most part agreements of wording. In some cases there are agreements of order. But for the most part what is in view is shared perspective, knowledge, or information, whether derived from direct literary contact or from common sources. In not a few cases the agreement is a matter of a common silence or suppression of information, or departures from what we find in the other Gospels. Some specific examples will be helpful. Neither John nor Luke forthrightly states that Jesus was baptized in the River Jordan by John (cf. Mark 1:9; Matt. 3:13), although Luke does refer to his baptism (Luke 3:21), which John does not mention. Both Mark and Matthew portray Jesus beginning his ministry with the announcement that the kingdom of God is at hand (Mark 1:15; Matt. 4:17; cf. the similar proclamation of John the Baptist in Matt. 3:2), but neither John nor Luke describes his message in this way. The stories of Jesus calling disciples are remarkably similar in Mark (1:16–20) and Matthew (4:18–22), but quite different in Luke (5:1–11) and John (1:35–42), although Luke and John also differ from each other. In fact, the Lukan call story is strangely paralleled by John's account of the appearance of the risen Jesus by the Sea of Galilee (John 21:1–14). Neither John nor Luke recounts a second miraculous feeding of a multitude, this time of only four thousand, as do Matthew and Mark. Nor do Luke or John describe a formal, nocturnal trial of Jesus before the Sanhedrin (Mark 14:53–65; Matt. 26:57–68), although Luke (Luke 22:66–71) contains elements of the Markan account and John gives evidence that he knows of it (John 18:24).

Some of the same personages are mentioned in Luke and John. The sisters Mary and Martha appear only in these two Gospels (e.g., Luke 10:38–42; John 11:1–44; 12:1–8), as does Lazarus (Luke 16:19–31; John 11:1–44; 12:1–11). Of course, it is only in John that Lazarus appears as a real person—rather than a parabolic character (Luke 16:19–31)—the brother of Mary and Martha. Similarly, only John and Luke think that Annas, as well as Caiaphas, might have been high priest at or about the time of Jesus' death (John 18:12–

24; cf. Luke 3:2; Acts 4:6). Although the Gamaliel of Acts 5 and the Nicodemus of John 3 are not the same person, they are both described as prominent Jewish teachers, and both in effect come to the defense of Jesus or his followers (cf. John 7:50–52).

There are marked similarities unique to Luke and John in the passion narrative. Only in these two Gospels does Pilate not once but three times pronounce Jesus innocent (Luke 23:4; 23:14–15; 23:22; cf. John 18:38; 19:4; 19:6). In Luke, Pilate proposes that he chastise (presumably scourge) Jesus and release him (Luke 23:16, 22), and his soldiers neither mock nor beat Jesus. In Luke (23:11), Jesus is mocked by Herod and his soldiers, and only by them, until the crucifixion (cf. Luke 23:36. According to Mark, followed by Matthew, Jesus is scourged and mocked immediately after Pilate has agreed to the death sentence (Mark 15:15–20; Matt. 27:26–31). John, like Luke, has no scourging or mocking after Pilate accedes to the crowd's demand for Jesus' death. Rather, in John (19:1–3), Jesus is scourged on Pilate's orders and then mocked in the course of the trial just before Pilate pronounces him innocent for the second time. Thus in John as in the suggestion of Pilate in Luke, the scourging represents an alternative to crucifixion, a much milder punishment. Also, in John (18:39–40) as in Luke (23:18–19), Barabbas is first mentioned by the crowd and then briefly described as a kind of after-thought, while in Matthew (27:15–26) and Mark (15:6–15) the governor's custom of releasing a prisoner and the circumstances of Barabbas's impris-onment are related, preparing for the question of Pilate to the crowd about Barabbas. Luke differs from John, however, in that as in the other Synoptics the crowd's choice of Barabbas leads directly to the decision to have Jesus crucified. Although there is no institution of the Lord's Supper in John's narrative of the Last Supper, the foot washing (John 13:1–11) is reasonably presumed to stand in its place. If so, there is a parallel difference in order from the Matthean and Markan accounts, where Jesus identified his betrayer, Judas, who has already connived with the authorities to betray Jesus, before the Last Supper (Mark 14:10–11, 17–21; Matt. 26:14–16, 20–25). In Luke (22:21–23) and John (13:21–30), Jesus identifies his betrayer only after the meal or after the foot washing, which in John takes place in the course of the meal (cf. John 13:2). But John differs from Luke also in that there is no mention of Judas's conniving with the authorities (cf. Luke 22:3–6), and one might infer that John thought it occurred only after Judas had departed from the supper (John 13:27, 30).

Needless to say, the list of the peculiar affinities and agreements between John and Luke could be prolonged and elaborated; these and others have been dealt with by the scholars we shall discuss. Understandably, those scholars who have argued or assumed that John knew Mark have thought it highly probable that he also knew Luke. But relatively few have maintained that he knew Luke but not Mark. Strikingly, Luke's verbatim agreements with John are fewer, particularly at points where Mark has verbatim agreements (see below, p. 102 and p. 105, n. 45). Luke's special material (L) seems not to be explicitly represented in John, although some of Luke's interests, such as Samaritans or the Samaritan mission, clearly are.

Obviously it is neither practical nor possible to review all the work done on John and Luke in this century, or even to touch on everything of significance. We shall attempt to make a representative presentation, discussing works that have raised important questions and offered distinct solutions, beginning with Julius Schniewind in 1914 and coming down to Robert Maddox in the early 1980s. Both, in different ways, represent the dominant position that developed during the middle portion of this century, from Gardner-Smith to Dodd, in that they regard the Gospel of John as importantly related to Luke yet at the same time not demonstrably dependent upon the Third Gospel.

## JULIUS SCHNIEWIND

Already in 1914, in a brief monograph on the parallel pericopes in Luke and John, Julius Schniewind concluded that there was no compelling reason to believe that John was dependent upon Luke.[2] How he came to such a conclusion, differing as it did from the majority opinion of the day, is worth observing. Because he regarded the comparison of the parallel pericopes to be the most urgent task, Schniewind devoted his monograph to a close analysis of agreements and disagreements in the following texts: the Baptist pericope (Luke 3:3–20; John 1:19–34); Peter's catch of fish (Luke 5:1–11/John 21:1–19); the centurion of Capernaum (Luke 7:10/John 4:46–54); the anointing (Luke 7:36–50/John 12:3–8); the entry into Jerusalem (Luke 19:28–40/John 12:12–19); the announcement of the denial (Luke 22:31–34/John 13:36–38); the arrest (Luke 22:39, 47–53/John 18:1–11); the denial of Peter and the trial before the Sanhedrin (Luke 22:54–71/John 18:12–27); the trial before Pilate (Luke 23:1–25/John 18:28—19:16); the crucifixion and burial (Luke 23:26-56/John 19:16–42); and the resurrection reports (Luke 24/John 20). These are not pericopes unique to Luke and John; with the exception of the

---

[2] Julius Schniewind, *Die Parallelperikopen bei Lukas und Johannes* (Hildesheim: G. Olms, 1958), an unaltered reprint of the original edition of 1914.

catch of fish and the Jerusalem appearance scenes, they are found also in the other Gospels. Schniewind is then looking for elements or details of these stories that only John and Luke share, and repeatedly he finds distinctive connections and agreements between John and Luke, which earlier scholars had sometimes observed. It is not surprising that he finds these clustered most thickly in the passion narratives and related material, for in the narrative of the public ministry John differs as much from Luke as from the other Gospels.

A long discussion of the denial of Peter and the Sanhedrin trial is the heart of this slim book.[3] The very fact that there is no formal, nocturnal Sanhedrin trial in either Luke or John is a major agreement of some consequence against Matthew and Mark. Luke, however, seems to use the Markan account, which he alters, while John is independent of it. Moreover, Schniewind finds it noteworthy that both Luke and John contain reports of hearings before Jewish authorities in the second half of the night (John 18:24) or on the following morning (Luke 22:66) and that these reports seem to complement each other. For example, in Luke specific charges emerging from the second meeting are reported to Pilate (Luke 23:2); in John they are not reported as such but are presupposed in the trial before Pilate (John 18:29–30, 33; 19:7). John does, however, report (John 18:24, 28) that Jesus was taken to Caiaphas after the hearing before Annas (a personage otherwise mentioned only in Luke 3:2 and Acts 4:6). Thus the Lukan and Johannine reports are complementary, for John's assumptions regarding the Jewish authorities' charges against Jesus point to his knowledge of an account of some sort of arraignment of Jesus before Caiaphas, which he mentions but does not relate. Luke's bare mention of Jesus being taken to the house of the high priest (Luke 22:54) is perhaps a vestigial trace of the Annas hearing in the Third Gospel. There is no mention of Annas or Caiaphas in Luke's pericope and indeed no account of a hearing. That hearing seems to have fallen out of the Lukan narrative, so that the denial scene becomes a unity in Luke (22:54–62), although it is not in John (18:15–18, 25-27). John's account of the Annas hearing (18:12–14, 19–24) makes Luke's mention of Jesus having been taken to the high priest's house intelligible.

Schniewind proposes on the basis of this sort of evidence, in which the Johannine version makes sense out of the Lukan, that there was a proto-Johannine account of these events available to both Luke and John. Thus a Johannine-sounding response of Jesus (but with no parallel in the Fourth Gospel) is found in Luke's account of the second hearing before Jewish authorities (Luke 22:67–68). (The RSV translates "If I tell you, you will not

---

[3] Ibid., 37–62.

believe; and if I ask you, you will not answer.") According to Schniewind, in this source Jesus was first led to Annas, as John (18:12–14) reports (cf. Luke 22:54). Peter followed him and the first part of his denial of Jesus then occurred (John 18:15–18). There ensued the hearing before Annas (John 18:19–23) and the dispatching of Jesus to Caiaphas (John 18:24; cf. Luke 22:66); next came the conclusion of the denial story and, finally, the hearing before Caiaphas (cf. Luke 22:66–71). Interestingly enough, Luke, who mentions both Annas and Caiaphas as high priests in Luke 3:2, does not name the high priest in reporting this second hearing before Jewish authorities (Luke 22:66–71); probably the appearance of both Annas and Caiaphas in his *Vorlage* had confused him. (Obviously, in omitting the Annas scene, Luke unified Peter's denial into a single scene.) In fact, only Matthew names the high priest of this trial scene Caiaphas (but cf. John 18:24, 28). Obviously, in Schniewind's view John cannot be said to depend upon Luke; the resolution of Lukan-Johannine relationships lies rather at the level of common tradition.

As we have just observed, Schniewind finds that more often than not John seems to reflect an earlier stage of the material common to his gospel and Luke's. In the Lukan account of the Roman trial Pilate says he finds no cause of guilt in Jesus immediately after the latter has responded quite ambiguously ("You say so.") to the question whether he is king of the Jews (Luke 23:4); such a response by Pilate is really inadequately motivated. In John, however, a similar statement by Pilate (John 18:38) occurs only after Jesus has responded fully to that question by way of explaining that his kingship is not of this world (John 18:36). The Johannine account makes the Lukan intelligible. Schniewind again suggests that there was a common tradition which we find in fuller, more satisfactory form in John than in Luke.[4]

Accordingly, the many parallels and contacts do not add up to a case for John's dependence upon Luke or for John's recollection of the other Gospel. Rather, they are the product of a shared oral tradition. Any verbal agreements occur at just those points one would expect in oral tradition, that is, the high points of the narratives. The common tradition of John and Luke can be seen more clearly in the passion narrative, although it is not confined there, as Schniewind argues in the remainder of the monograph.[5] As to John's relation

---

[4] Ibid., 63–64.

[5] Hans Klein, "Die lukanisch-johanneische Passionstradition," *ZNW* 67 (1976): 155–86, has taken up aspects of Schniewind's work, using much of the same evidence to define more precisely the relation of Luke and John in the passion narrative. Klein takes it to be generally agreed that the passion account that John possessed was the most primitive. He argues that Luke had not only the Gospel of Mark but a separate passion tradition showing obvious affinities with the Gospel of John. His investigation of such similarities then leads to the conclusion that Luke and John possessed a common passion source (G = *Grundschrift*), ultimately derived from, but not the same as, the primitive passion source that Mark used. Luke employed Mark (not Mark's source) and G, while John had G only (not Mark or Mark's source).

to the Synoptic Gospels generally, Schniewind will say only that he presupposes them without depending upon them.

## F. C. GRANT

More than twenty years after the appearance of Schniewind's monograph, but apparently without knowledge of it, the American scholar F. C. Grant published an important article in which he asked, "Was the author of John dependent upon the Gospel of Luke?"[6] The article is a useful inventory of the evidence, for Grant collects and examines the passages in which John is often alleged to have drawn directly upon Luke rather than (or in addition to) Mark, for example: the saying about disciple and master (Luke 6:40/John 13:16, 20); the anointing of Jesus by a sinful woman (Luke 7:36–50/John 12:1–8); Mary and Martha (Luke 10:38–42/John 11:1); and Satan's entering into Judas (Luke 22:3/John 13:27). In all, Grant considers some thirty instances.

Grant's analysis is not as thorough as Schniewind's (whom he does not cite) and does not take the discussion of the problem further exegetically. Nevertheless his conclusions are not unimportant. Like Schniewind he finds no reason to posit a direct, literary dependence of John upon Luke. Rather, he believes that John knew Q, making use of some of its sayings, L, and a special Lukan passion source, as well as Mark, whose use can be taken for granted. On the whole, the contacts or affinities do not require us to think that John knew and drew upon the Third Gospel in its present form.

Moreover, Grant makes the interesting proposal, which is plausible if not demonstrable, that some, if not all, of the verbatim similarities between John and Luke, particularly in the Jerusalem appearance narratives, may be accounted for as the result of textual assimilation.[7] Thus Luke 24:22–24, and also 24:37, 39–43, which bring Luke closer to John, are regarded as early glosses assimilating Luke to the Fourth Gospel, although there is no extant manuscript evidence to support this view. There are, however, analogous cases in which manuscript evidence exists. For example, Luke 24:12 (cf. 24:36, 40) is found in most major manuscripts but is missing from Codex Bezae and the Itala and has been widely regarded as an assimilation to the Johannine account (John 20:1–10). (In the 26th edition of Nestle-Aland, however, it has been

---

[6] F. C. Grant, "Was the Author of John Dependent Upon the Gospel of Luke?" *JBL* 56 (1937): 285–307.

[7] Ibid., 303–6.

restored to the text, reflecting the judgment that it was original in Luke.) Otherwise, Grant is not at all embarrassed about the lack of manuscript evidence, which he thinks would have long since disappeared.

Such emendation as he suggests may, so to speak, cover a multitude of sins. Can one adequately control such conjectures, reasonable though they may be? The question is a serious one, as the lack of control is obvious. Nevertheless the free handling of the text during the earliest decades in which the New Testament books circulated is a matter to be reckoned with. The critical apparatus reveals that there is ample evidence for textual assimilation in extant manucripts, and, as Grant points out, there is no reason to think it was any less common during that earliest period from which no manuscript evidence survives. Indeed, in the period when the concept and the reality of the canon were being established it was likely more common. The broader implications of this view of the assimilation of the texts of John and Luke are obvious. Streeter invoked assimilation to account in part for the agreements of Matthew and Luke against Mark and preserve the integrity of the Markan hypothesis.[8] Grant now calls upon it to explain, at least in part, verbatim agreements between John and Luke. Why not invoke assimilation to explain the similarities between John and any one or all of the Synoptic Gospels, without resorting to the traditional view of literary dependence? Some assimilation in all probability took place before any of our extant manuscripts of the Gospels were written down. John's canonical authority was the last to be accepted. Presumably John would have been subject to assimilation for a longer period and would likely have been changed to conform to the Synoptics. Yet assimilation might also move in the other direction, as Grant suggests. But how much assimilation of John to the Synoptics (or vice versa) affected the form of the text is one of those imponderables about which one can at best hazard a guess. To deny such assimilation is to go against the grain of probability, but the more one invokes it to solve exegetical problems, the less convincing such solutions are likely to seem.

Although Grant might well have taken advantage of Schniewind's work, and arguably should have, the fact that he did not becomes fortuitously significant. Working independently, Grant comes to virtually the same conclusion that Schniewind embraced, namely, that the numerous affinities between John and Luke cannot be explained adequately on the premise that John knew and used Luke. Rather, the two evangelists drew on a common or related source or sources. That John knew, or knew about, Mark is scarcely

---

[8] Streeter, *The Four Gospels*, 306–29.

questioned. Grant assumes John's use of Mark,[9] while Schniewind concedes that John presupposes the other Gospels. As for the relation between John and Luke, however, both Schniewind and Grant are impressed by the difficulty of understanding how the text of the one could be based on that of the other. In other words, John's specific differences from Luke make it seem unlikely that he was using that Gospel as his source. Both Grant and Schniewind antedate Gardner-Smith, but both reason quite similarly to him and to Dodd and others who followed. Gardner-Smith would, of course, ask why it is necessary to suppose that John knew even Mark.

## JOHN A. BAILEY

In the same year that Dodd's book appeared, John A. Bailey published a study of the traditions common to the Gospels of Luke and John, which he had undertaken as a Basel dissertation under Oscar Cullmann. Bailey finds that John drew upon the Gospel of Luke, as well as upon tradition common to both, and therefore could not have been written earlier than the 80s of the first century.[10] Although Bailey notes the works of Schniewind and Grant, as well as Gardner-Smith's book, he nevertheless regards it as certain that John knew both Luke and Mark and obviously takes this to be still the dominant consensus of scholarship.[11]

Bailey begins his investigation with a comparison of Luke 7:36–50 with John 12:1–8 (the anointing of Jesus' feet by a woman), for he believes that the evidence of these parallel pericopes proves that John knew not only Lukan tradition but Luke's gospel. Moreover, while granting that the context of the stories is different in the two Gospels and that the verbal similarities are inconclusive, Bailey insists that the remarkable contacts between John's account and Mark's (14:3–9) make it absolutely certain that John used Mark's text "directly as a source."[12] When this is recognized, it becomes clear also

---

[9] Grant, "Was the Author of John Dependent Upon the Gospel of Luke?" 303–7. Apparently Grant regards John's use of Mark to be a safe assumption, referring to the "proof" of J. Weiss, *Das älteste Evangelium: Ein Beitrag zum Verständnis des Markus-Evangelium und der ältesten evangelischen Überlieferung* (Göttingen: Vandenhoeck & Ruprecht, 1903), 97ff. Yet Weiss's own contribution is less a proof than a neat statement of the generally held hypothesis.

[10] John A. Bailey, *The Traditions Common to the Gospels of Luke and John*, NovtSup 7 (Leiden: E. J. Brill, 1963), vii. A convenient summary of Bailey's results may be found in Kysar, *The Fourth Evangelist and His Gospel*, 56–58.

[11] Bailey, *Traditions*, 4 n. 2.

[12] Ibid., 2. These similarities include the 300 denarii as the price of the ointment; the location of the incident at Bethany at the beginning of the passion narrative; the reproach to Jesus against the woman because of her extravagance; Jesus' statement about the poor; and the use of the extremely rare word *pistikos*. On the comparison of Luke 7:36–50 with John 12:1–8, see pp. 1–8.

that John has drawn two elements from Luke as well, the anointing of the feet (in Mark it is the head) and the drying with the hair, and that any difficulties in the present text may be understood as a result of this careful and purposeful conflation of his sources. Furthermore, the reference to Martha's serving in John 12:2 is based on Luke 10:38ff.; John has added it to be sure the reader will identify the woman mentioned here and in John 11 with the same characters who figure in Luke. But John is not dependent on Mark and Luke alone. Bailey posits the existence of a cycle of traditional stories about Mary and Martha, one of which has been taken up into John, another into Luke. The information that the name of the woman who anointed Jesus was Mary was probably drawn from such an oral source and incorporated by John into his story so that there could be no mistaking her identity with the sisters mentioned also in Luke. Despite his acknowledgment of a common tradition underlying Luke and John, Bailey is quite certain that the many agreements between Luke 7:36–50 and John 12:1–8 can only be explained on the basis of John's direct, literary dependence upon Luke.

Turning to a comparison of the Baptist material,[13] Bailey notes that only Luke and John report the speculation of onlookers over whether John himself was the Messiah (Luke 3:15–16/John 1:19–27). The statement to this effect in Luke 3:15 is regarded as the composition of the third evangelist. If at this point John's material could be shown to be derivative from Luke's redactional statement, it might then be inferred that John was dependent upon the Third Gospel. Yet Bailey judges the differences between John and Luke at this point to be too great to be explained in this way. Rather, both Luke and John derive this information independently from oral tradition. This assignment of one set of similarities to direct literary dependence and another to common tradition is typical of Bailey's work. Sometimes, as in the resurrection narratives of Luke 24 and John 20 and 21, the same Johannine pericope, or at least the same complex, is said to be composed both of elements drawn from the Third Gospel and of other materials drawn from common tradition.[14] Precisely Bailey's objectivity in refusing to press all the related material into the same Procrustean bed of direct dependence of John upon Luke has, however, led to a serious question about his thesis.

In his review of Bailey, Pierson Parker (who himself had just published an article on the Johannine-Lukan connection when Bailey's book appeared) asks whether for no apparent reason John would have likely turned at one

---

[13] Ibid., 9–11.
[14] Ibid., 85–102.

point to the Gospel of Luke and at another to Lukan tradition in the composition of his gospel.[15] Furthermore, Parker feels that Bailey's unequivocal assertions about John's use of Luke's Gospel are not adequately supported by the evidence he musters. He also thinks it regrettable that Bailey does not take into account the work of Gardner-Smith and Dodd. (Although Bailey cites Gardner-Smith, he does not really debate his thesis; doubtless Dodd's book appeared too late to be considered.) Quite apart from any judgment about its validity, however, it may be that Bailey's book was simply born out of season, for the tide of critical opinion was already moving in the opposite direction. Verbal and other similarities, which to an earlier generation and to Bailey clearly signaled John's dependence on the other Gospels, had now ceased to seem compelling as evidence of copying or conflation. Yet on neither side was anyone able to come forward with objective criteria for testing whether or not similarities were or were not the result of John's copying, or at least recalling, the other Gospels. Bailey's suggestion that John's dependence on specifically Lukan redaction would prove dependence on the Third Gospel was a move in the right direction. But, as we shall see, the determination of what is Lukan or synoptic redaction would prove to be no small problem in itself.

Despite Parker's question to Bailey, the latter's conclusion that John uses Luke but also shares earlier traditions with him is not in principle far-fetched. John would have known Luke as an equivalent source, a peer, not as a canonical and authoritative book in a class by itself, so to speak. Moreover, if John drew upon Luke (and Mark) from memory, as Bailey thinks,[16] his merging of Lukan elements with other material becomes intelligible. Nevertheless there are other difficulties, which are of two sorts. First, if John knew canonical Luke (or Mark), why did he ignore so much of it, particularly the distinctive Lukan material? Such a question could be applied to the Gospels as a whole, but it is also applicable to each individual set of parallel pericopes, such as the anointing of Jesus. The other question has to do with how specific agreements or parallels are assessed as to origin. For example, can it be made convincing that the woman's anointing of the feet of Jesus, rather than his head, and her wiping them with her hair could only have been derived from

---

[15] Pierson Parker, *JBL* 85 (1966): 508–9, Bailey's book was apparently not widely reviewed, but Wilhelm Wilkens in his review, *TZ* 19 (1963): 297–99, remains unconvinced of John's direct dependence upon Luke.

[16] Bailey, *Traditions*, 4 n. 2.

the Gospel of Luke? Or is it not entirely likely that there were several pre-canonical versions of this evidently popular story?[17]

## PIERSON PARKER

Typical of the trend away from dependence theories was Parker's own article, published at the same time as Bailey's book, in which he made a comprehensive survey of the agreements and other points of contact between Luke and John.[18] Parker then took inventory of the agreements or points of contact of John with Mark and Matthew individually and found twenty-six points of contact with Matthew only and nineteen with Mark, but 124 with the Third Gospel! Yet he does not conclude that the relatively large number of affinities between Luke and John allows the inference that the fourth evangelist used Luke or, indeed, any of the Synoptic Gospels. That John apparently assumed his readers would know parts of the gospel story that we know only from the Synoptics does not necessarily mean that he (or his readers) knew them from the Synoptics. As is well known, John also tells synoptic stories (e.g., 2:14ff.; 4:46ff.; 12:12ff.) as if his readers had never before heard them. To insist on John's dependence on the other Gospels is to ignore the role of preaching, discussion, debate, and oral tradition generally in the church: "Oral tradition is fully adequate to produce the features John shares with the other gospels. The differences, on the other hand, are often inexplicable on the assumption of a direct literary relationship."[19] The large number of agreements between John and Luke are to be explained as the result of a special oral tradition peculiar to them. Moreover, Parker concludes with the speculation, and it can scarcely be much more than that, that the fourth evangelist and Luke were somehow, somewhere, associated with each other in the early Christian missionary enterprise.

Parker's article obviously represents a growing body of opinion in the 1960s, according to which John was not dependent upon Luke, or indeed upon any

---

[17] Brown, *The Gospel According to John (i–xii)*, 449–52, maintains that Luke 7:36–50 and John 12:1–8 represent two separate incidents (and stories). The second is found in its purest form in Mark 14:3–9. The Lukan story of the first incident has been influenced by the Markan account of the second, while the Johannine account of the second has been influenced by the Lukan account of the first. (But Brown does not believe there is a direct, literary relationship between John and Luke.) Joseph A. Fitzmyer, *The Gospel According to Luke (i–ix)*, Anchor Bible (Garden City, N.Y.: Doubleday & Co., 1981), 686, opts for one original or basic story that has, in the oral tradition, found three different forms: the Markan, the Johannine, and the Lukan.

[18] Pierson Parker, "Luke and the Fourth Evangelist," *NTS* 9 (1962–63): 317–36.

[19] Ibid., 333.

of the Synoptic Gospels. Thus in his review of Bailey's book we see a collision of consensuses. Parker already saw, however, that to affirm John's independence of canonical Luke leaves one with the question of how the many points of contact between John and Luke are to be explained. He later suggested that Luke and the Gospel of John share certain distinctly Judean traditions and interests. In a fascinating, if at points complex, article he pointed out how this common background manifests itself in a series of agreements between the Gospel of John and the Acts of the Apostles, which Parker believes was composed before canonical Luke (but not before Proto-Luke; cf. Acts 1:1).[20]

There is a sense in which Parker's comparison of Acts and John remains at the level of "raw data," in that he makes no effort to factor in the differences of genre and the fact that in Acts Jesus is dealt with by allusion or in the barest of summaries. Nevertheless his findings are extremely interesting and potentially significant, however they may be explained. His survey suggests that Acts not only agrees with John over a wide range of rather diverse data but frequently agrees with John against the Gospel of Luke. (This actually means in many cases against Mark, for Luke in such cases often simply reflects knowledge of Mark.) Some examples will illustrate the thrust of Parker's work.

Only in John (1:20) and Acts (13:25) does John the Baptist say "I am not he" (i.e., the Christ), and only in John and Acts is he *not* called the Baptist.[21] Only John (10:23) and Acts (3:11; 5:12) mention Solomon's porch. Both John and Acts mention a Philip frequently. In John, this Philip is a disciple (presumably one of the Twelve); in Acts, he is apparently Philip the deacon (Acts 6:5) and evangelist (Acts 8:5), not one of the Twelve, although this distinction is not explicitly made.[22] In John and Acts only are Jesus' miracles called signs in a positive sense (e.g., John 2:11; Acts 2:22 and passim). Only John and Acts omit mention of Jesus' institution of the Eucharist at the Last Supper.[23] Only in John (20:17) and Acts (1:1–11) is the ascension of Jesus clearly and explicitly mentioned or described.[24] Moreover, as the Son of man

---

[20] Pierson Parker, "When Acts Sides with John," in *Understanding the Sacred Text: Essays in Honor of Morton S. Enslin on the Hebrew Bible and Christian Beginnings*, ed. John Reumann (Valley Forge, Pa.: Judson Press, 1972), 201–15. Parker elaborated the evidence for a relationship between the Gospel of John and Acts in "The Kinship of John and Acts," in *Christianity, Judaism, and Other Greco-Roman Cults: Studies for Morton Smith at Sixty*, ed. Jacob Neusner (Leiden: E. J. Brill, 1975), *Part One: New Testament*, 187–205. Cf. also Parker's "Mark, Acts, and Galilean Christianity," *NTS* 16 (1969–70): 295–304; and idem, "The 'Former Treatise' and the Date of Acts," *JBL* 84 (1965): 52–58.

[21] Parker, "When Acts Sides with John," 203.

[22] Ibid., 204.

[23] Ibid., 205.

[24] Ibid., 206.

he is exalted and seen in the opened heavens (John 1:51, cf. 6:62; Acts 7:56).[25] From there, and only there (i.e., after his death and exaltation), he gives the Spirit.

A number of the agreements distinctive to Acts and John have to do with Jesus' teaching.[26] For example, parables (*parabolai*) are mentioned in neither Acts nor John. In neither is Jesus portrayed speaking of riches or adultery. In neither does he set aside Jewish dietary laws. In fact, in Acts 10 (vv. 12–15) it becomes clear that Peter knows nothing of such laws having been set aside and must himself be instructed. Obviously there is no room in the Acts summaries for any of Jesus' parables to be told. Nevertheless it is striking that the feature of Jesus' teaching so prominent in the Synoptics, and regarded by many scholars as most characteristic of him, is not mentioned in Acts' summaries of his ministry. Certainly faith is an important theme of Jesus' teaching throughout the Gospels. Yet it must be significant that the verb occurs nearly a hundred times in John and nearly forty times in Acts, but fewer than a dozen times in any of the Synoptics. Obviously it occurs in connection with the missionary preaching of Acts, but this fact may suggest a similar missionary background or purpose of the Fourth Gospel. The same may be said of the relatively frequent use of "witness" (*martyria*) terminology in John and Acts, together with the description of Jesus (John) or the apostles (Acts) speaking boldly (*parrēsia*).

Certain theological affinities may also be observed. The Holy Spirit plays a large role in both Acts and John, and it is given only by the risen Jesus and at his behest. Both Acts and John lack the characteristically apocalyptic language of much early Christian eschatology. Yet both speak quite explicitly of the return of Jesus himself (Acts 1:11; John 14:18).[27] Unlike the synoptic tradition, Acts and John do not speak in the third person of the coming of a Son of man figure, who is not necessarily Jesus, as modern exegesis had discerned. Christologically, Acts and John agree in calling Jesus savior (*sōtēr*), a term which otherwise appears only in the Lukan infancy narratives among the Gospels. Perhaps more significant, however, is the fact that only John (6:14; 7:40) and Acts (3:22; 7:37) appear to identify Jesus with the Mosaic prophet of Deuteronomy 18.[28]

Although Parker does not put it in exactly these terms, there is a kind of ethnic awareness distinctive of John and Acts. The term "Jew" or "Jews"

---

[25] Ibid., 208.

[26] Ibid., 206–7.

[27] Ibid., 208.

[28] Ibid., 209.

(*Ioudaioi*) appears dozens of times in both John and Acts as against a handful of occurrences in the Synoptic Gospels and a modest number elsewhere, mostly in the Pauline epistles. The word for Romans or a Roman (*rōmaios*) occurs only in John and Acts in the New Testament. The term *hellēn* (a male Greek) appears only in John and Acts among the narrative books of the New Testament (otherwise it appears in the Pauline corpus), although the feminine form (*hellēnis*) is found once, in Mark (7:26).[29]

Whatever one makes of this collection of data of various sorts and significance (and its implications are not immediately obvious), it is probably too sizable and significant to be dismissed or written off to sheer coincidence. Referring to his earlier proposals, Parker suggests that the Book of Acts and an earlier version of the Gospel were written before the canonical Gospel of Luke and were based on a southern, Judean tradition akin to the Gospel of John.[30] In this connection he has observed that the role of Galilee is diminished in both John and Acts. In John, Jesus is, of course, more frequently in Judea or Jerusalem, while in Acts the missionary summaries (e.g., Acts 1:8) characteristically omit mention of Galilee. In the present Gospel, then, Luke strives to reconcile this earlier tradition with the Markan. In seeing such signs of Luke's Gospel attempting to reconcile John and Mark, Parker adumbrates an important insight of Lamar Cribbs, whose proposal we shall next review.

## F. LAMAR CRIBBS

Cribbs has placed Johannine-Lukan relationships in a fresh perspective by questioning the generally held assumption that any relationship or line of dependence must run from John to Luke; that is, John must be regarded as dependent upon Luke or Lukan tradition. In an important *JBL* article, Cribbs made a surprisingly strong case for the lines of influence or dependence running in the opposite direction, with Luke somehow dependent upon John.[31] This is not to say that Luke must have known John in its present form but only that he knew a form of the Johannine tradition, or perhaps an earlier form of the gospel than that which now lies before us. As we have seen, this

---

[29] Ibid., 210.
[30] Ibid., 214.
[31] F. Lamar Cribbs, "St. Luke and the Johannine Tradition," *JBL* 90 (1971): 422–50; and an extended and elaborated version of that work, idem, "A Study of the Contacts That Exist Between St. Luke and St. John," *Society of Biblical Literature: 1973 Seminar Papers*, ed. George MacRae (Cambridge, Mass.: Society of Biblical Literature, 1973), 2:1–93.

position was already adumbrated by Schniewind, who found, for example, in the accounts of the hearing before Jewish authorities reason to think that John was closer than Luke to their primitive, common source.

While Cribbs amasses a variety of evidence of differing magnitude and weight, his basic argument is relatively simple. Luke shows a strong tendency to depart from, alter, or omit the Markan (or Markan/Matthean) tradition, which he follows for much of his Gospel, at those points where it is contradicted or otherwise called into question by the Fourth Gospel:

> The fact that Luke agrees quite closely with Matthew and Mark in those pericopes that he shares only with these two co-evangelists . . . , but makes numerous divergencies from the Matthean/Marcan traditions in the direction of the Johannine tradition in almost every pericope that he shares with all three of his co-evangelists would seem to suggest that this is a critical problem that should be re-examined.[32]

Quite noteworthy and significant is the fact that Cribbs approaches the problem from the standpoint of Luke rather than John. That is, instead of beginning with John and asking whether that Gospel did or did not draw directly upon Luke at those points where it shows affinities with it, he begins with Luke and asks what phenomenon is associated with that Gospel's affinities with the Gospel of John. The answer is departure from the Markan (or Markan-Matthean) tradition. Thus it is a reasonable, if not a necessary, inference from Luke's departures from the other Synoptics in agreement with John that these departures were occasioned by his use of John or of Johannine tradition. In a manner of speaking, Luke took John seriously where it collided with his major narrative source. (John's agreement with Luke against Mark/Matthew would not, on the other hand, seem nearly so striking, since John, unlike Luke, does not otherwise follow Mark closely.)

These agreements of John and Luke against the other Synoptics are familiar to students of the problem and certainly not insignificant. For example, Luke and John agree in presenting only one report of Jesus' feeding of a large crowd (John 6:1–15; Luke 9:10–17) against Matthew and Mark, who report two feedings. Only Luke and John report speculation over whether John the Baptist was himself the messiah (Luke 3:15; John 1:20), and only in John (1:20; 3:28) and Acts (13:25) is John portrayed as denying that he is the Messiah. Neither Luke nor John explicitly reports that Jesus was baptized by John, as do Matthew and Mark. Strikingly, neither Luke nor John reports an

---

[32] Cribbs, "St. Luke and the Johannine Tradition," 426.

evening meeting of the Sanhedrin that condemns Jesus to death. In this connection, Cribbs observes that the use of Old Testament testimonia also reveals a significant pattern.[33] In pericopes with no Johannine parallels (i.e., triple tradition), Luke produces eleven of twelve quotations that are found in Matthew and Mark. Yet in the twenty-odd pericopes that are common to John as well as to the Synoptics, Luke with one exception reproduces only those Old Testament quotations that Matthew and Mark have in common with John. There are eighteen Old Testament quotations in these pericopes, but only three (cf. Luke 3:4 par.; 19:38 par.; 23:34 par.) are found in all four Gospels, and only in Luke 19:46 does the third evangelist share a quotation with Matthew and Mark but not with John.

Luke's order of events in large blocks of material is closely parallel to Mark's (Luke 3:1—6:19 = Mark 1:1—3:19; Luke 8:4—9:17 = Mark 3:31—6:44; Luke 9:18—50 = Mark 8:27—9:41; Luke 18:15—24:11 = Mark 10:13—16:8), but Luke's order tends to diverge from Mark's at just those points where Mark and John conflict. Thus, for example, although John has the foot washing instead of the institution of the Lord's Supper, Luke's order of events at the Supper is closer to John's than it is to Mark's.[34] Cribbs also finds that Luke's wording is usually close to Mark's (or Matthew's) in the 47 pericopes of the triple tradition for which there is no Johannine parallel. Where there is a Johannine parallel, however, there are frequent and wide departures from the Markan or Matthean wording in Luke's text, often in the direction of the Gospel of John.[35] Occasionally one finds that in the reporting of some event on which John contradicts or otherwise clashes with Mark, Luke will give yet another rendition or version.[36] Thus Luke's version of Jesus' calling of the disciples (Luke 5:1–11) differs on the one hand from Mark's and Matthew's and on the other from John's, as does his handling of the trial of Jesus before Jewish authorities (Luke 22:66–71). The latter is a nocturnal sitting of the Sanhedrin in Mark and Matthew, while in John only an evening hearing before Annas is reported. Like the other Synoptics, Luke reports a meeting of the council of elders (Sanhedrin), but on the following morning, rather than in the evening of the arrest, and Luke does not report the testimony of witnesses that gives the Markan-Matthean account the aura of a formal trial. Also Matthew and Mark place Jesus' public ministry in Galilee but John has

---

[33] Cribbs, "A Study of the Contacts," 23–24.

[34] Ibid., 9–20, 50. Cribbs claims that of the fourteen deviations from Markan order in the Lukan passion, eleven put him in agreement with John (p. 47).

[35] Ibid., 12–20, 80, and passim. Cribbs finds major Lukan departures from Mark-Matthew in nineteen of the twenty pericopes of the quadruple tradition (p. 16).

[36] Ibid., 16–17.

it mainly in Judea; Luke places it in the whole of the Jewish territory (4:14–15; cf. 4:44; 5:17; 6:17; 7:17).

Could John have known the Gospel of Luke? Cribbs thinks not, observing that John generally lacks parallels to those major sections of Luke (1:1—2:52; 9:51—18:14) that are distinctive of that Gospel as well as to Luke's special passion material (Luke 23:6–12, 28–31, 39–43). At the same time, however, there are frequent and significant agreements of Luke with John, which include sequence, wording, or factual information, particularly in the parts of their passion narratives that run parallel. John may lack such parallels to peculiarly Lukan material as would immediately suggest his dependence upon the Third Gospel as it lies before us.[37] But when one approaches the question from the opposite, Lukan side, one finds many indications of Luke's having been influenced by Johannine material.

Cribbs's findings are nevertheless not without anomalies. For example, he points out that of the number of close verbal agreements between John and Mark, few are to be found in comparable form in the Gospel of Luke.[38] (Yet at other points Luke has verbal similarities to John that Mark lacks.) It seems unlikely to Cribbs that Luke, if he had used Mark as his primary source and in turn been used by John, would have by coincidence omitted so many of those Markan sentences or phrases that John would later pick up. True enough, but it is also hard to conceive of Luke, if he had a tendency to conflate Johannine and Markan material, as having omitted such instances where his sources showed verbatim agreement. Since there is a difficult coincidence in either case, this bit of evidence can only be regarded as indecisive, although it is typical of the problem of John and the Synoptics generally: the evidence is sometimes ambiguous.

Lamar Cribbs, who passed away without being able to bring his work to fruition, was an anomaly in contemporary biblical research. A pastor rather than an academic, he was not able to work near a university library, and he held no advanced degree in the field. Yet his scholarship does not suffer from lack of erudition, thoroughness, or imagination. Neirynck, in his *Forschungsbericht*, takes note of the comprehensiveness of Cribbs's inventory of the agreements between Luke and John and suggests that in his 1979 monograph Cribbs may have backed away from his original thesis that Luke knew an early version of John (or Johannine tradition), quoting a concluding statement in which Cribbs advances his thesis as one of several possibilities (including

---

[37] Ibid., 6.
[38] Ibid., 42.

John's knowledge of Luke or their use of common sources).[39] Neirynck's inference is logical, but one should bear in mind that Cribbs's paper was prepared for an SBL seminar and was apparently intended to lay out the evidence without prejudice to any theory. Thus, for example, Cribbs takes no position on synoptic relationships. Much of the evidence that Cribbs assembled in what turned out to be his last work actually supports his thesis. Where all Gospels run parallel, Luke as a rule deviates from Mark (and Matthew) at just those points where John presents an alternative or contradictory account. To the best of my knowledge, no one has pursued Cribbs's thesis further, whether by way of confirmation, refutation, or testing. But, as we have seen, his work takes up and expands upon the insights and perspectives of Schniewind and Parker, among others, who on close examination of Lukan and Johannine texts found the assumption that John presupposes Luke, rather than the other way around, a questionable working hypothesis.

## ROBERT MADDOX

There were several major contributions to the study of the question of John and the Synoptics in the 1980s, but in this chapter we shall deal only with Robert Maddox, who in *The Purpose of Luke-Acts* devotes a chapter to "The Special Affinities of Luke and John" as a way of illuminating that subject.[40] In doing so, he takes a position on the broader question of the relation of John to the Synoptics. Maddox's work is well suited to conclude this stage of our history of the problem, for it accurately represents the consensus on John's independence of the Synoptics that was attained in the 1960s as well as his independence of Luke specifically. Therefore it will be worthwhile to describe the views of Maddox in some detail.

Maddox rightly observes there have been two basic answers to the question of why John differs so radically from the Synoptic Gospels: (1) he knew them but drastically rewrote them so as to bring out new insights; and (2) he drew

---

[39] See Neirynck's *Forschungsbericht*, "John and the Synoptics: 1975–1990," to be published in the proceedings of the Colloquium in the BETL series. (In the Colloquium papers, see p. 10 and n. 128.) See also F. Lamar Cribbs, "The Agreements That Exist Between Luke and John," in *Society of Biblical Literature: 1979 Seminar Papers*, ed. Paul J. Achtemeier (Missoula, Mont.: Scholars Press, 1979), 1:215–61. The latter is an exceedingly closely packed collection of the concrete and specific data of Johannine-Lukan relations, which needs to be carefully examined, and perhaps corrected and refined, but it should prove to be a valuable source for future research.

[40] Robert Maddox, *The Purpose of Luke-Acts*, FRLANT 126 (Göttingen: Vandenhoeck & Ruprecht, 1982), 158–79. (For the works of Dauer, Heekerens, and Thyen, which bear upon Johannine-Lukan relations, see chap. 6.)

on independent but overlapping oral tradition.[41] Josef Blinzler's *Forschungs-bericht*[42] showed clearly that from Holtzmann (1869) to Gardner-Smith (1938) almost everyone agreed that Clement of Alexandria had been right in regarding John as a supplementary gospel intended to show the spiritual meaning of the "physical," synoptic story of Jesus. Since Gardner-Smith, all that has changed, however, for he argued strongly and, most thought, persuasively for John's independence of the Synoptics. Maddox believes his views gained such wide acceptance in part because they allowed for a view of the Fourth Gospel that credited it as a historical witness, but mainly because of a growing aware-ness of the role and importance of oral tradition in the early church. Blinzler, however, dissented from Gardner-Smith's position on three grounds: (1) John's apparent assumption that the reader would know certain persons or events as presented by Mark; (2) the agreement in order of such events as John has in common with Mark; and (3) eight verbatim agreements that suggest that John was copying Mark's text.

Maddox does not believe that any of these arguments is finally convincing.[43] As to knowledge of personages being assumed on the basis of Mark, he notes that Nicodemus, not mentioned in Mark, is explained in John but that Na-thaniel, also not mentioned in Mark, is not. The implication is that the iden-tification or nonidentification of a figure when introduced is not a good guide to what other canonical documents, if any, an author assumes the reader will know. Maddox might have mentioned that Pontius Pilate is first mentioned in Mark in 15:1 without being identified. Presumably any Christian reader of the Gospel would know who he was. (Matthew 27:2 remedies this deficiency by identifying Pilate as governor.) The argument from common order is a bit stronger. Yet precisely where Mark and John share the greatest amount of material over a broad span of the narrative, that is, in the passion account, John diverges widely from Mark (often to agree with Luke), and his differences are not all easily understood as based on John's theological or literary purpose. Even the verbatim agreements are not best explained by John's use of the Markan text. For example, the agreement in John 12:3/Mark 14:3, "myrrh of pistic nard, very costly" (*murou nardou pistikēs polutimou/polutelous*), stands in the midst of unaccountable disagreements or divergences. (One might observe, for example, the difficulty of explaining how or why John converted Mark's perfectly clear statement about the purpose of the anointing in Mark

---

[41] Ibid., 158.

[42] Blinzler, *Johannes und die Synoptiker*, 16–19; cf. Maddox, *The Purpose of Luke-Acts* 159–60.

[43] Maddox, *The Purpose of Luke-Acts*, 160–62.

14:8 into Jesus' puzzling remark in John 12:7.) Maddox concludes that common oral tradition affords a better explanation of these relatively few verbal agreements.

It is satisfactory to view Luke as using, departing from, or correcting Mark, but this is scarcely the case with John. On such a view, John would seem to change Mark in ways that do not obviously suit his purposes. Thus, if John intends to play down the role of the Baptist vis-à-vis Jesus, as he clearly does, why should he portray him working concurrently with Jesus (cf. John 3:24)? To have him off the scene as he is in Mark, as well as in Luke, would serve John's purpose better. One might also ask why John substitutes for Mark's call story, in which Jesus acts imperiously and alone, one in which John is instrumental in sending his own disciples to Jesus. Some Johannine incidents such as the entry into Jerusalem are obviously the same as those described in Mark or the Synoptics, but in other cases there is a question whether we are even dealing with the same story: Peter's confession; the official's son or, as in Matthew and Luke, the centurion's servant. Maddox concludes, "In the light of these considerations, I believe the probability lies with Gardner-Smith's argument."[44]

Turning to John's relation to Luke, Maddox observes that it differs from his relation to Mark. "There are no cases of exact verbal correspondence between John and Luke like the eight between John and Mark."[45] (In fact, as Cribbs has shown, there are some notable instances of verbatim agreement. For example, compare John 12:3b with Luke 7:38b; John 12:13b with Luke 19:38a; and John 20:19b with Luke 24:36b. Luke, however, characteristically lacks just those that are most impressive in Mark.) Often John and Luke share common information or points of view, sometimes over against the other Gospels, sometimes independently of them. Maddox groups these positive relationships under three heads: common material, common geographical perspective, and common theological perspective.

Under common material Maddox isolates first what he calls small coincidences of fact or imagery. For example, Jesus' speaking of a grateful master who causes his slaves to recline at dinner and then serves them (Luke 12:37) calls to mind Jesus' act of washing the disciples' feet at the Last Supper (John 13:4). Much more significant, however, are a series of larger narratives with

---

[44] Ibid., 162.
[45] Ibid., 162. Maddox is referring to those listed by Blinzler, *Johannes und die Synoptiker*, 55–56: John 6:7 and Mark 6:37; John 12:3 and Mark 14:3; John 12:5 and Mark 14:5; John 12:7 and Mark 14:6; John 18:18 and Mark 14:54; John 18:39 and Mark 15:9; John 5:8 and Mark 2:11; John 14:31 and Mark 14:42.

similar contents or ideas. Maddox gives Schniewind's list of eleven,[46] which include episodes distinctive of John and Luke, such as the story of a miraculous catch of fish (John 21:1–14/Luke 5:1–11) or of a resurrection appearance of Jesus to the Twelve (John 20:19–22; Luke 24:36–41, 47–49), as well as others with parallels to Mark (John 12:3–8) or Q (John 4:46–54) but with some distinctive features in common with Luke. Among these narratives, agreements in or about the passion predominate. There are also interesting agreements of order between John and Luke within the passion narrative, as Cribbs has shown in great detail. Peter's denial is predicted at the supper in Luke 22:31–34 and John 13:36–38 but on the way to Gethsemane in Mark 14:26–31 and Matthew 26:30–35. Similarly, Judas's betrayal is predicted after the institution of the Lord's Supper in Luke (22:21–23) and after the comparable foot washing in John (13:21–30). Earlier in the narrative only Luke and John have Peter's confession follow directly upon the feeding of the five thousand, whereas in Matthew and Mark much other material intervenes.

Perhaps most striking is the fact that only in Luke 23:2 and John 19:12–15 do the Jewish authorities explicitly charge Jesus with sedition.[47] In Mark (15:10) and Matthew (27:18) these authorities are said to be motivated by envy, although it is implied, but implied only (by Pilate's question), that Jesus has claimed to be king of the Jews. There are, of course, other interesting agreements between John and Luke only in the trial before Pilate: Pilate's threefold declaration of Jesus' innocence; the scourging of Jesus either proposed as an alternative punishment (Luke 23:16) or carried out before a verdict is rendered (John 19:1, 2), not presented as the customary Roman preliminary to execution. Only in John and Luke is the cry of dereliction from the cross (Mark 15:34/Matt. 27:46) omitted.

Very tantalizing is the apparent web of relationships between Luke and John in the narratives concerning Mary, her sister Martha, and their brother Lazarus.[48] All three names appear only in these two Gospels. In Luke, of course, no brother named Lazarus is mentioned, but there is a Lazarus in the parable of Luke 16:19–31, the only character named in any of Jesus' parables. This Lazarus is, of course, preserved to eschatological life somewhat like the Lazarus of John 11, who is raised from the dead. On the other hand, the Johannine Lazarus returns to conditions of earthly life and is apparently subject to death (John 12:10), while the rich man of Luke's parable, Lazarus's opposite number, is denied his request to return to warn his brothers (Luke 16:27–

---

[46] Maddox, *The Purpose of Luke-Acts,* 163.

[47] Ibid., 164.

[48] Ibid., 165–67.

31). Mary and Martha seem to fill comparable roles in the two Gospels, although in different narratives. At dinner, Martha serves (John 12:2; Luke 10:40), while Mary is at Jesus' feet, either to listen to his teaching (Luke 10:39) or to anoint and wipe his feet (John 12:3) with her hair. In the Lukan anointing story a nameless woman anoints Jesus' feet and wipes them with her hair (Luke 7:38). Obviously there are many and complex relationships, which Maddox believes admit of no simple resolution, such as that John altered the Markan story under the influence of Luke. The view that he did attributes the anointing of the feet and the wiping of the myrrh in John to Lukan influence upon the Markan story. But these putative alterations lack adequate theological or literary motivation. More plausible is the view that the similarities of the Johannine version to the Lukan and Markan are the result of common or overlapping oral tradition. The same is, in Maddox's view, true of the story of the miraculous catch of fish in Luke 5:1–11 (where it is a call story) and John 21:1–14 (where it is a resurrection story).[49]

In some of the stories in which John and Luke share the same or similar special materials they may not appear to manifest common interests, although in the denial that the Baptist is the Messiah and the attribution of sedition to Jesus just such interests do seem to emerge. In the instances of common geographical or theological perspective, however, Maddox discerns "similar points of view and convictions about the meaning of the gospel story."[50] Thus Judea and Jerusalem are of great importance in both John and Luke.

Only if one reads Luke in the light of Matthew and Mark does it seem that in the Synoptics Jesus' ministry took place mostly in Galilee. Actually, after Luke 9:51 Jesus is no longer in Galilee but in Samaria on the way to Jerusalem, and already in Luke 4:44 Jesus is said to be preaching in the synagogues of Judea. Twice in the three Lukan references to Samaria or Samaritans (Luke 10:33–35; 17:11–19) they appear in a favorable light, but Mark does not refer to Samaria and in Matthew Jesus forbids his disciples to go there (Matt. 10:5). Luke's interest in Samaria, reflected in Acts as well as in the Gospel, is real and stands alongside an obvious interest in Jerusalem and Judea and a relative lack of interest in Galilee (mentioned as a locus of the church only in Acts 9:31 and conspicuously absent in the missionary charge of Acts 1:8).[51] In these respects, Luke is much closer to John than to the other Synoptic Gospels, for John, of course, refers to Judea as Jesus' own country (*patris*) in 4:43–45 and emphasizes Jesus' visits to Jerusalem at the time of Jewish

---

[49] Ibid., 167.
[50] Ibid., 168.
[51] Ibid., 168–70.

festivals. Most of Jesus' public ministry takes place in Judea. Luke apparently cannot match John's Judean traditions but nevertheless edits his material or sources to make Jesus' ministry appear to center much more largely in the south than do the other Synoptic Gospels.

John's and Luke's common interest in Jerusalem, the center of Judaism, is commensurate with their concern about questions of the relationship of Jews, Gentiles, and Christians in God's plan.[52] Luke and John agree that the Jews' failure to give heed to Jesus is of a piece with their failure to heed Moses and the prophets (cf. Luke 16:29–31 and John 5:46–47). John sums up the effect of Jesus' public ministry to his own with a quotation from Isaiah 6:9–10: "He has blinded their eyes and hardened their heart. . . ." Luke has Paul employ exactly the same Isaiah quotation to the same effect at the end of his public ministry in Acts 28:26–28. In both John and Luke, "Israel" as a theme is closely related to Christology. That in neither John nor Luke Peter's confession is set at Caesarea Philippi in gentile territory is indicative of the fact that both, more than Matthew and Mark, restrict the access of Gentiles to Jesus until after the resurrection. The gentile mission is a post-resurrection phenomenon; Jesus' ministry was to Israel. The death of Jesus marks a crucial turning point, for he thenceforth enters into his glory (Luke 9:31–32; 24:26; John 7:39; 12:16, 23; 13:31–32). Accordingly, Jesus' ascension is prominent in both John and Luke, although it is handled differently. But for both it is associated with the gift of the Holy Spirit; and in John, as in Luke, Jesus bestows the Spirit on his disciples, equipping them for mission (John 20:21–22). For Luke, the Spirit is invoked as an aid to faithful testimony under persecution (Luke 12:11–12; 21:14–15), and in this it is not unrelated to the role of the Johannine Paraclete (John 14:16, 26; 16:7–11). Moreover, although he does not call the Holy Spirit *paraklētos*, Luke speaks of the church's comfort (*paraklēsis*) in the Holy Spirit.[53] The similar views of the Spirit's role in John and Luke are accompanied by some significant agreement on eschatology. Both John and Luke emphasize, albeit in different ways, the eschatological fulfillment that has already come about in and through Jesus. Luke preserves a lively futurist expectation, it is true, but this has not totally disappeared from John (5:28–29; 6:39–40; etc.).

In fact, Maddox has been able to point to significant agreements between Luke and John over a range of central theological topics. How are these to be accounted for or explained? Maddox is inclined to see the common

---

[52] Ibid., 170–72.
[53] Ibid., 173. See Acts 9:31.

traditions, common geographical interests, and the kinship in theology as rooted in the south, that is, Judea, and arising from "the memories of Judaean disciples who followed Jesus in Judaea during his lifetime and who formed the core of the Judaean churches after his resurrection."[54] This Judean tradition stands over against the Galilean, so strongly represented in Matthew, Mark, Q, and, in a sense, by Jesus himself. Along with this Judean locus and tradition, John and Luke also attest the existence and vitality of Samaritan churches. Interestingly enough, although distinctive Judean traditions are relatively rare in the Gospel of Luke, which appropriates a good deal of Mark and Q, they are much more prominent in Acts. While Maddox is inclined to trace the traditional roots of the material and emphases common to Luke and John to a southern, Judean origin, he sees no compelling reason to locate the finished documents there.[55] In the case of the finished forms of both Gospels, we are dealing with the culmination of a development, rather far removed from its traditional origins. Probably Luke lodges the justification of the writing of his work in the distinctive perspective with which he will embue it, a perspective rooted in a southern, Judean and to some extent Samaritan, point of view. This he shares with the Fourth Gospel.

Maddox does not refer to, and presumably does not know, Parker's contribution to the study of the relationship of John and Acts particularly. Parker's collection of these parallels and affinities would, however, afford an interesting complement to Maddox's work. For Parker's contention, based on his research, is that Acts preserves a more ancient level of tradition and agreement with the Johannine tradition and that Luke's Gospel accommodates that tradition and perspective with the Markan. This position can be maintained without invoking some version of the Proto-Luke hypothesis, to which Parker himself adheres. However that may be, there is an interesting coincidence between Maddox's conclusion and Parker's evidence—all the more intriguing because they are independent of each other.

Maddox's book, then, represents a significant consensus of scholarly opinion on the relationship of John to the Synoptics that had already emerged ten to fifteen years earlier. Moreover, his view of John's indirect relationship to Luke is one that had also been evolving, in part independently, alongside the consensus on John and the Synoptics generally. This, therefore, marks a good breaking point in our narrative, although significant works on John and Luke have been published since. Increasingly, works published in the 1980s tend

---

[54] Ibid., 174; cf. 174–76.
[55] Ibid., 175.

to see a closer, more direct, literary connection between John and Luke, as well as between John and the other Synoptics. We shall hold them in abeyance, however, as we turn to another specific issue or area that has figured importantly in discussions of John and the Synoptics, namely, the question of whether there was available to Mark, and perhaps to other evangelists, a primitive, pre-gospel, passion narrative.

# 5

# The Renaissance
# of the Problem: Passion
# Narratives

The very recent history of New Testament scholarship, like any very recent history, is difficult and hazardous to write. Time usually produces a consensus at least about what was important, if not who or what was correct. As we have observed, the problem of John and the Synoptics was not regarded as a severe problem from late antiquity until the nineteenth century. Even after the rise of biblical criticism, the traditional view that John knew and used the Synoptics enjoyed wide respect and adherence, even—and perhaps especially—where the Fourth Gospel was no longer taken to be the work of John the son of Zebedee. This dominant viewpoint on their relationship maintained itself until seriously challenged on the one side by Windisch, who argued that John did not approve the Synoptics, and on the other by Gardner-Smith, who argued that John did not know them. Gradually the position that John was independent of other gospels established itself and for a couple of decades could be aptly characterized as the dominant view. In all probability, it still is, in that most scholars who have worked on the Fourth Gospel in the last quarter of a century have assumed that position. But there is little question that we are now seeing a resurgence of interest in the relationship of John and the Synoptics, characterized by a revival of the traditional view that John knew and used the Synoptic Gospels in the composition of his own.

In this connection, there has been an intensification of the redaction-critical line of questioning. One asks, or emphasizes the importance of asking, whether John's Gospel incorporates, or betrays evidence of knowing, the redactional work of Mark or of any of the synoptic authors as it can be identified within their respective Gospels. If John incorporates Markan, Matthean, or Lukan redaction, he must have known these Gospels and not merely their tradition.[1] A definite positive, or negative, determination on this matter should settle the question for good. So far, at least, the redaction-critical solution has not led to uniform conclusions in the way one might have anticipated because of the difficulty in reaching agreement on what is redactional and what is traditional in the synoptic narratives. Nevertheless, scholars will undoubtedly continue investigations and debates along these lines.

Attention has recently focused on the passion and to some extent the resurrection narratives, since here the similarities between John and the Synoptics are most numerous. Because there are many parallel episodes, the task of comparing John to the Synoptics with a view to finding whether synoptic redaction has been absorbed into John ought to prove feasible. Of course, the remarkable parallels in the passion accounts have in much modern research been explained as the result of John's and the Synoptics' dependence upon a common primitive passion narrative antedating any of the Gospels. The existence of such a narrative was an important ingredient of the view that John was not directly dependent on the Synoptics. The relationship of their respective resurrection narratives is considerably different from that of the passion account, but it has also been the subject of intense interest. Whereas in the passion John goes along with the Synoptics, which in their turn move together, in the resurrection accounts the synoptic episodes are each quite different. All the Gospels report the discovery of the tomb empty, but beyond that it is only John that agrees with any of the others. (Mark, of course, ends at that point without a resurrection appearance.) Each of John's episodes has a Lukan or Matthean parallel of sorts.

The scenes of appearances of Jesus to the Twelve in John 20:19–29 and Luke 24:36–43 have strong affinities, and the account of the appearance of Jesus to Mary Magdalene (John 20:14–18) outside the tomb is paralleled by his appearance, briefly narrated, to two unnamed women as they hurried away from the tomb in Matthew 28:9–10. Of course, Mark's longer ending reflects knowledge of John (chap. 20 only!). John 21, moreover, curiously supplies the unfulfilled expectations aroused by Mark 16:7 (14:28): Jesus has gone before the disciples to Galilee. They see him; Peter is restored. Obviously there are distinctly Johannine elements in John 21 (above all, the appearance of the Beloved Disciple), but it is equally obvious that we are here dealing

---

[1] This was the method employed by Helmut Koester in his noteworthy monograph, *Synoptische Überlieferung bei den apostolischen Vätern*, TU 65 (Berlin: Akademie Verlag, 1957), 1–3. The lack of specific redactional traits of the canonical Gospels led Koester to the conclusion that the Apostolic Fathers did not depend on our gospel canon for their Jesus tradition.

with older traditional elements related to the Synoptics (cf. Luke 5:1–11). In this connection it is worth noting that the *Gospel of Peter,* at the point it breaks off, also anticipates a Galilean appearance and in a way that is not obviously dependent on either Mark or John.

If we judged only on the basis of the resurrection narratives, we might well imagine that John deliberately brought together, elaborated, and reconciled what he found in Matthew and Luke. Or, we might view John as a conflation of what is found, or should be found, in the Synoptics. The fact that John's Gospel otherwise differs so markedly from the Synoptics, while at the same time it is so difficult to conceive of a plausible Johannine redaction of them, gives pause to such a theory. Yet the affinities between John and the Synoptics in the resurrection accounts are indeed striking and of a different nature from those we encounter elsewhere, even in the passion. It is not surprising that they have been invoked on the side of the renascent position that John indeed knew the Synoptic Gospels.

## REDACTION-CRITICAL APPROACHES TO THE PASSION NARRATIVES AND THE QUESTION OF A PRIMITIVE SOURCE

One of the first scholars to insist upon the importance of determining whether John betrays knowledge of Markan redaction was Norman Perrin. In a paragraph in his *Introduction,* Perrin stated succinctly and conveniently basic elements of a case in favor of John's knowledge of Mark:

> For a long time the general opinion of New Testament scholars was that the passion narrative existed as a connected unit before the Gospel of Mark was written, and it was easy and natural to think that John had known and used a version of that pre-Markan narrative rather than the Gospel of Mark. But today the tendency is to ascribe more and more of the composition of the passion narrative to the evangelist Mark himself and to doubt the very existence of a pre-Markan and non-Markan passion narrative extensive enough to have been the basis for the Gospel of John. A particular consideration is the fact that the trial before the High Priest (John 18:19–24) is set in the context of the denial by Peter (18:15–18, 25–27), as it is also in the Gospel of Mark. But there is a strong case that Mark himself originally composed this account of the trial at night before the Jewish authorities and then set it in the context of the story of Peter's denial. If so, the evangelist John must necessarily have known the Gospel of Mark.[2]

---

[2] Norman Perrin, *The New Testament, An Introduction* (New York: Harcourt Brace Jonavich, 1974), 228–29. The same paragraph is maintained in the 1982 revision, p. 334. (See above, chap. 3, n. 121.)

A major basis and justification for Perrin's observation is the research of one of his former students, John R. Donahue. Donahue's dissertation, *Are You the Christ?*, a redaction-critical study dealing with the place and composition of the trial narrative in Mark,[3] concludes that the scene as such is the evangelist's composition. Mark may have used earlier tradition, but the implication of Donahue's work is that the generally held view that Mark based his passion account on a continuous passion source is at best an unnecessary hypothesis. If Mark knew no traditional passion narrative but presumably composed the first such account, how much less likely is it that John knew such a tradition? Although Donahue did not actually treat Johannine-Markan relations in this volume, the implications seem clear. In a subsequent study in a volume of essays on the passion in Mark edited by Werner H. Kelber and written mostly by others of Perrin's students, Donahue follows Perrin's argument in suggesting that John may well have known the Markan passion account.[4] Other essays by Kim Dewey, Werner Kelber, and John Dominic Crossan take the same or related positions on similar grounds. John knew the Markan passion narrative, which is Mark's own composition, and therefore presumably Mark's Gospel as a whole.

Subsequently, in a major treatise on orality and textuality in the communication of the gospel, Kelber has marshaled arguments against the existence of a pre-Markan passion narrative.[5] No more than in the account of Jesus' public ministry did Mark have in the passion a continuous traditional account. The very "tightly plotted story" which many have seen as evidence for an early narration, often thought to be close to the historical reality itself, is taken to be evidence rather of Mark's own deliberate and self-conscious composition. Moreover, disagreement among the experts who attempt to define the source

---

[3] John R. Donahue, *Are You the Christ? The Trial Narrative in the Gospel of Mark*, SBLDS 10 (Missoula, Mont.: Scholars Press, 1973).

[4] Werner H. Kelber, ed., *The Passion in Mark* (Philadelphia: Fortress Press, 1976), 1–20, esp. 9–10.

[5] Werner H. Kelber, *The Oral and the Written Gospel: The Hermeneutics of Speaking and Writing in the Synoptic Tradition, Mark, Paul, and Q* (Philadelphia: Fortress Press, 1983), 184–226, esp. 195–99, on the passion narrative as textual rather than oral medium. "If we recognize the densely *literary* nature of Mark's passion narrative, why do we continue searching for an *oral* setting?" (p. 195). But does the literary nature of the text, if that is indeed its nature, preclude an oral, and therefore a cultic, setting? Of course, there are also cultic texts.

Interestingly, in *The Society of Biblical Literature One Hundred Seventh Annual Meeting Seminar Papers* (Cambridge, Mass.: Society of Biblical Literature, 1971), 2:503–85, there is a lengthy seminar report, "Reflections on the Question: Was There a Pre-Markan Passion Narrative?" The authors, Werner Kelber, Anitra Kalenkow, and Robin Scroggs, differ in their judgments. Scroggs agrees with Bultmann that such a source existed; Kalenkow thinks there was at least a traditional structure or pattern; Kelber is not convinced that any such traditional account existed. Although the consensus represented by Scroggs receded in the 1970s and early 1980s, it did not die, as the later works of Trocmé and Green show (see below).

is grounds for doubting its existence. Certainly results have been diverse, but what can be said of Mark's putative passion source can be said of many, if not most, of the "results" of the application of historical criticism to the Bible. Whether one is persuaded by Kelber will depend largely on what one makes of his arguments regarding the dichotomy of oral and written in the communication of the gospel.

Conclusions similar to Kelber's were reached by Frank J. Matera, whose redaction-critical analysis did for Mark 15 what Donahue's did for Mark 14.[6] Matera displays and accentuates evidence of Markan redaction in the Markan account of Jesus' trial before Pilate, execution, and burial. To the question of how active Mark was "in forming the narrative or connecting it to read as a continuous story," Matera ultimately answers that he was very active indeed. The works of Eta Linnemann and others are cited as chipping away at the form-critical consensus in favor of a primitive passion narrative by showing how the interests of Markan theology are expressed in and through the evangelist's redaction.[7] Matera's own contribution is to show how Markan stylistic, linguistic, and theological elements permeate the narrative. As is the case with the earlier part of the Gospel, such evidence is particularly noteworthy in the interstices between, or within, episodes. Matera judiciously avoids claiming that his research disproves the existence of a pre-Markan passion source, although he himself is clearly of the opinion that in the passion as well as the public ministry Mark has tied together individually transmitted units of tradition. As much as one may want to affirm Matera's skepticism of rather divergent scholarly efforts to reconstruct a pre-Markan passion source,[8] one will also wonder whether what is true for the source-critical goose is true also for the redaction-critical gander. That is, if source-critical results cannot escape the shadow of dubiety, can redaction criticism proceed with a greater measure of certainty?

The difficulty with the redaction-critical method of analysis as applied to Mark is inherent in the Markan material. Since we do not have the tradition that Mark used, we can only infer its form, extent, and character. With how much confidence, then, can one distinguish tradition and redaction? The association of the denial of Peter with the trial before the high priest may be, as Perrin suggested, the result of Mark's composition. Yet even if it is, who is to say that this combination can only mean that it is Mark's original idea as

---

[6] Frank J. Matera, *The Kingship of Jesus: Composition and Theology in Mark 15*, SBLDS 66 (Chico, Calif.: Scholars Press, 1982).

[7] Ibid., 2.

[8] Ibid., 4.

well? (Possibly Mark had two traditional stories that he knew belonged to-gether.) Only the view that it is his original idea requires that John should have gotten it from Mark. Otherwise, John may be cited as evidence against Mark's originality in making this combination. Moreover, there are significant differences from Mark in John's rendition, which are not easily explicable as expressions of Johannine theology. John's account of Jesus' appearance before the high priest is almost completely different and, as commentators have noted, less theologically freighted than Mark's. Because of this, the contention that Mark's composition was original and John depended on Mark is, at this point, less than compelling.[9] Is it, then, far-fetched to suggest that John and Mark know from tradition both the trial scene and its association with the denial?

As Clifton Black has shown, Markan redaction criticism may in practice owe more to the historical and other presuppositions of its practitioners than to the canons of the method itself.[10] A method that seeks the rationale and necessities of an author's composition naturally tends to see the hand of the author at work in the formation and arrangement of material. Thus redaction criticism has a built-in bias in favor of the conscious intent or purpose of the author. By the same token, form criticism or tradition history quite naturally sought the meaning and coherence of texts, and particularly the passion narrative, in the putative purpose and setting of the material in the community (especially the cult) and its functions. It is not surprising that the founders of the form-critical method, Rudolf Bultmann and Martin Dibelius, argued for the existence of a traditional cultic passion narrative antedating the compo-sition of any Gospel. On these terms, Mark and John could have had access independently to such a narrative tradition or to its variant recensions. The existence of John's narrative, differing as it did from Mark's, became at the same time evidence for the earlier account(s).

Dibelius's arguments for the existence of such a passion narrative are ex-egetically based. For example, Mark 14:1–2 suggests that Jesus was arrested before the Passover feast. Yet according to Mark's own understanding, the Last Supper was itself a Passover meal (Mark 14:12), and so there is a tension between Mark and what must be presumed to be his traditional source.[11] Be that as it may, Dibelius is already predisposed to seek such a source in the early tradition because of his view of the necessities of the church and its

---

[9] See further, Robert Tomson Fortna, "Jesus and Peter at the High Priest's House: A Test Case for the Relation Between Mark's and John's Gospels," *NTS* 24 (1977–78): 371–83.

[10] C. Clifton Black, *The Disciples According to Mark: Markan Redaction in Current Debate*, JSNTSup 27 (Sheffield: JSOT Press, 1989).

[11] Martin Dibelius, *From Tradition to Gospel*, trans. B. L. Woolf (New York: Charles Scribner's Sons, 1934), 180–81. The first German edition was published in 1919.

preaching: "For what we know of the Christian message makes us expect a description of the whole Passion in the course of a sermon, at least in outline."[12] He goes on to point out that every formulation of the early preaching (i.e., the kerygma) mentions the crucifixion and resurrection. Bultmann's analysis is typically more complex and proceeds by a kind of *via negativa*. Bultmann identifies individual units (e.g., the Last Supper, Peter's denial) that did not belong to the earliest narrative but, in a sense, presuppose it and have been fitted into it.[13] Like Dibelius, he locates the motivation for the development of such a narrative in the early kerygma or preaching: "For what led to a coherent narrative . . . was above all the kerygma, as we know it in the prophecies of the Passion and Resurrection in Mk. 8:31; 9:31; 10:33f. and in the speeches of Acts."[14] Georg Bertram's full-scale form-critical study of the entire passion narrative followed by but a year or two the publication of the fundamental works of Dibelius and Bultmann.[15] Bertram's characterization of the passion as a cult narrative representing an early, oral stage in the development of the Christian tradition, particularly the preaching, was fully in accord with the insights and perspectives of his predecessors. Needless to say, such a view of the existence and motivation for a primitive passion narrative could be accommodated exceedingly well in the classic case for the primitive kerygma centered on the cross and resurrection as developed by C. H. Dodd in *The Apostolic Preaching and Its Developments*.[16] Joachim Jeremias, generally regarded as more conservative than the radical Bultmann or even the more moderate Dibelius, also posited the existence of such a primitive narrative, taking his cue from the existence of parallel, but apparently independent, accounts in Mark and John.[17]

Hazardous though it may be to draw causal connections, it is nevertheless the case that the advent of redaction criticism and the newer literary criticism has been accompanied by an erosion of the consensus about a pre-Markan

---

[12] Ibid., 178–79.

[13] Rudolf Bultmann, *The History of the Synoptic Tradition*, trans. John Marsh, rev. ed. (Oxford: Basil Blackwell, 1968; translated from 1931 German ed.), 275–79.

[14] Ibid., 275.

[15] Georg Bertram, *Die Leidensgeschichte Jesu und der Christuskult: Eine formgeschichtliche Untersuchung*, FRLANT, new series 15; entire series 32 (Göttingen: Vandenhoeck & Ruprecht, 1922). Earlier, John's use of some independent passion traditions was acknowledged. Perhaps typical was Maurice Goguel, *Les sources du récit johannique de la passion* (Paris: Librairie Fischbacher, 1910), who concluded that John used some independent tradition in contact with Mark's source and some material taken from the Synoptics, to which he added his own compositions (p. 103).

[16] C. H. Dodd, *The Apostolic Preaching and Its Developments* (London: Hodder & Stoughton, 1936).

[17] Joachim Jeremias, *The Eucharistic Words of Jesus*, trans. Norman Perrin (New York: Charles Scribners Sons, 1966), 89–96.

or pre-gospel passion narrative. Perrin and his former students and colleagues are representative of this trend in North America. As for Europe, we have already mentioned the monograph of Eta Linnemann.[18] Yet on the Continent the older, form-critically inspired view is still well represented. Certainly it is reflected in Ferdinand Hahn's study of the Johannine passion narrative published the same year as Linnemann's monograph (1970).[19] Hahn views the Johannine narrative as parallel with, but not derivative from, the synoptic. Along with contrasts with Mark, there are special affinities with Luke that point to the use of a common tradition. The pre-Johannine passion tradition began as early as the report of the meeting of the Sanhedrin (John 11:47; cf. Mark 14:1). Through John 17 the report is heavily interlarded with the evangelist's distinctive material, but from the account of the arrest of Jesus (John 18:1–11) onward one finds the relatively complete, traditional narrative. The same general point of view is found in Hans Klein's study of the Johannine and Lukan passion narratives published a half dozen years later.[20] Klein maintains that the Johannine and Lukan narratives are based not directly on Mark but on a common source (G), which in turn was based on the passion source (or *Vorlage*) of Mark but contained other material. Hence the agreements between Luke and John.

Probably the more widely held opinion on a Markan passion source is still better represented by Rudolf Pesch's espousal of a pre-Markan source in his influential commentary[21] and by the collection of essays on the synoptic passion narrative edited by Meinrad Limbeck[22] than by those who doubt or deny the existence of a traditional passion narrative antedating Mark's Gospel.

---

[18] Eta Linnemann, *Studien zur Passionsgeschichte*, FRLANT 102 (Göttingen: Vandenhoeck & Ruprecht, 1970), 171: "Wir haben den Nachweis geführt, dass der Passionsgeschichte des Markusevangeliums kein zusammenhängender Bericht zugrunde lag. Sie ist von Anfang bis Ende vom Evangelisten aus selbständigen Einzeltraditionen komponiert."

[19] Ferdinand Hahn, "Der Prozess Jesu nach dem Johannesevangelium," in *Evangelisch-Katholischer Kommentar zum Neuen Testament, Vorarbeiten* (Neukirchen-Vluyn: Neukirchener Verlag, 1970), 2:23–96.

[20] Klein, "Die lukanisch-johanneische Passionstradition," 155–86, reprinted in the work edited by Limbeck (n. 22 below), 366–403. (On Klein's thesis, see above, chap. 4, n. 5.) On Lukan-Johannine relations, note also the earlier work of E. Osty, "Les points de contact entre le récit de la passion dans Saint Luc et dans Saint Jean," in *Mélanges J. Lebreton, RSR* 39 (1951): 146–51, who suggests a personal relationship between the evangelists John and Luke!

[21] Rudolf Pesch, *Das Markusevangelium*, Part 2: *Kommentar zu Kap. 8, 27—16, 20*, Herder's theologischer Kommentar zum Neuen Testament (Freiburg: Herder, 1977), 1–27. Pesch has staunchly defended his reconstruction and early dating of Mark's source in "The Gospel in Jerusalem: Mark 14:12–26 as the Oldest Tradition of the Early Church," in *The Gospel and the Gospels*, edited by Peter Stuhlmacher (Grand Rapids: Wm. B. Eerdmans Publishing Co., 1991), 106–148.

[22] Meinrad Limbeck, ed., *Redaktion und Theologie des Passionsberichtes nach den Synoptikern*, Wege der Forschung 481 (Darmstadt: Wissenschaftliche Buchgesellschaft, 1981).

In his introductory essay for *Redaktion und Theologie des Passionsberichtes nach den Synoptikern*, Limbeck mentions that Linnemann, Kelber, and G. Schille reject a pre-Markan source and simply observes that critical opinion in general has not been persuaded.[23]

Since the appearance of the Pesch commentary and the Limbeck volume, Till Arend Mohr has published his massive Basel doctoral dissertation (1982, but basically completed in 1980) on the Johannine and Markan passion narratives.[24] As the author indicates at the outset, the goal of the work is principally to illumine the Markan account. (Mohr promises a second volume on the Johannine passion.) The Johannine narrative is then examined primarily with the Markan account in view, and Mohr concludes that John's account is basically independent of Mark. Although they rely on different renditions of a primitive passion account, John's, not Mark's, is the earlier. Mark's version of the source has been subject to a pre-Markan redaction and augmentation even before its incorporation into the Second Gospel. Both Mark and John had the source in written form.[25] By and large, traces of Markan redaction and even pre-Markan redaction do not appear in John.[26] The chief evidence that would prove John's dependence on Mark is thus missing. Therefore it is all the more surprising that Mohr repeatedly asserts that John knew the Synoptics and confidently states that he wrote in order to supplement *(ergänzen)*, deepen, and correct them. Interestingly enough, neither Gardner-Smith nor Windisch is cited in the extensive bibliography, nor for that matter are Boismard and Neirynck. Mohr actually amasses a great deal of evidence that would support Gardner-Smith's view that John wrote without knowing the Synoptics. Although Mohr thinks John intended to supplement or correct the Synoptics, he does not adequately meet Windisch's objections to that traditional view. In fact, his major effort is directed toward showing John's independence of the Synoptics, not his knowledge of them. Perhaps it is not surprising, then, that he appears to have achieved greater success in that undertaking than in the other.

The question of a primitive passion narrative (that Mark used) has been set in a new perspective by John Dominic Crossan, who finds such a source not within Mark's narrative, or John's, but in the *Gospel of Peter*.[27] With certain

---

[23] Ibid., 2.

[24] Till Arend Mohr, *Markus- und Johannespassion: Redaktions-und traditionsgeschichtliche Untersuchung der markinischen und johanneischen Passionstradition*, ATANT 70 (Zurich: Theologischer Verlag, 1982).

[25] Ibid., 404–9.

[26] Ibid., 347.

[27] John Dominic Crossan, *The Cross That Spoke: The Origins of the Passion Narrative* (San Francisco: Harper & Row, 1988); cf. idem, *Four Other Gospels: Shadows on the Contours of the Canon* (Minneapolis: Seabury/Winston, 1985).

other scholars, notably Helmut Koester,[28] Crossan has abandoned the presumption that the canonical Gospels are earlier than the apocryphal and proceeds to analyze and compare *Peter*, of which we have only a fragment of the passion and resurrection narratives, with Mark and the other Synoptics. In *Peter*, there are striking similarities to, or reminiscences of, the canonical account, which Crossan attributes to later editing or emending on the basis of those Gospels, but the basic framework is not derivative, and is said to be quite ancient and primary. The original narrative included the crucifixion and burial, the placing of a guard at the tomb, and a distinctive account of the resurrection itself. From the canonical Gospels have been added Joseph of Arimathea's role in the burial, the women's encounter with a young man at the tomb, and the beginning of an account of the risen Jesus' appearance to the disciples at the sea. The primitive narrative is obviously mythological, unhistorical, and anti-Jewish, having been constructed on the basis of Old Testament motifs rather than historical traditions or recollections. Mark and the other evangelists have domesticated and historized this narrative, but their verisimilitude cannot·be equated with history—quite the contrary!

The fourth evangelist was also influenced by this *Cross Gospel*, as Crossan calls it, as well as by the canonical Gospels,[29] but John has no other, independent source. Crossan's work certainly shows that the idea of an early, pre-gospel passion source used by our evangelist is not dead. He has revised it in a new and provocative form. Whether it better accounts for the canonical passion narratives or they for it is a question that in all likelihood will be sharply debated. Interestingly enough, Crossan seems to share with others who deny to John any independent passion tradition the view that there was only one such original and independent passion narrative. It was not Mark's, however, but Peter's. One might ask, on form- or tradition-critical premises, whether there would not likely have been more than one such passion tradition or more than one recension of a common tradition.

While the 1980s saw Crossan present an ingenious thesis that is certainly unusual, other, more conventional, attempts to understand the passion narrative as a product of the church and its cult, antedating any written gospels, have continued. In a brief monograph entitled *The Passion as Liturgy*, Etienne Trocmé has advanced the thesis that the passion narrative had liturgical roots, specifically in the Passover celebration of early Jewish Christians at which the

---

[28] Helmut Koester, "Apocryphal and Canonical Gospels," *HTR* 73 (1980): 105–30.
[29] Crossan, *The Cross That Spoke*, 17–21.

death of Jesus was commemorated.[30] Inasmuch as his death occurred at Passover, such a commemoration would have been appropriate. It is then quite natural to imagine that the narrative of Jesus' passion and death would have been recited on that occasion, and eventually written down. Subsequently, Joel B. Green published a much longer work on the subject of the narratives of the death of Jesus in which he strongly reasserted the form- and tradition-critical perspective.[31] Green analyzes the passion narrative of each Gospel with a view first of all to ascertaining literary dependence and relationships.

It is not surprising that a keystone of Green's argument is his analysis of the Johannine passion, carried through in discussion with scholars, particularly M. Sabbe, who have espoused John's dependence on the Synoptic Gospels. In three test cases, the anointing of Jesus (John 12:1–8), the foot washing (John 13:1–30), and the Jewish trial of Jesus (John 18:13–27), Green maintains that John's narratives are not derived from and do not presuppose the Synoptics. Thus the Fourth Gospel becomes a witness for an independent rendition of the narrative of Jesus' passion, and there is reason to push behind the Markan, or synoptic, version to inquire about the narrative's traditional and cultic roots. This is exactly what Green then does. After an analysis of the place of the passion in Mark and Mark's redactional policy he has chapters entitled "The Passion in the Early Church: Form-Criticism Revisited" and "The Sitz im Leben for the Early Passion Narrative." Green identifies this setting as the celebration of the Lord's Supper, in which the focal point is Jesus' death and the salvation of humankind that it signifies. (Green rejects Trocmé's proposal on grounds that we lack evidence of an early Christian Passover celebration.) One cannot overlook the fact that the radical method of an earlier day, form criticism, now becomes the instrument of a more conservative criticism. This is not necessarily a point against Green's thesis, however, for it may simply confirm the appropriateness of the form-critical interest and perspective. The question of the literary relationships among the extant gospel passion narratives cannot be divorced from an interest in the origin and function of those narratives, presumably in the life and cult of the early church.

---

[30] Etienne Trocmé, *The Passion as Liturgy: A Study in the Origin of the Passion Narratives in the Four Gospels* (London: SCM Press, 1983). Trocmé's argument at the level of literary analysis is tied to his rather unique view that the Markan passion narrative (Mark 14–16) is a later addition to the original Gospel. See his *Formation of the Gospel According to Mark* (London: SPCK, 1975). It is not, however, dependent on that analysis in principle.

[31] Joel B. Green, *The Death of Jesus: Tradition and Interpretation in the Passion Narrative*, WUNT 33 (Tübingen: J.C.B. Mohr [Paul Siebeck], 1988), originally a Ph.D. dissertation at the University of Aberdeen, Scotland, with I. Howard Marshall.

Now to reiterate, by way of summary, the relevance of the primitive passion narrative hypothesis to the relationship of John and the Synoptics. Characteristically, scholars who believe that Mark created the passion narrative, whether out of separate traditions or out of whole cloth (usually the former), also assume that his narrative was the sole archetype. Thus John must have appropriated it for the passion narrative of his Gospel. Although this is a logical way of reasoning, it may be worthwhile to ask whether it is necessary or airtight. Is it necessary, on the premise that Mark composed his own passion narrative (presumably out of traditions available to him), to suppose that he alone did so and that his passion narrative must then have been the sole source of the Gospel of John as well as of those of Matthew and Luke? (On the other hand, if Mark drew upon an earlier traditional passion narrative, the chances are that other evangelists, especially Luke and John, could have availed themselves of that or other, related passion traditions.) It does not actually follow, however, that if Mark created the first passion narrative (or at least his own passion narrative), no one else could have done so independently. John might have done so, but whether John knew and used Mark's, or the Synoptics', would have still to be determined on the basis of comparative redaction-critical and similar studies; that would also be the case if John had used a traditional source. There is a sense in which such study remains haunted by the ghost of the primitive passion source, but the existence of such a source, even if it could be taken for granted, would not decide the issue of John and the Synoptics. Is John's redaction best explained against the background of such a source or against the Synoptics? The possibilities are not mutually exclusive and need to be tested in individual pericopes before a blanket judgment is made. In this regard, the work of Anton Dauer becomes significant, for he has devised a method of testing for the occurrence of a tradition and of synoptic redaction in John that holds out hope of not being infected by the investigative presuppositions.


## ANTON DAUER

Biblical scholars have generally assumed that oral tradition preceded the writing of gospels or other narrative documents and then died out. But are the grounds for that assumption firm? In an important study now more than two decades old, Anton Dauer has questioned this assumption on the basis of a close analysis of the Johannine passion account. Dauer's monograph on the Johannine passion narrative breaks new ground in the discussion of John and the Synoptics in setting forth a method of deciding whether contacts between John and the Synoptics are based on a literary relationship or on an oral tradition.[32]

Limiting himself to John 18–19, the Johannine passion, Dauer subjects it and parallel synoptic texts to very intensive scrutiny. His method is closely analytical and inductive. He does not begin with a dominant insight or working hypothesis, nor with an analysis of breaks or sutures in the text, although the latter figure in his analysis. Rather he closely examines the Johannine text, always with a view to determining its relationship to the synoptic parallels, observing style and speech, the author's compositional technique (seams, redactional transitions, etc.), and expressions of Johannine theology. Obviously, narrative elements that do not exhibit a high incidence of Johannine style, speech, or thought become prime candidates for a pre-gospel source, especially when evidence of the evangelist's redactional activity is also present. Affinities with the Markan and other synoptic accounts within the putative source material tend to confirm rather than call into question the identification of the source. The source can be expected to show affinities with the Synoptics. In fact, most of the affinities with the Synoptics occur in passages that on other grounds are assigned to the source rather than to the fourth evangelist.

In the case of each pericope or complex, the attempt to isolate the source is followed by an analysis and explanation of the parallels or contacts with the Synoptic Gospels.[33] At this stage of his research, Dauer's working hypothesis is that John does not draw directly or primarily upon the Synoptics. This is finally not a methodological weakness, however, for, having isolated the Johannine source, it would have been theoretically possible for him to conclude that it was, or in some part was, derived from Mark. Dauer does not, however, reach this conclusion. Instead, his analysis repeatedly confirms the conclusion that John is not directly or primarily dependent upon one or more of the other Gospels. The verbal agreements and other contacts are outweighed by many differences, which cannot be accounted for out of the

---

[32] Anton Dauer, *Die Passionsgeschichte im Johannesevangelium: Eine traditionsgeschichtliche und theologische Untersuchung zu Joh 18, 1—19, 30*, SANT 30 (Munich: Kösel-Verlag, 1972), originally a dissertation with Rudolf Schnackenburg at Würzburg. Dauer cites with approval (pp. 60–61 nn. 218, 219; and elsewhere) the earlier work of Nils A. Dahl, "Die Passionsgeschichte bei Matthäus," *NTS* 2 (1955–56): 17–32, esp. 22, and Peder Borgen, "John and the Synoptics in the Passion Narrative," *NTS* 5 (1958–59): 246–59, esp. 251. Note also the discussion between Borgen and Ivor Buse: Buse, "St. John and the Marcan Passion Narrative," *NTS* 4 (1957–58): 215–19, criticized by Borgen (op. cit.) for not taking the later Synoptics into account, and Buse, "St. John and the Passion Narratives of St. Matthew and St. Luke," *NTS* 7 (1960–61): 65–76, in which he responds. Neither Borgen nor Buse takes John to be dependent on the Synoptics directly; nor does Dahl, for that matter.

[33] Dauer, *Passionsgeschichte*, 21–61, on the arrest of Jesus. See pp. 22–41 for the isolation of the source; and pp. 49–61 for the relation of the source to the (later) synoptic evangelists.

evangelist's theology or other interests. These differences are, in fact, among the hallmarks of the author's source. Yet one of the results of Dauer's investigation is that the synoptic contacts lie mainly in the Johannine passion source, not in the material attributed on other grounds to the evangelist.

Because Dauer's work is so detailed and his method inductive, any general description of it will inevitably appear abstract and perhaps colorless. It may be useful to describe briefly how Dauer proceeds in a specific instance. The arrest of Jesus (John 18:1–11) will afford a good example.[34] A phrase-by-phrase examination leads to the conclusion that John 18:1–3 is derived by John from a traditional source. As even a glance at the gospel parallels will show, most of the content of this section is without parallel in Mark or the other Synoptics. Yet it serves a necessary role in introducing the account, setting the scene, describing the personae, and so forth. Nor does it show particularly Johannine stylistic characteristics or theological interests. By contrast, the entire section of John 18:4–9, which has no real parallel in the synoptic account, is replete with Johannine stylistic and compositional characteristics and bears his theological signature. To begin with, instead of being identified by Judas's kiss, Jesus takes the initiative in his own arrest (John 18:4). Moreover, the text makes it explicitly clear that Jesus knows fully what is transpiring. After the arresting party have fallen upon the ground (18:6) and Jesus has asked a second time, "Whom do you seek?" (18:7), they finally say, "Jesus of Nazareth," to which he responds *egō eimi* (18:8). Typically, Jesus has complete knowledge and control of the situation. The concluding statement (18:9), which speaks of the fulfillment of the word Jesus has spoken, is again Johannine in its formulation and content. In 18:10, however, we have the incident of the striking of the high priest's servant's ear, paralleled in all the Synoptics, which in John has a resolution (18:11) paralleled only in Matthew (26:52): Jesus tells Peter (so identified in John only) to put away his sword. (Dauer, unlike the Aland *Synopsis*, takes John 18:12 to be the beginning of the hearing before the high priest rather than the conclusion of the arrest.)

A striking fact is now observed: the most distinctive contacts of John's account with the Synoptics are with Matthew or Luke separately rather than with Mark. The fact that the description of the blow to the servant's right ear (John 18:10) closely parallels Mark 14:47 is not taken to confirm John's knowledge and use of Mark but rather his use of a parallel tradition, to which Dauer ascribes both proper names (Peter, Malchus) that appear only in the

---

[34] Ibid., 21–61.

Johannine version.[35] But, among other things, only Matthew and John agree in having Jesus order the sword to be put away (Matt. 26:52/John 18:11).[36] Apart from the word for sword (*macheiran*, acc.), there is, however, little verbatim agreement between them. At the same time, only Luke and John agree in describing the place where the arrest will take place as a customary meeting place. There is at this point (Luke 22:39/John 18:2) no verbatim agreement at all in their descriptions. In each case the wording is very different. John writes, "Jesus gathered there frequently with his disciples." Luke has, "Going forth he went as usual (*kata to ethnos*) to the Mount of Olives, and his disciples followed." Here John's statement lies in what has otherwise been determined to be his source. Strangely, only Luke and John also fail to name the place Gethsemane, and only they specifically mention the disciples as coming with Jesus (Luke 22:39/John 18:1).[37] In each of the cases mentioned, Dauer concludes that Matthew or Luke is responsible for the item in question (or lack thereof), that is, it appears in his redaction and was not drawn from a special source or tradition to which John also might have had access.

What conclusion may be inferred from this state of affairs? John has hardly copied Matthew and Luke; there are too many differences from either or both. Moreover, these contacts, and the vast majority of others Dauer will find, appear in parts of the Johannine narrative ascribed on other grounds to the traditional source. Did the source, or its author, know and copy the Gospels of Matthew and Luke? Again, the paucity of verbatim agreements and the seemingly haphazard nature of the points of contact make such a conclusion appear unlikely. Rather, the Gospels of Matthew and Luke specifically, not just the traditions they embody, seem to have influenced the continuing oral tradition, which in turn has been taken up into the Johannine source. Thus, one must conjure with what Dauer calls the interweaving of oral and written sources: not only do gospel writers draw upon oral tradition, as well as upon one another, but written gospels influence the continuing oral tradition. In some such manner, the influence of the written Synoptic Gospels, particularly Matthew and Luke, affected the formation of the Johannine passion source (whether written or oral).

As we have just seen, Dauer repeatedly invokes the principle, based on redaction-critical analysis, that the editorial compositions of one document found in another imply the use of the former document, not merely the tradition it embodies, by the author of the latter. To find even hints of, or

[35] Ibid., 44–46.
[36] Ibid., 51–52.
[37] Ibid., 53–56.

allusions to, the editorial work of Matthew or Luke in John (i.e., John's source) strongly suggests that the Gospel of John somehow, or at some level, reflects familiarity with the Gospels of Matthew and Luke, not just the traditions they contain. As a principle of exegetical logic this is impeccable and should be applicable to Mark as well as to John. If John shows signs of being influenced by Markan redaction, John must have known Mark's Gospel.

In fact, we now arrive back at the redaction-critical insight that Perrin stated so cogently. We have, however, already noticed some problems it presents, for there is considerable uncertainty in identifying redactional over against traditional material in Mark. In the case of Luke and Matthew, the problem is less severe, inasmuch as we have in Mark and Q what most scholars take to be their primary sources. Yet even there it is difficult to obtain certainty, much less agreement among scholars. In his review of Dauer's work, Raymond E. Brown observed that of six contacts with Luke in John 18:1–3, 10–11, all of which Dauer assigns to Lukan redaction, Vincent Taylor assigns three certainly to a pre-Lukan passion narrative, two probably to that source, and one to redaction.[38] This is not taken to mean that Dauer's work is subjective and of no value. Nevertheless, Brown has dramatically illustrated that confidence in its results is contingent upon the certainty with which redactional elements in the Synoptics can be identified. Even in instances where those elements can be identified with great certainty, however, there remains at least the one further imponderable that the distinction between redaction and tradition is not airtight; they need not be mutually exclusive categories. That is, to take an example from current discussion, even if the bracketing of the trial of Jesus by Peter's denial is redactional in Mark (or in John), it does not follow that their juxtaposition is a free creation of the evangelist. It may be based on memory, that is, tradition. If John makes the same juxtaposition, he may know what Mark also knew, but it does not necessarily follow that he could have known it only from Mark.[39]

Nevertheless Dauer, in developing earlier insights of Nils A. Dahl and Peder Borgen, whom he credits,[40] has posed intriguing questions about the character of any contacts or connections between the Fourth Gospel and the other canonical Gospels. Must they in every case depend on copying? Does the tradition necessarily move *von Schreibtisch zu Schreibtisch*, or from one document to another, even after gospels have been written? The curious combination of John's wide divergencies from the Synoptics in conjunction with

---

[38] Raymond E. Brown, *JBL* 92 (1973): 608–10.
[39] See Fortna, "Jesus and Peter at the High Priest's House."
[40] See n. 32 above.

his putative source's apparent knowledge of some of their redactional material and language suggests to Dauer that the Synoptic Gospels have influenced the oral tradition upon which the Johannine account is based (perhaps the Johannine source—Dauer is not sure whether the pre-Johannine narrative was written). This is a refinement of the frequent suggestion that John knew the Synoptics at a distance, so to speak, and quoted them from memory. As such, it will be a useful and necessary ingredient of any future discussion of the problem of John and the Synoptics as well as of their passion narratives.

As Dauer points out, the passion tradition or source that he finds in the Fourth Gospel has much in common with the source proposed by Bultmann in his commentary as well as with those of Ferdinand Hahn and Robert T. Fortna. (There are more references to Bultmann in Dauer's index than to any other scholar.) The work of Hahn and Fortna appeared too late to be incorporated into Dauer's monograph, but they are treated separately in an appendix.[41] All four efforts to delineate a passion source, despite some differences, have in common the result that the Johannine passion source runs parallel to the synoptic, conveys most of the same episodes, but differs in ways that cannot easily be accounted for in terms of the fourth evangelist's theology or style. But Dauer also has affinities with C. H. Dodd, who preferred to speak of oral tradition rather than a written source, and in principal with Dodd's predecessor Percival Gardner-Smith. Thus Dauer's work stands in a burgeoning tradition of scholarship which he endeavors to refine, particularly in his ingenious explanation of the relationship of the Johannine passion source to the Synoptic Gospels.[42]

---

[41] On Fortna, see above, pp. 71–73; on Hahn, p. 118.

[42] Dauer's method has been extended to the Johannine farewell discourses by Takashi Onuki, "Die johanneischen Abschiedsreden und die synoptische Tradition: Eine traditionskritische und traditionsgeschichtliche Untersuchung," *Annual of the Japanese Biblical Institute* (Tokyo: Yamamoto Shoten, 1977), 157–268. For such items as Jesus' prophecy of the betrayal (John 13:21–22, 26–27), the words of institution of the Eucharist (albeit not given in the Gospel), Jesus' announcement of the scattering of the disciples (16:1, 32) and the denial of Peter (13:36–38), and Jesus' final struggle in prayer (12:27–28; 14:30–31; 18:11), as well as others, there was a Johannine tradition, used by the evangelist, parallel to the Synoptics. Onuki finds, as did Dauer in the passion, that the Johannine source shows evidence of synoptic influence, and not just by synoptic tradition but by distinctively redactional elements, particularly of Mark and Luke.

Dauer himself has now applied basically his same method of analysis to Luke (see below, chap. 6) and to the trial before Jewish authorities. His paper, "Spuren der (synoptischen) Synedriumsverlandlung im 4. Evangelium: Das Verhältnis zu den Synoptikern," is in the proceedings of the 1990 Louvain Colloquium, *John and the Synoptics*, ed. Denaux.

## ROSEL BAUM-BODENBENDER

While Dauer stands in a scholarly tradition in which the passion narrative used by John is perceived as having many affinities with the synoptic, Rosel Baum-Bodenbender breaks out in a new direction. In her Mainz dissertation, *Hoheit in Niedrigkeit: Johanneische Christologie im Prozess Jesu vor Pilatus (Joh 18, 28—19, 16a),*[43] Baum-Bodenbender intends primarily to make a contribution to the understanding of Johannine Christology, but a large part of her work is devoted to the source question. Her results, so far pertaining only to Jesus' trial before Pilate, are almost the obverse of those of Dauer and the scholarly tradition he represents. According to her theory, the original stratum of the Johannine narrative is not parallel to the Synoptics but consists rather of just those distinctively Johannine elements which the Synoptics lack. Baum-Bodenbender is skeptical of the basis of the stylistic criteria used by Dauer to separate out the traditional source from the work of the evangelist. Moreover, she questions the historical implications of Dauer's thesis. If John's source was influenced by Matthew and Luke toward the end of the first century, when is the Gospel of John itself to be dated? In other words, is it not being pushed too late? Ferdinand Hahn's view that John's dependence on the Synoptics is superfluous to the understanding of his text is likewise questioned.[44] The issue of John's relation to the synoptic narratives must not be prematurely closed, for it is important for understanding the distinctive theological character of the Johannine passion.

For our purposes we may bypass Baum-Bodenbender's worthwhile literary analysis of John 18:28—19:16a as a whole to deal with her source proposals, which comprise the major part of her dissertation.[45] As we have already suggested, she discovers behind the trial scene a source that consists of the more distinctly Johannine elements of the narrative (e.g., 18:33, 36–38), which exegetes such as Bultmann, Dauer, and Fortna had assigned largely to the evangelist just because of the presence of clearly Johannine motifs. Those parts of the narrative in which the clearest affinities to the Synoptics appear (e.g., 18:39—19:6) are assigned by Baum-Bodenbender to the later redaction,

---

[43] Rosel Baum-Bodenbender, *Hoheit in Niedrigkeit: Johanneische Christologie im Prozess Jesu vor Pilatus (Joh 18, 28—19, 16a),* Forschung zur Bibel 49 (Würzburg: Echter Verlag, 1984).

[44] Ibid., 10–16 (on Dauer); 16–19 (on Hahn). Hahn, "Der Prozess Jesu nach dem Johannesevangelium," as we have seen, more or less assumes the widely held view that John's similarities to the Synoptics in the passion are based on common tradition rather than a direct literary relationship.

[45] Baum-Bodenbender, *Hoheit in Niedrigkeit,* 97–231 ("Untersuchung der Entstehungs-geschichte der Erzählung vom Prozess Jesu vor Pilatus").

whose purpose was precisely to conform John's account more closely to the other Gospels. (Contrariwise, most of that portion was assigned by Bultmann and Fortna, as well as by Dauer, to the source, the synoptic-like traits confirming its traditional character.[46]) The thoroughly Johannine source is independent of the Synoptic Gospels. The redactional additions, on the other hand, reflect knowledge of those Gospels.

The analyses and results of many other commentators are, in effect, stood on their heads, in that Baum-Bodenbender holds what is distinctly Johannine as more primitive and what is less so as a later attempt to conform John to the broader tradition. She sets forth her position with many keen exegetical and related insights, as we shall observe. At the same time, her perspective on Johannine origins and development (as well as source criticism) diverges sharply from the one commonly held today, particularly in English-language scholarship. To put her position succinctly, the Johannine trajectory does not move toward Gnosticism but away from it; not away from a common synoptic tradition but toward it. Baum-Bodenbender's thesis is not, however, based on such general considerations but arises out of close analysis of the text. Her method is that of the older literary criticism. She looks first for seams in the texts, for tensions, breaks, or doublets that might indicate the existence of more than one literary stratum. An understanding of her thesis requires some grasp of its detail.

Initially two major breaks in the narrative are noted.[47] The first is after the general introduction (John 18:29-30), which prepares the reader for the whole trial but not specifically for Pilate's opening question, "Are you the King of the Jews?" (18:33), which in the context remains unmotivated. Thus the transition from introductory setting of the scene to Pilate's question is a problem. Second, after Pilate says that he finds no guilt in Jesus (18:38), Pilate's offer to release him, presumably as a criminal (to whom the crowd prefers Barabbas), is a non sequitur. Had he been found innocent, he should have been released forthwith. Similarly, the flagellation of Jesus (19:1) is in this context unmotivated. (In Luke, the offer to chastise Jesus explicitly stands in lieu of further punishment.) Moreover, when Pilate for the third time (John 19:6; cf. 19:4) finds no crime in Jesus, the narrative obviously has not moved beyond the point we found it in 18:38b (Pilate's first pronouncement of Jesus'

---

[46] On Bultmann, see D. Moody Smith, *Composition and Order of the Fourth Gospel*; 46–47; 49–50. Fortna, *The Gospel of Signs*, assigns only those aspects of 18:33, 36–38 which are parallel to the Synoptics to the Gospel of Signs (122–28, 243). He assigns 18:39–40 to the source, with 19:1–3, 6 (vv. 4 and 5 are attributed to the evangelist).

[47] Baum-Bodenbender, *Hoheit in Niedrigkeit*, 105–9.

innocence), so the transition from the first scene (18:29–38) to the second (18:39—19:6) is also problematic.

Besides these two major breaks, Baum-Bodenbender finds nearly two dozen other problems.[48] For example, after Pilate's question (John 18:33), 18:34 and 35 easily fall away, and if they were absent, they would not be missed. Jesus' answer comes only in 18:36ff. The Jews' crying "again" (*palin*) in 18:40a is problematic, for to that point in the narrative they have not cried the first time. (But in the parallel Mark 15:13 the crowd cries out "again.") In the immediate context of 19:4 Pilate's words would seem to be addressed to the soldiers (cf. 19:2). Only in the broader context is it clear that they must be addressed to the Jews. In 19:16 the trial ends abruptly, with no actual verdict from Pilate. He hands Jesus over to "them" (*autous*), which in the immediate context can only mean the Jews, although it is clear from 19:23 that the (Roman) soldiers crucify Jesus. Moreover, we find narrative doublets.[49] There are two scenes in which Jesus is led outside the praetorium by Pilate (19:4–6; 19:13–16); twice Pilate tells the Jews to take Jesus themselves and try him (18:31) or crucify him (19:6).

On the basis of such problems, and many more that she cites, Baum-Bodenbender suggests that there is good reason to doubt that there is an originally unified narrative in or underlying John 18:28—19:16a. More likely, this narrative complex was not a literary unity and has a long and perhaps complicated compositional history, which she now intends to unravel.

The introductory scene between Pilate and Jesus' adversaries (18:29–30) does not really introduce Pilate's initial question to Jesus as to whether he is King of the Jews (18:33), yet it is integrally related to 18:31–32, which requires the immediately preceding verses to make sense.[50] Verses 29–32 form a coherent sense unit, v. 28 aside. But 18:31–32 does not prepare for Pilate's questions any more than what precedes. Moreover, 18:29–32 as a whole forms no integral connection with 18:34–35, Jesus' counterquestion to Pilate, which requires the question of v. 33, although it is easily dispensable. Yet 18:34–35 functions to take up and tie together vv. 29–30 and 33 and is thus secondary to them. Both vv. 30 and 35 speak of Jesus' having been delivered by the Jews to Pilate (although in 19:16 Jesus will seemingly be delivered by Pilate to the Jews!), and apparently belong to the same narrative level. If so, vv. 29–32 and 34–35 were apparently inserted into an older narrative, represented by vv. 33 and 36–38. Taken together, 18:29–32, 34–35 form no

---

[48] Ibid., 109–22.
[49] Ibid., 122–24.
[50] For the following, ibid., 125–39.

coherent whole but are intelligible only with 18:33, 36—38, the original narrative layer. Probably this narrative included also an introduction in which Jesus was brought to Pilate, of which elements survive in v. 28. If this much can be established, we gain some basis on which to separate further an older narrative stratum (A) from a later (B). What Baum-Bodenbender proposes so far is based on internal literary (source) analysis only, but she anticipates that it will be confirmed by comparison with the Synoptics, the affinities with the Synoptics falling in the secondary level B.

With this expectation, Baum-Bodenbender turns to John 18:39—19:7.[51] John 18:39—40, the Barabbas incident, fits neither with what precedes nor with what follows. Instead of Pilate simply allowing Jesus to go free, as one would expect after 18:38, inasmuch as he has declared Jesus innocent, he makes an offer of amnesty for Jesus. The Jews, of course, reject Jesus in favor of Barabbas. But vv. 39—40 lead to no further developments in the narrative; we are not even told what happened to Barabbas. (In Mark 15:6—15 there is a much fuller account of the Barabbas incident, which concludes with specific mention of the freeing of Barabbas and the delivery of Jesus for crucifixion.) Probably 18:39—40 is a redactional addition rather than a part of the original narrative.

The beating and mocking of Jesus (John 19:1—3) also seems incongruous at this point.[52] It presupposes a guilty sentence (as, in fact, in Mark and Matthew)—just the opposite of 18:38. In that sense it agrees with what might have been expected (i.e., the sentence of condemnation) in 18:39—40, yet is not specifically said; but it certainly does not agree with the narrative context of 18:(28) 33, 36—38, in which Pilate pronounces Jesus innocent. The whole section of 19:1—6 forms a coherent narrative, of which v. 5b ("Behold the man") is the climax and v. 6 the conclusion. Thus 18:39—19:6 presupposes a unified narrative standpoint, according to which Jesus has been pronounced guilty. It does not agree with the older Johannine tradition of 18:38, according to which Pilate declared Jesus innocent. On the other hand, 19:7 resumes the narrative line that was dropped with 18:38. Jesus has been declared innocent and the Jews now protest. In such fashion, Baum-Bodenbender continues to sort out the remainder of the narrative of the trial.[53]

Comparison with the Synoptic Gospels then confirms the results of strictly internal literary analysis. Affinities with the Synoptics lie mainly, although not exclusively, in level B. In pursuing her comparison, Baum-Bodenbender

---

[51] Ibid., 140—47.
[52] For the following, ibid., 142—46.
[53] Ibid., 147—62.

first gathers all the parallels between John and the Synoptics in the trial scene,[54] recognizing that a parallel with the Synoptics is not itself a sure sign of literary dependence.[55] But if one finds the same words, the same syntactical structure, and verbal parallels extending over whole clauses or sentences, the conclusion of literary dependence can scarcely be avoided.[56] The question is then only the direction of the dependence.

It is not surprising that Baum-Bodenbender begins this stage of her evaluation of the gathered Johannine-synoptic parallels with 18:39—19:6, where she has found such parallels to be most numerous. At the same time, this section is, on the basis of her literary critical analysis, clearly a later, redactional addition to the original Johannine source.

In the brief Barabbas account (John 18:39–40), most of John's words are either identical with the Synoptics or have the same meaning.[57] Baum-Bodenbender counts only four words that are not somehow related to the Synoptics. That is prima facie evidence of a literary relationship. Moreover, that the crowd cries out "again" is completely incongruous in John, since they have not cried out previously.[58] Could the "again" be picked up from the Markan parallel (Mark 15:13)? (One might observe that the "again" is actually not well motivated in Mark; Luke drops it. But that could be all the more reason for thinking that John picked it up inadvertently from Mark.) Insofar as John's abbreviated account here departs from Matthew/Mark, which it may presuppose, it follows Luke's. For example, in John and Luke, Pilate's offer to release Jesus leads instead to the crowd's demand for Barabbas, who has heretofore not been mentioned. In Mark and Matthew, on the other hand, it is first stated that according to custom the governor would release one prisoner at the feast and that Barabbas was being held. In Mark, the crowd requests Pilate to grant the usual amnesty to one prisoner. (In Matthew, Pilate offers the choice of Barabbas or Jesus.) Thus Luke and John agree against Matthew and Mark in holding the characterization of Barabbas in second place, so to speak, after the question of Jesus' release, which is put first. Also, only Luke and John use the construction "This one . . . Barabbas" (*touton . . . ton Barabban*) in describing the criminal. Thus there is a considerable verbal and sense agreement between John and the Synoptics on the Barabbas incident, but precisely where John departs from Matthew and Mark he agrees with Luke.

---

[54] Ibid., 180–83.
[55] Cf. ibid., 186.
[56] Ibid., 187.
[57] Ibid., 188–92.
[58] Ibid., 191.

The similarities between John and the Synoptics continue in the narrative of events subsequent to the Barabbas incident,[59] but John puts the flagellation of Jesus (19:1) before the condemnation. By way of contrast, Mark and Matthew have it afterward, while Luke (23:16) relates that Pilate suggested he would punish Jesus and let him go free. Thus Luke and John, albeit in different ways, include this element of flagellation within the trial rather than at or after its conclusion.[60] In the account of the mocking of Jesus (John 19:2–3) there are close verbal similarities to Matthew, and especially to Mark (15:17–19). John 19:3b is reminiscent of Mark 14:65. In this section again the verbal similarities are too close to be a matter of chance, while the differences may be understood as stylistic variations. John 19:5a corresponds (again) to Mark 15:17; John 19:6a to both Mark 15:13 and, in the doubling of the demand to crucify Jesus, its Lukan parallel 23:21. The three statements of Pilate declaring Jesus' innocence (John 18:38; 19:4; 19:6), of course, parallel three very similar statements in Luke (23:4, 14, 22). A direct literary relation may be difficult to prove, but Baum-Bodenbender believes that John has taken this motif over from Luke. The pattern of strong similarities to the Synoptics, with divergences from Matthew and Mark in agreement with Luke, recurs repeatedly (a phenomenon that, we observed, Cribbs had emphasized).

Following this method of combining old-fashioned literary analysis of the Johannine account and comparison with the Synoptic Gospels, Baum-Bodenbender finds the results to be mutually confirmatory. Eventually the two levels of the narrative are completely identified and separated.[61] To A, the original, Johannine source, belong 18:33, 36; 19:7–11a, most of 13–15; with elements of this source detectable in 18:28a, c; 19:1, 16a as well. To B, the redactional additions (presupposing A), belong 18:29–32, 34–35; 18:39—19:6a; 19:11b–12c; as well as 18:28b and 19:14a. The many parallels between B and the Synoptics are most reasonably explained as based on the redactor's knowledge of them. There are, however, also parallels between A and the Synoptics (e.g., Pilate's question to Jesus in 18:33), but these can be explained on the basis of common tradition. To sum up: the coincidence of aporiae leading to the discrimination of two levels, with the higher incidence of agreement with the Synoptics in the level that is perceived as creating the aporiae while remaining dependent on the other (remaining) level, generates Baum-Bodenbender's distinctive hypothesis.

---

[59] Cf. ibid., 192–200.
[60] Ibid., 193.
[61] Ibid., 226–31.

Her literary theory, which moves from analysis of the Fourth Gospel to comparison with the Synoptics, appropriately finds further confirmation in the theology of the two layers.[62] The original narrative A is characterized by a high Christology *(Hoheits-Christologie)* which interprets Jesus' death as his triumphal return to the Father and victory over the world. With the high Christology goes the Johannine dualism and corresponding soteriology. The redactional level B is not a continuous narrative and is scarcely conceivable apart from A.[63] It cannot be understood in its own terms and should not be thought of as theologically opposed to A. The author of B really agrees with and accepts the theology of A and only seeks to qualify it.[64] His "Behold the man" (19:5 = B) complements the affirmation of Jesus' divine Sonship (19:7 = A), so that flesh as well as glory are emphasized. Thus high Christology is balanced with a Christology of lowliness *(Niedrigkeits-Christologie)*. While characteristic elements of the synoptic passion narrative are worked in by B, the hostility of the Jews is accentuated further.

At this point Baum-Bodenbender sets her research over against the current tension in Johannine theological interpretation characterized by the opposed positions of Bultmann and Käsemann.[65] Clearly, she finds that her analysis tends to support Bultmann, particularly with respect to the final redaction. Käsemann's position looks, on Baum-Bodenbender's terms, more like the point of view of the original source A. Indeed, Käsemann's interpretation has proceeded from texts in which A's position predominates. (Perhaps ironically, while her assessment of Johannine theology fundamentally agrees with Bultmann's, her source analysis is considerably different.)

Baum-Bodenbender's analysis is extended to and confirmed by history-of-religions considerations.[66] The question of how John is related to Gnosticism is still very much debated, although there can be little doubt of the existence of the relationship, even if it takes its rise from and is subsequent to the Fourth Gospel itself. The strongest affinities with Gnosticism or gnosis are found in the source, level A, where expressions such as "this world," "witness to the truth," and "hearing Jesus' voice" abound.[67] With its Christology of lowliness, the redaction (B) deliberately counters this gnostic dimension.[68] In this respect,

---

[62] As Baum-Bodenbender anticipates, ibid., 236.

[63] Ibid., 263–64.

[64] Ibid., 268–70.

[65] Ibid., 274–88.

[66] Ibid., 289–348, esp. 295–306, where Baum-Bodenbender shows that Bultmann, Schnackenburg, and Käsemann agree in seeing an important relation of the Fourth Gospel to gnosis, but radically disagree in understanding the nature of that relationship.

[67] Ibid., 324–28.

[68] Ibid., 328–31.

B lies close to the purpose and character of the Johannine Epistles. Baum-Bodenbender's view of the purpose and function of the Epistles is very much like Raymond E. Brown's, who, however, is never mentioned in this connection.[69] In all probability the Johannine tradition took its rise in an area where gnostic ideas were gaining currency; thus the gnostic or proto-gnostic character of level A. The redaction of the Gospel (B) and the Johannine Epistles attempt to check the drift toward Gnosticism without denying the high positive Christology of the source. Although she grants that this proposal remains hypothetical because of the lack of extra-New Testament sources for Gnosticism, Baum-Bodenbender nevertheless clearly believes that the congruence of literary criticism, theological analysis, and history-of-religions considerations support not only the plausibility but the truth of her proposals.

Baum-Bodenbender's analysis is brilliantly conceived and executed. How far it can be convincingly applied throughout the Gospel is a question that remains to be answered. Probably the predisposition of most scholars has been to assume that the Synoptic Gospels and the synoptic tradition are prior to, and in some sense the basis of, the Johannine, even if John did not know or use the Synoptic Gospels themselves. Moreover, throughout most of the passion narrative (18:1—19:42), indeed through the account of the empty tomb (20:1–10), John's basic narrative elements are parallel to the Synoptics. It may be that in other episodes of the passion one could delineate a proto-Johannine source, upon which the synoptic-like elements rest, as Baum-Bodenbender has done with the trial before Pilate.

Whether this could be done as successfully, that is, without seeming to perform a tour de force, seems to me at least doubtful. Obviously, the trial before Pilate is permeated with distinctly Johannine composition or redaction, and it is difficult to ferret out or separate the traditional elements. Dauer did not attempt to restore the source with exactitude, mainly because of the extent to which John seems to have rewritten his material. Of course, for Dauer, as for others, similarity to the Synoptics has been a criterion for identifying the traditional source.[70] Baum-Bodenbender has thrown this whole procedure into question, but she has astutely chosen the episode where the Johannine element is most extensively integrated with the backbone of the narrative. Accordingly, it is more difficult to extract a framework of synoptic-like elements. On the other hand, in a simpler episode or pericope such as the arrest

---

[69] Ibid., 331–42, for Baum-Bodenbender's view. For Raymond E. Brown's, see his *Community of the Beloved Disciple* (New York: Paulist Press, 1979) and his commentary, *The Epistles of John,* Anchor Bible 30 (Garden City, N.Y.: Doubleday & Co., 1982).

[70] Dauer, *Passionsgeschichte,* 119–45.

(18:1–11) or the burial (19:38–42, not treated by Dauer), the clearly Johannine elements are more readily recognizable and are not required to preserve the basic story or plot. For example, Dauer's analysis of the arrest, to which we have already referred, finds the Johannine element in 18:4–9, while the remainder of the account (18:1–3, 10–11), where the parallels with the Synoptics are located, provides all that is necessary for the story itself and is with good reason deemed traditional.

While Baum-Bodenbender's source theory is, to the best of my knowledge, original, it is not without parallel, and there are congenial proposals that have to do with other aspects or parts of the Fourth Gospel. Early on, Hartwig Thyen had expressed the view that the final redaction of John involved assimilation of this rather different Gospel to the synoptic type, citing Bultmann as still basically correct in this regard. Moreover, in some distinction from his teacher Bultmann, Thyen came to regard the final redaction of the Gospel as significantly more extensive than the latter thought and proposed calling the final redactor the evangelist.[71] Two of Thyen's students, Wolfgang Langbrandtner and Hans-Peter Heekerens, have presented doctoral dissertations that in different ways propose a similar view of Johannine origins, in which the affinities with the Synoptic Gospels belong at the end of the Gospel's development rather than at the beginning.[72] Moreover, this general position accords rather well with Ernst Käsemann's argument that the Gospel of John represents a naively docetic view of Jesus and is therefore theologically significantly different from the Synoptics. While Käsemann does not commit himself to any specific theory of the development of the Gospel, he regards the whole process of its acceptance and canonization by the church as an attempted hermeneutical assimilation of it to the other Gospels and to an emerging orthodoxy, in which its distinctive edge and contours are lost from

---

[71] See Hartwig Thyen, "Johannes 13 und die 'Kirchliche Redaktion' des vierten Evangeliums," in *Tradition und Glaube: Das frühe Christentum in seiner Umwelt. Festgabe für Karl Georg Kuhn zum 65. Geburtstag*, ed. G. Jeremias, H. W. Kuhn, and H. Stegemann (Göttingen: Vandenhoeck & Ruprecht, 1971), 343–56. For Thyen's view of the later assimilation of the Fourth Gospel to the Synoptics, see his "Aus der Literatur zum Johannesevangelium," *ThR* 42 (1977): 211–70 (3. Fortsetzung), esp. 226–27, 252.

[72] Heekerens will be treated below, pp. 165–67. For Wolfgang Langbrandtner's view of a dualistic gnostic-like *Grundschrift* and later more "orthodox" redaction in the Fourth Gospel, see his *Weltferner Gott oder Gott der Liebe: Der Ketzerstreit in der johanneischen Kirche: Eine exegetisch-religionsgeschichtliche Untersuchung mit Berücksichtigung der koptisch-gnostischen Texte aus Nag-Hammadi*, BBET 6 (Frankfurt am Main: Peter Lang, 1977), esp. 106–21. Interestingly enough, Langbrandtner compares the theology of the source with Käsemann's and Luise Schottroff's interpetation of the Gospel of John, and that of the redaction with "conservative" exegetes such as Schnackenburg (pp. 120–21). As we noted, Baum-Bodenbender made a similar observation, based on her source analysis, about Käsemann and Bultmann (above, p. 134).

view.[73] Thus Baum-Bodenbender's thesis finds its niche in a certain strain of Johannine source criticism and interpretation.

The brilliance of Baum-Bodenbender's thesis and analysis notwithstanding, a case may still be made for the primitive character of most parallels to the Synoptics in the Johannine passion narrative. Nevertheless it would be unfair to prejudge too quickly the prospects for successfully extending her proposal throughout the passion narrative and the Gospel. Baum-Bodenbender and Dauer represent opposite and alternative ways of understanding the development of the passion narrative, worked out with great care and thoroughness on the basis of differing premises and initial insights and correlated with divergent views of the direction and development of Johannine theology. Both scholars, differing as they do, are nevertheless representative of much recent research in important respects. First, they agree in principle that there was a proto-Johannine passion narrative basically independent of the Synoptics. Together with even so radical or original a critic as Crossan, they do not accept the recently revived view that John's narrative is simply based upon Mark's. Thus, although they also reckon with important synoptic influences on the Johannine passion, they agree (also with Crossan!) that such influence was not primary but indirect (Dauer) or secondary (Baum-Bodenbender).

---

[73] Käsemann, *The Testament of Jesus*, esp. 74–78.

# 6

# *The Dissolution of a Consensus*

More than two decades ago, Archibald M. Hunter wrote, "In 1938 Gardner-Smith was a lone voice protesting John's independence; in 1968 his view may almost be said to represent 'critical orthodoxy.' "[1] A decade or so later, Frans Neirynck could still say that "the prevailing view in Johannine scholarship is undeniably that of John's independence, and J. Blinzler, as well as C. K. Barrett and W. G. Kümmel who continue to defend dependence on the Gospel of Mark, acknowledge the remarkable shift in exegetical opinion inaugurated by the little book of P. Gardner-Smith (1938)."[2] Yet Neirynck went on to indicate his own dissent from that consensus, and in his 1990 Louvain Colloquium *Forschungsbericht*, he could point to a growing body of exegetical opinion that was challenging the once prevailing critical orthodoxy.

Whether another major shift in scholarly opinion on this issue has occurred, or is about to occur, is in my opinion still uncertain, but there is no question that the Gardner-Smith consensus is now significantly eroded. As we have observed, some uncertainty about the existence of a pre-gospel passion tradition or narrative(s), upon which Mark and John could have drawn independently, has been a contributing factor. Perhaps more important is the identification of traces of the redactional work of individual synoptic evangelists in the Fourth Gospel. The search for such reflection of synoptic redaction in John continues. Of equal importance, however, is the recurring recognition,

---

[1] Archibald M. Hunter, *According to John: The New Look at the Fourth Gospel* (Philadelphia: Westminster Press, 1968), 14.

[2] Neirynck, "John and the Synoptics," in *L'Evangile de Jean*, 73.

based on literary analysis, that John presumes a knowledge of the gospel story.

The seminal literary-critical study of R. Alan Culpepper addresses the question of John and the Synoptics only tangentially, if at all. It is all the more significant, therefore, that when Culpepper asks, "Does the reader know the story of Jesus, or parts of it, before it is told?" he can respond, "The gospel suggests an affirmative answer."[3] Clearly the reader is expected to know already of Jesus' resurrection (John 2:22) even as the story is being narrated. Among other things, the implied reader knows also about John the Baptist's imprisonment, the presence of the Spirit, the synagogue ban, the fear of the Jews, the anointing of Jesus by Mary (11:2), and probably the betrayal of Jesus by Judas. Probably the evangelist also (or better, the implied author) knows that Jesus was born in Bethlehem and was a descendant of David (cf. 7:41–43). "If so, this is one of the few instances where his irony depends on information which is never given to the reader (cf. 7:52; 11:48). Because one of the author's favorite devices is to allow Jesus' opponents to speak the truth unawares, the balance is in favor of the assumption that the author and his readers know the tradition of Jesus' birth in Bethlehem."[4] Do they know it from Matthew or Luke? The answer will likely depend on a view of Johannine-synoptic relations formed on other grounds.

The way in which the fourth evangelist introduces, or fails to introduce, characters could provide an important key, particularly if he introduces characters not known from the Synoptics but does not introduce characters known from them. As we earlier observed, however, there is no consistency in the matter. He introduces the Beloved Disciple, Lazarus, and Nicodemus, who do not appear in the Synoptics, but he also introduces Joseph of Arimathea, Caiaphas, and Annas, who do appear there.[5] In a number of places John seems to presuppose his readers' knowledge of the Twelve, particularly their commissioning as such (4:38; 6:70; 15:15–16; 17:18). "The choosing of the Twelve begins in the first chapter, but it is not completed, and their commissioning does not come until 20:21–23." The passages just noted "retain an anachronic force through their location in the narrative and cumulatively point to a scene of appointment and commissioning which has been omitted."[6] In other words, it is as if John fails to narrate the commissioning of the Twelve

---

[3] R. Alan Culpepper, *Anatomy of the Fourth Gospel: A Study in Literary Design*, New Testament Foundations and Facets (Philadelphia: Fortress Press, 1983), 222. See pp. 222–23 for what the implied reader is expected to know.

[4] Ibid., 170.

[5] Cf. ibid., 216.

[6] Ibid., 59.

until the end and then does not narrate their appointment because he can presuppose his readers' knowledge. From what source? Does his procedure make the best sense if his readers can be presumed to know already about the appointment and commissioning of the Twelve? Quite possibly. It is worth noting, however, that Paul seems to presuppose his readers' familiarity with the Twelve (1 Cor. 15:5) at a time when no gospels had been written.

Other examples might be adduced, but these suffice to show how the evangelist (or implied author) seems to assume his reader's knowledge of the story of Jesus, which the Christian reader through the centuries has known from the Synoptic Gospels. It is then only a few brief steps to the conclusion that John must have known the story from the same source. The factors giving pause before such a conclusion are basically two: first, John's unaccountable differences from and contradictions of the synoptic accounts and, second, the possibility that other no longer extant gospels or traditions, or even a living memory, could have supplied this knowledge. To say that John need not have known anything other or more than the Synoptics—and thus to apply Ockham's razor—does not in itself mean that he must have gotten his information from them.

As early as the mid-1970s, however, the consensus that was reached in the 1960s had given way to a more ambivalent picture, and in a certain sense that ambivalence was represented in the more complex conclusions of Boismard regarding Johannine-synoptic relations generally and of Dauer and Heekerens on Johannine-Lukan relations. All three find that there was an original and independent Johannine tradition or source, but that the present Gospel, indeed, the Gospel as it left the hands of the fourth evangelist himself, already reflected knowledge of the Synoptic Gospels.

## M.-E. BOISMARD

M.-E. Boismard, longtime professor at the Ecole Biblique in Jerusalem, has been interested in the origin and development of the Fourth Gospel for over four decades. At one point Boismard proposed that the Gospel of John had been redacted by Luke![7] Although he later abandoned this proposal, it was an early expression of his insight and position that the Gospel of John as we

---

[7] M.-E. Boismard, "Saint Luc et la rédaction du quatrième évangile (Jn, iv, 46–54)," *RB* 69 (1962): 185–211.

know it indeed contains synoptic elements but that they are secondary and not constitutive of the Gospel in its primal form.

The position ultimately attained by Boismard finds definitive expression in his massive commentary (part of a three-volume *Synopse des quatre Evangiles*), which is largely devoted to source-critical matters.[8] A. Lamouille is the coauthor of this book and G. Rochais is named as collaborator, but it is safe to assume that Boismard, despite his modesty, provided the inspiration and basic direction of the work. Situated as he is in Jerusalem, the center of the Holy Land, and in the Ecole Biblique, the great center of Roman Catholic biblical archaeological work there, it is perhaps not surprising that Boismard's work has a quasi-archaeological character. That is, in method and procedure it constitutes a kind of literary stratigraphy of the Fourth Gospel! As we shall see, the basic question about this undertaking is not whether it is ingeniously conceived and executed but whether such a precise delineation of sources and redaction is finally feasible. Does Boismard set out to discover more than can ever be known? Bultmann's source, displacement, and redaction theory once seemed complex enough, but it is relatively simple in comparison to Boismard's. Boismard's overall theory is truly remarkable in the way it accommodates not only traditional views of gospel origins (e.g., an early form of Matthew was prior to Mark and was a source of Mark) but also many of the insights of Boismard's scholarly predecessors (e.g., Bultmann, Fortna).

Boismard's reconstruction of the origin and development of the Fourth Gospel should be set in the context of his overall view of gospel origins. Suffice it to say that in his opinion each Gospel except Luke is the product of at least three distinct stages of composition. (John has four, including the final redaction by someone other than the evangelist.) Matthew, Mark, and John are based ultimately on primal documents denominated A, B, and C respectively. (In addition, there is also the primal document Q.) Each then goes through an intermediate stage of composition before reaching its final form. Luke, however, has no distinctive primal document but begins, so to speak, at the intermediate stage (Proto-Luke) at which point it is composed out of Q, Document B (primal Mark), Document C (primal John = John I), and intermediate Matthew. It is intermediate Mark whose incorporation into the final redaction of Matthew and Luke gives rise to the Markan hypothesis. But already intermediate Mark has been influenced by Document A (primal Matthew), so that the ancient church view of the priority of Matthew survives.

Frans Neirynck has diagramed Boismard's theory of gospel origins (p. 143) so that it becomes quite easily comprehensible, while at the same time its

---

[8] M.-E. Boismard and A. Lamouille, with the collaboration of G. Rochais, *L'Evangile de Jean.*

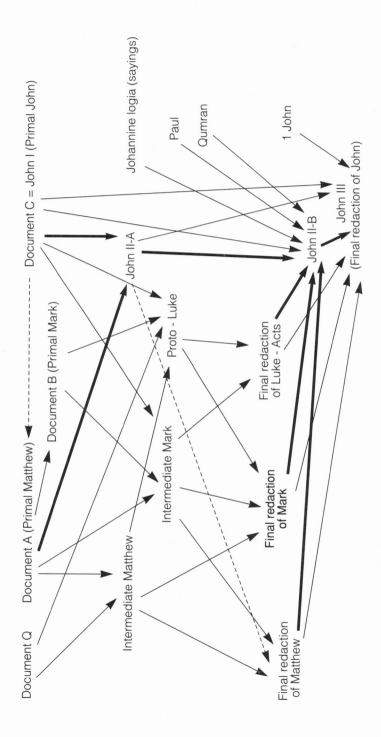

BOISMARD'S THEORY OF GOSPEL ORIGINS

complexity may be clearly seen.[9] As one moves from left to right in the diagram, or from Matthew to John, relationships become increasingly complex, and the diagram of Johannine development and interrelationships surpasses all others in complexity.

As can be seen, the basis of the Gospel of John is one of Boismard's four primal documents, Document C, called also John I.[10] From this original document the present Gospel developed by stages within the Johannine school. Document C began at 3:23, 25 (3:24 is obviously a later emendation) with John baptizing at Aenon near Salim. For the next episodes of this document, Boismard moves back to the account of Jesus and John in chapter 1, then on to the appearance of Jesus in Samaria (chap. 4). After Jesus begins his ministry in Samaria, he moves south to Galilee, performing three signs there (2:1–11; 4:46–54; 21:1–14). Subsequently he goes to Jerusalem for the Feast of Tabernacles (material from chaps. 7; 8; 9; 11; and 12 belongs to Document C), which turns out to be the occasion of his arrest, trial, and death. After his death, Jesus appears to his disciples by the sea, in a scene Boismard derives from John 6; 20; and 21, using as a model and justification for his reconstruction the parallel in Luke 24:36–43. In Document C, Jesus celebrates the Last Supper at Bethany rather than at Jerusalem. The Samaritan ambience of Document C accounts for the fact that here Jesus is apparently understood and hailed as the prophet like Moses (Deuteronomy 18), not the Davidic messiah. The eschatology is futuristic; the return of Jesus (14:1–3) is expected. Needless to say, this strange gospel shows few enough affinities with the Synoptics, although its one-year pattern is closer to Mark than to canonical John, and scarcely requires any one of them as its source. It recounted none of the great discourses of Jesus and only five of his signs, none of which was derived from the Synoptics. In Document C, Jesus' principal foes are the chief priests, who had actually been a party to his crucifixion. Written in Palestine, probably in Aramaic, near the middle of the first century, it was utilized by Luke (Proto-Luke) and to a lesser degree by Mark. John the son of Zebedee may have been the author, but we cannot know for sure.[11]

---

[9] Frans Neirynck, with the collaboration of Joël Delobel et al., *Jean et les synoptiques: Examen critique de l'exégèse de M.-E. Boismard,* BETL 49 (Louvain: Louvain University Press, 1979), 9. The diagram is reproduced from Neirynck's work with permission of the publisher.

[10] Boismard, *L'Evangile de Jean.* See pp. 10–11 for a summary description of the theory; pp. 16–19 for the restored text of Document C, pp. 19–25 for discussion of the reconstruction; also pp. 45–46 on the relation to the Synoptics.

[11] Ibid., 67–68. A case can also be made that Lazarus, whom Jesus was said to love, was the Beloved Disciple and author of this earliest version of the Gospel of John. At the stage of John II–B, the author of this document is identified as the Beloved Disciple (21:24).

Document C was then revised by another author, again in Palestine and probably before the Roman war (A.D. 66–70). It preserved the original order of the older gospel but added to it such things as the story of the calling of Andrew and Peter, several of the discourses of Jesus, and two miracles from the synoptic tradition, namely, the feeding of the multitude (6:1–14) and the healing of the man by the pool (5:1–9). Still, this author did not know the Synoptic Gospels themselves; he gets these two stories from Document A (primal Matthew!). At this level, which Boismard calls John II-A, distinctly Jewish (i.e., Davidic) as distinguished from Mosaic and Samaritan, messianic categories were introduced. Now "the Jews" have become the principal enemies of Jesus.[12] John II-A influenced the final redaction of Matthew (e.g., John 12:14–15 and 7:40–42 = Matt. 21:4–5, 9–11; John 1:40–42 = Matt. 16:16–18).

More than a couple of decades later, the same author who had composed John II-A (probably the Elder John) moved from Palestine to Ephesus, where he revised his earlier work (again in Greek) in view of his changed situation and needs (John II-B).[13] Now the hostility of the synagogue had led to the expulsion of Jewish Christians, and the principal enemies of Jesus were the Pharisees, who had become increasingly important in the Jewish community after A.D. 70. No longer is the author innocent of the Synoptic Gospels; indeed, he now knows and uses them all. He also introduces the scheme of Jewish festivals into the Gospel and now gives primacy to the Feast of Passover, prominent, of course, in the Synoptics, in place of Tabernacles, which had loomed so large in Document C. Indeed, we now have three Passovers in the Gospel. These Passovers point to Jesus' death and resurrection, and by introducing this scheme John hopes to counter and put down Jewish usages (Sabbath, circumcision, feasts) among Christians. At this stage various changes in the order of the narrative take place. Most of John 15 and 16 were added at this stage as well as John 21, the final chapter. Not only does John II-B know the Synoptic Gospels; he now comes under the influence of Luke-Acts in particular but also of the letters of Paul and of the Qumran writings. The Gospel as it leaves the hands of the author at this stage is essentially the Gospel of John as we have it now. The transition from futuristic to realized eschatology, which had begun in John II-A, is now complete. Jesus himself is no longer merely the Jewish messiah; he is Son of God and, indeed, God.[14]

---

[12] Ibid., 57; cf. pp. 25–35 for text and discussion of II–A; also pp. 46–47 on the relation to the Synoptics.

[13] Ibid., 68–70 on the identity of the author of II–A and II–B. Boismard here also discusses the change in settings.

[14] Ibid., 35–45, for text and discussion of II–B; also pp. 47–48 on the relation to the Synoptics; on date, place, and identity of the author, pp. 68–70.

But there was yet a subsequent redaction of the Fourth Gospel, this one carried out by another author, the third in the sequence (John III). Also a member of the Johannine school, he knew John II-A and inserted into his recension material especially sayings (e.g., 3:31–35) not used in II-B. It was this redactor who unaccountably revised the order of John 6 and 5, giving us the present arrangement, which has so puzzled exegetes. This redactor, of course, also knew the Synoptic Gospels. Moreover, he knew 1 John as well (it had been penned already by the author of John II-B) and inserted sayings from it into the Gospel (e.g., 1 John 4:9 in John 3:16a, 17; 1 John 5:20b in John 17:3).[15]

Even such a brief summation allows us to see what a grand scheme of development has been conceived by Boismard. The Gospel of John reflects knowledge of the Synoptics but only in the last two stages of its composition. Yet not only the final redactor (stage III) knows the Synoptics but also the evangelist himself (stage II-B). How does Boismard justify and defend this scheme? He sets it out at the beginning of his *Commentaire*, then discusses criteria and method, and finally proceeds to extricate the sources from the text in the process of exegesis. In discussing criteria for source criticism, Boismard presupposes the familiar litany of aporiae that have given rise to literary-critical solutions since the time of Schwartz and Wellhausen (e.g., the seeming displacement of John 6 and 5; Jesus' command of 14:31 to arise, followed by a continuation of the discourse and a prayer; etc.).[16] He discusses a number of indications of sources or strata: obvious glosses or notations; doublets; evidence of displacement or dislocation; stylistic criteria, of which he has assembled an enormous catalogue; and text-critical problems. To these may be added theological criteria, such as the different valuation of signs at various points in the Gospel. Despite the work done on stylistic criteria, Boismard recognizes their ambiguity, for authors or editors could have easily imitated the style of their sources.

Notwithstanding the care taken with method and criteria, the work is apparently grounded upon a basic insight or working hypothesis: namely, that the Fourth Gospel is too different from the Synoptics—and unaccountably different from them—to be understood as having been derived from them. On the other hand, the similarities with the Synoptics are too extensive to preclude some sort of direct literary relation, which is located at a rather late

---

[15] Ibid., 44–45, for discussion of John III; also p. 48 on sources; for date, place, and identity of author, p. 70.

[16] For aporiae, ibid., 9–11; for general criteria of literary criticism, pp. 12–16; for specific stylistic traits of the various strata, pp. 63–67.

stage in the Gospel's redaction history. A via media must be envisioned, and Boismard and his colleagues have done just that. We should bear in mind that Boismard set out, not primarily to solve the problem of John and the Synoptics per se, but to understand the development of the Fourth Gospel in the light of the difficulties it presents, keeping the question of its relationship to those other Gospels always in view. Boismard represents a continuation of the tradition of Bultmann and Brown, in that he still sees the influence of the Synoptics as entering the picture late in the redaction history of the Gospel. Yet it now impinges directly upon the evangelist, not merely upon secondary redactors.

Since in a real sense Boismard's methods and conclusions represent the culmination of a consensus that we saw beginning with Gardner-Smith and developing through the work of other scholars such as Dodd, Bultmann, and Brown, it may seem odd and even misleading to present him under the rubric of "The Dissolution of a Consensus." Nevertheless the culmination of the consensus in Boismard contained within it the seeds of its own dissolution, as Frans Neirynck clearly saw. While on Boismard's terms, the basis of John's account is independent of the Synoptics, the present form of the Gospel is not. Not only the final redactor knows the Synoptics, but such knowledge must be attributed to the evangelist himself at the stage of his final revision of his work. Once such knowledge of the Synoptics, which now must be described as more than peripheral, is conceded, how can one be sure it is temporally secondary in the process of composition rather than basic? By what right does one assign priority to hypothetical sources when a significant relationship to still extant documents must be granted? As we shall see, Neirynck was quick to seize upon what we have described as the ambivalence in Boismard's work and to urge upon him a reconsideration of the point at which the Synoptics became a factor in the composition of the Fourth Gospel.

## FRANS NEIRYNCK: HIS CRITIQUE OF BOISMARD AND HIS OWN POSITION

Even as M.-E. Boismard has served at the Ecole Biblique in Jerusalem, Frans Neirynck has presided over New Testament studies at the Catholic University of Louvain. In their professional careers and in their institutions, they represent two poles of modern, liberal Catholic biblical scholarship, now unsurpassed in erudition and methodological sophistication. Neirynck has turned his attention to the relationship of John to the Synoptics in the last two decades, having earlier made major contributions to synoptic research. Boismard's interest in the Fourth Gospel can be traced back to the beginning of his scholarly career in the late 1940s.[17] Each now espouses the view that the canonical form of the Gospel of John reflects significant knowledge of the Synoptic Gospels. As we have seen, Boismard believes that the Gospel of John is based on an independent tradition but that in the later stages of its composition history it has been significantly influenced by the Synoptic Gospels themselves, not just synoptic-like tradition. Neirynck, on the other hand, has come to the conclusion that the fourth evangelist took the Synoptic Gospels as his point of departure, so to speak. (In fact, at an early point in his investigations Neirynck seems to have regarded John as based on a more or less independent tradition related to the Synoptic Gospels.[18]) The Synoptic Gospels were then basic sources of the Fourth Gospel. In the development of his own position, Neirynck has frequently been in conversation and debate with his Jerusalem colleague, and in 1979 published a major volume in which he analyzed the literary-critical theory of Boismard's *L'Evangile de Jean*.[19] In order to get at Neirynck's point of view, it will be useful to examine his critique of Boismard.

At the outset, Neirynck observes with satisfaction that Boismard's position differs from that of a number of recent commentators, in that he takes the evangelist himself (II-B) rather than the later, final redaction, to have been influenced by the Synoptic Gospels.[20] Earlier, he had seen the direct influence of the Synoptics upon John occurring only at the level of the final "post-Johannine" redaction, but now it is moved back one stage. Moreover, in Boismard's revised position the so-called signs source has fallen out of the picture. Instead, the miracle stories are assigned either to Document C or Document A (the no longer extant source of Matthew). Proto-Luke has apparently become superfluous as a source of John, inasmuch as the final recension of the evangelist (II-B) is influenced by the Synoptic Gospels themselves. Neirynck can only applaud Boismard's recognition that the evangelist himself knows and uses the Synoptics. In his view the commentary has the

---

[17] For example, an early article of Boismard's is "Le chapitre XXI de Saint Jean: Essai de critique littéraire," *RB* 54 (1947): 473–501.

[18] Frans Neirynck, "Les femmes au tombeau: Etude de la rédaction matthéenne," *NTS* 15 (1968–69): 168–90, esp. 189: "Thus, it seems to me a reasonable hypothesis that the accounts of the burial and of the empty tomb are based on a tradition similar to the synoptics, and even, as certain precise resemblances seem to suggest, a tradition formed in part from our Synoptic Gospels" (translation mine). This article is reprinted in *Evangelica, Gospel Studies—Études d'évangile: Collected Essays*, ed. F. Van Segbroeck, BETL 60 (Louvain: Louvain University Press, 1982), 273–96.

[19] See n. 9 above.

[20] Neirynck, *Jean et les synoptiques*, 15.

great merit of placing that whole problem at the center of the discussion.[21] Neirynck's basic question and criticism is whether, given knowledge of the Synoptics, it is necessary to suppose that John based his narrative on a more primitive gospel (Document C = John I) and composed an earlier version of his Gospel (II-A) without knowledge of them.

While affirming the contribution Boismard has made in assembling and classifying more than four hundred Johannine stylistic characteristics, and recognizing Boismard's caution in the use of these for purposes of source criticism, Neirynck is nevertheless dubious of even their limited value for that purpose. Circularity is difficult to avoid; and the classification of a characteristic as "non-Johannine" because it is "synoptic," when the fourth evangelist (II-B) was himself influenced by the Synoptics, creates ambiguities. How does one know that a synoptic characteristic has not been absorbed into John's style? Such reservations about the fruitfulness of stylistic characteristics in source criticism take very specific form in his arguments against the proposal that the evangelist used a hypothetical Document C in the composition of the initial recension of his Gospel.[22] Neirynck examines four passages in which Boismard detected that source: the empty tomb (20:1–10); the beginning of the denial of Peter (18:15–16); the cleansing of the temple (2:13–22); and the anointing at Bethany (12:1–11). Neirynck's criticisms are as detailed as Boismard's own analysis, but his fundamental objections can be simply stated. In every case the two agree that the Synoptic Gospels have influenced the Johannine narrative at some point. The question is always at what point. By attacking the stylistic, linguistic, and contextual grounds on which Boismard separates Document C (II-A or II-B), Neirynck calls into question the existence of these hypothetical sources or literary strata prior or external to the evangelist himself. He then suggests that the explanation of the existing text of John on the basis of his use of Mark or the Synoptics is equally possible and, in view of the fact that these are extant rather than hypothetical documents, to be preferred. Once the existence of synoptic influence is granted, how can one be sure it did not lie at the beginning, rather than only at the end, of the development of the Johannine accounts?

In Boismard's view, the numbered signs (2:1–11; 4:46–54; as well as 21:1–14) formed a section of Galilean miracles at the beginning of the account of Jesus' ministry in Document C. (Thus there is no longer any need for a miracle

---

[21] Ibid.; cf. 21.
[22] Ibid., 71–91.

source per se.) Boismard thinks that John II-B removed the miracle of the catch of fish in 21:1–14 from the Galilean ministry (Document C; cf. Fortna's *The Gospel of Signs*) to its present position at the end of the Gospel. In doing so, he combined it with a primitive appearance scene by the lake in Galilee, which in Document C and II-A had followed the appearance to Mary Magdalene. In an amazingly complex and subtle analysis, Boismard has derived this appearance not only from parts of John 21:1–14 but from elements of Luke 24:28–43 (albeit in Jerusalem!) and the synoptic account of Jesus walking on the sea, for which it was a source. Moreover, elements of this primitive narrative can be detected in John 6:19bd, 20a. It is not surprising, in the measure that this analysis is subtle and complex, that it is also unconvincing to Neirynck, who fails to see the need or the legitimacy of positing John's dependence on one of Luke's sources as well as on the final version of that Gospel. (Boismard thinks that both Luke and John depend on this common source, Document C, which turns up in Proto-Luke, as well as John II-A; but John II-B also knows the Gospel of Luke per se.) For Boismard, the "pure fish story" identified in John 21:2, 3, 4a, 6 is the common source of John 21:1–14 (where II-B has combined it with the appearance story) and Luke 5:1–11. Yet if even in Boismard's view the redactor of John 21 (II-B) knows the Gospel of Luke, Neirynck asks whether it is really necessary or helpful to suppose that he also knew a source that he shares with Luke. Neirynck obviously regards Boismard's effort to distill a third Galilean sign from 21:1–14 as most dubious and vulnerable and is no more convinced that the first and second Cana miracles of 2:1–11 and 4:46–54 can safely be ascribed to a more primitive source, whether a *semeia* source or Document C, from which they were derived by the evangelist at the level of John II-A. "The point of departure of all *semeia*-source theories, that is to say, the grouping of the two narratives at the level of pre-Johannine tradition, remains an undemonstrable hypothesis."[23]

Nor is Neirynck persuaded by Boismard's arguments that along with Document C, John (at the stage II-A) used the ultimate source of Matthew (Document A), from which he took the stories of the healing of the blind man and the feeding of the multitude. According to Boismard, the motifs of sin and the Son of man which appear in 5:1 ff. are, like the story itself, derived from Document A, and not from Mark, since these stories were incorporated at the level of II-A, before the evangelist knew the Synoptics. Of course, later on (II-B), he did know and was influenced by the synoptic accounts. Neirynck's

---

[23] Ibid., 174.

basic argument against Boismard's proposal at this point is again that once synoptic (Mark's) influence upon John is granted, it is unnecessary and superfluous to deduce from the Johannine text on stylistic and other grounds a primitive form of the story that does not show Mark's influence. The same principle applies to Boismard's attempt to show that the multiplication of the loaves in John is based on an originally independent account (again Document A) which only secondarily (level II-B) was influenced by Mark. "Boismard has made a great step forward by accepting the dependence of John upon the Synoptic Gospels in their present form," writes Neirynck, but "he ought to ask himself whether the knowledge of the same Synoptics does not explain equally the elements of the Johannine text which he still attributes to a level of pre-synoptic redaction (John II-A) or to a primitive Gospel (Document C)."[24] Perhaps after diagraming Boismard's complex theory of Gospel origins, Neirynck could not at this point resist diagraming his own, which is simplicity itself, a quadrilateral with one Gospel at each corner and one line bisecting it in order to connect John to Mark as well as to Matthew and Luke!

On reflection, it is not surprising that Neirynck does not find Boismard convincing. Boismard's theory of Johannine origins, one aspect of a complete theory of Gospel origins, is so detailed and complex as to suggest that in its totality it could never attract an appreciable consensus of scholarly opinion. Is there adequate reason to think, as Boismard seems to believe, that, given the Johannine text, along with the synoptic texts that bear some relation to it, we can coax from them the secrets of their origins, development, and relationships? At many, if not most, of the points at which Neirynck undertakes a critical analysis of Boismard, he is able to make telling points, in no small part because Boismard in attempting so detailed a reconstruction has given many hostages to fortune.

Raymond E. Brown, who demurs from accepting Boismard's theory, nevertheless points out that, insofar as it touches the Fourth Gospel, this theory moves in the same direction as, or reflects, a broad spectrum of recent research.[25] Quite remarkable, for example, are the affinities between Boismard's Document C and Fortna's *Gospel of Signs*. (Of course, Boismard has been able to read Fortna, but his viewpoint is not derivative from Fortna's work.) Boismard has, of course, gone much further in the direction of separating literary strata and assigning them to the developmental history of the Fourth Gospel than most scholars would be willing to do. Nevertheless, in objecting to

---

[24] Ibid., 389.
[25] See Raymond E. Brown's excellent review, *CBQ* 49 (1978): 624–28, esp. 627–28.

Boismard's procedure Neirynck is calling into question the direction of much current Johannine scholarship.

The fact that both Boismard and Neirynck accept John's knowledge, and to a greater or lesser extent his use, of the Synoptic Gospels is significant. As we have already observed, much of the force of Neirynck's criticism of Boismard derives from his asking the latter why, since he acknowledges that use at one redactional level, he must posit other more basic narrative sources, particularly when those sources themselves have noteworthy affinities with the Synoptics. Boismard believes that the case for John's secondary (as opposed to fundamental) use of the Synoptics can be clearly established, while Neirynck questions Boismard's significant qualification or limitation of the role the Synoptics play. Neirynck's own view of Johannine origins is only now being developed, although he has made clear that he believes it can be shown that John not only knew the Synoptics but made them the basis of his narrative. Presumably, Neirynck believes that John can be explained mainly in terms of its relationship to the Synoptics, although even he leaves open the possibility that John knew other traditions.[26] On the other hand, Boismard's elaboration and defense of his own position seem to be grounded in an initial perception of the independence of the Johannine narratives and Gospel. The Gospel of John does not on the face of it appear to be derived from the Synoptics, as much as it may at some points show synoptic influence. In this respect, Boismard still stands in the tradition of scholarship represented in different ways by Gardner-Smith, Dodd, Bultmann, and Raymond E. Brown, while Neirynck no longer does. Thus, while the agreements between Boismard and Neirynck are real, the differences are more significant.

Neirynck's publications on John and the Synoptics neither began nor ended with his book-long response to Boismard. In large part, however, they consist of lengthy and detailed responses to the work of other scholars who regard John's dependence upon the Synoptics as nonexistent, questionable, or secondary. To view his perspective and procedures more concretely, it may be useful to compare briefly his understanding of the sources and composition of John 20:1–18 with Boismard's. I give the text, as Boismard apportions it to sources, according to the RSV, changing it slightly to conform to Boismard's French translation, which in particular honors the historical present tense, a characteristic of Document C. (In his *NTS* article on 20:1–18, Neirynck simply gives the Greek.) The underlining is Neirynck's, who, of course, does not agree

---

[26] See Neirynck's Louvain Colloquium *Forschungsbericht* in *John and the Synoptics,* ed. Denaux.

with Boismard's source and redaction analysis.[27] The underlining indicates parallels to the Matthean and Lukan narratives that Neirynck takes to be the sole source of the Johannine narrative. (The broken rule indicates a more remote relationship to the putative synoptic source.) The plural forms in parentheses represent Boismard's Document C.

COMPOSITE OF THE ANALYSIS OF
BOISMARD AND NEIRYNCK

| C | II-A | II-B | III |
|---|---|---|---|

(1)  Now on the first day of the week

Mary Magdalene comes

(they came) to the tomb early

while it was still dark,

and she (they fem.) sees (see) the stone had been taken away from the tomb.

(2)  So she (they) runs (run) and goes (go) to Simon Peter and to the other disciple,

the one whom Jesus
loved,

and she (they) says (say) to (him)

them

"They have taken the Lord out of the tomb, and we do not know where they have laid him."

(3)  <u>Peter</u> then <u>came out</u>

with the other disciple, and they went to the tomb.

(4)  They both ran. But the other disciple <u>ran</u> first, more quickly than Peter

and came

first

<u>to the tomb,</u>

(5)  <u>and, stooping, he sees the linen cloths</u>

lying there;

but he did not go in.

(6)  Then Simon Peter comes, following him, and went into the tomb, and he sees the linen cloths

lying

(alone)

---

[27] Boismard's discussion is, of course, found at the appropriate point of his commentary (*L'Evangile de Jean,* 453–66). The charts showing his breakdown of the text are on pp. 453 and 459; I have combined them. For Neirynck, see his "John and the Synoptics: The Empty Tomb Stories," *NTS* 30 (1984): 161–87. Cf. also his presidential address, "John 21," *NTS* 36 (1990): 321–36. His display of the text is found in Neirynck, "John and the Synoptics: The Empty Tomb Stories," 179–80.

| C | II-A | II-B | III |
|---|---|---|---|
| (7) | | and the napkin, which had been on his head, not lying with the linen cloths, but rolled up in a place by itself. | |

(8)        Then the other disciple, who reached the tomb first also went in and he saw and believed.

(9)        For as yet they did not know the scripture, that he must rise from the dead.

(10) (And he returned)

       Then the disciples went back home again.

       (home.)

(11) But Mary stood

       near the tomb,

       outside, weeping,

(12)        and as she wept, she stooped to look into the tomb, and she sees two angels in white, sitting, one at the head and one at the feet, where the body of Jesus had lain.

(13)        And these say to her: "Woman, why are you weeping?" She says to them: "They have taken away my Lord, and I do not know where they have laid him."

(14)        Having said this

       she turned around behind and saw Jesus standing

       but she did not know that it was Jesus.

(15)        Jesus says to her: "Woman, why are you weeping? Whom do you seek?" She, supposing him to be the gardener, says to him: "Milord, if you have carried him away, tell me where you have laid him, and I will take him away."

(16)        Jesus says to her: "Mary." Turning, she says to him

       in Hebrew,

       "Rabboni!"

       (which means Teacher).

(17)        Jesus says to her: "Touch me no more, for I have not yet ascended to the Father; but go to my brothers and say to them: "I am ascending to my Father and your Father, to my God and to your God."

(18)        Mary Magdalene

       (and she) goes announcing to the disciples: "I have seen the Lord(.)"

       and that he said these things to her.

We shall first discuss Boismard's complex analysis and then return to Neirynck. Boismard notes the obvious Johannine parallel to the synoptic accounts of the discovery of the empty tomb and the striking parallel between John 20:2–10, the visit of Peter and the Beloved Disciple to the tomb, and Luke 24:12 (long considered textually doubtful). Many interpreters have taken John 20:2/3–10 to be a later Johannine insertion into a traditional narrative. But Boismard believes, rather, that within John 20:1–10 is preserved a single, brief, older narrative (Document C = John I), to which Luke 24:1–2, 12 also attests, of women discovering the empty tomb. John II-A then added to this primitive account the figure of the other disciple (only later identified by the redactor, John III, with the Beloved Disciple, although elsewhere the Beloved Disciple appears at stage II-B), who accompanies Peter. Then John II-B reduced the number of women to just one, Mary Magdalene, and added the description of the grave cloths that evokes the Lazarus scene. By naming her Mary Magdalene, a name she did not bear in the original account (C), John II-B reconciles this story with the Synoptic Gospels, which he knows. John II-B also adds v. 9, which by its reference to the necessity of understanding the Scripture corrects the sign theology of v. 8, where the other disciple sees and promptly believes. This assignment of v. 9 to II-B is confirmed by several stylistic characteristics, particularly the *oudepō* (not yet), the perfect *ēdeisan* (had known); the reference to *graphē* (scripture). The unusual (for II-B) use of *anastēnai* instead of *egeirein* for Jesus' resurrection is explained by the influence of Acts 17:2–3. Since only John II-B knows Acts, this is said to confirm Boismard's attribution.

The genuineness of Luke 24:12, the brief notice of Peter's going to the tomb, is affirmed, despite the fact that it is missing in Codex Bezae, and taken to attest Luke's use of a tradition common to John, which is none other than Document C. Luke 24:12 (cf. also 24:24) thus becomes an important aid in discovering Document C in John 20:2–10. (Thus textual criticism comes into play in an important way, since Luke 24:12 has significant verbatim agreement, particularly with John 20:5a.) The fact that Luke 24:12 contains elements of Lukan style ("Peter arose"; "he went home wondering at what had happened") means it could hardly have been added by a later scribe. Such Lukanisms would, however, scarcely have been removed by John. More likely they were added by Luke to a (common) source that John also knew. The fact that Luke 24:12 (cf. John 20:5) contains a historical present not characteristic of Lukan style ("he sees"; *blepei*) confirms the origin of this statement in a pre-Lukan source. Moreover, elements of the introduction to the empty tomb story are found in John 20:1b and Luke 24:2.

John II-A (first recension of the evangelist proper) has in v. 2 introduced the other disciple into the account (cf. 18:15–16 where the introduction of this figure is earlier attributed to II-A). He turns up again in vv. 3b, 4, and 8, also from II-A. That there has been an insertion by John II-A into this source at vv. 5 and 6 also is indicated first of all by the occurrence of the expression "he sees the linen cloths lying" (note historical present as in Luke 24:12) at the beginning of v. 5 and the end of v. 6. (The phrase is taken up in v. 6, after the insertion, from the source in v. 5.) Peter and the Beloved Disciple now perform the same action. Verse 8 is assigned to John II-A as well on the strength of the recurrence of the mention of the other disciple. Stylistic and other considerations are said to buttress the argument for source separation, for example, the mention of the other disciple himself (who belongs to II-A and II-B, not to Document C), and the "however" (*mentoi*) of v. 5. The theology of faith based on signs (v. 8) is, moreover, typical of II-A, but it is then qualified in v. 9 (II-B). And so it goes; we are merely sampling Boismard's style of argumentation, but it already becomes clear how contextual, stylistic, and theological considerations fit together.

Turning briefly to the account of Jesus' appearance to Mary Magdalene at the tomb (20:11–18), Boismard immediately senses that in this appearance of Jesus to Mary we have an element of the oldest tradition (Document C), which can be identified in John 20:11a, 14b, and 18a: a brief account of the appearance of Jesus to Mary outside the tomb. It is somewhat surprising that Boismard emphasizes John's differences from the Matthean story of Jesus' encounter with the two women outside the tomb (28:9–10) and is reluctant to claim that they are related.

The identification of this oldest element is, however, assisted by the recognition of later, redactional additions. Already in v. 11b the repetition of the verb "to weep" contained in Document C, as well as the entire expression "then while she was weeping," suggests a redactional addition. In fact, vv. 11b–14a function to bring the Johannine account into line with the Synoptics, as the angel addresses Mary; so this addition is attributed to II-B, the stage at which the evangelist knew the Synoptic Gospels. The section vv. 14b–17, 18b, apart from recognizable redactional additions by II-B, is, however, assigned to level II-A. But Boismard admits the difficulty of distinguishing II-A from II-B, inasmuch as they were both composed by the same author, albeit decades apart.

The beauty and strength of Neirynck's criticism of Boismard, as well as his own proposal, is its simplicity. Boismard's source-critical theory has a wonderful consistency and logic, which, although a sine qua non of its being true, does not guarantee its truth. Neirynck, whose skepticism of Boismard's theory we have already noted, offers a competing analysis of John 20:1–18, in which he simply makes a case for John's dependence on the Synoptics (Luke 24:12 and Matt. 28:9–10) for the two parts of his narrative, that is, 20:1–10 and

20:11–18.[28] Essentially, Neirynck keeps pressing the question of why, once John's knowledge of the Synoptics is granted at any stage or level, it should be necessary to posit other sources of his accounts.

In an earlier article, Neirynck had shown how Matthew 28:9–10, the story of Jesus' encounter with the women outside the tomb, can be understood as a Matthean editorial composition.[29] The principal argument against this view always refers to the existence of John 20:11–18, the appearance to Mary Magdalene, said to be based on a similar and related tradition. Now Neirynck seeks to show that the Johannine account can be read more intelligibly as an elaboration and retelling of the Matthean story.[30] The logic of his argument is impeccable: if Matthew composed 28:9–10 on no traditional basis, and if John can best be understood against that background, John must have known Matthew's Gospel, and other putative sources become superfluous. John has carried forward what was already occurring in Matthew, the displacement of the angelophany (John 20:11–13) by the appearance of Jesus himself. As one can observe by noticing Neirynck's underlinings in the text above, essential elements of Matthew's brief narrative recur in that of John, albeit mostly in different forms. It is, of course, scarcely possible that Matthew redacted and compressed John; on the other hand, that John created his dramatic narrative and gave to Mary Magdalene the central role is easily imaginable.

If one considers the earlier part of the narrative (John 20:1–10), something similar can be seen happening.[31] First of all, Neirynck agrees with Boismard that Luke 24:12, which describes Peter's visit to the empty tomb of Jesus, is a part of the original text of Luke. Here, even more than in the case of the appearance of Jesus to Mary (or the two women) the similarities to John (20:3–10) are striking, including one notable verbatim agreement with John 20:5. That the stooping and looking in are ascribed to the Beloved Disciple and not to Peter is what one might expect in the Fourth Gospel. But might not John and Luke have known the same tradition, which John redacted rather extensively in accord with his own interests? Neirynck points out three Lukanisms in 24:12 (*anastas*; *thaumazein* + accusative; *to gegonos*) that are not paralleled in John. Moreover, non-Lukan traits are found in 24:12 as well, notably *parakuptein* and *othonion*, both of which occur in John 20:5 and seem more at home there, as well as the historical present *blepei* which also occurs in John 20:5. But John, in using Luke, would have dropped the three

---

[28] Neirynck, "John and the Synoptics: The Empty Tomb Stories," 161–87.
[29] Neirynck, "Les femmes au tombeau: Etude de la rédaction matthéenne."
[30] Neirynck, "John and the Synoptics: The Empty Tomb Stories," 166–71.
[31] Ibid., 175–79.

Lukanisms, which did not suit his style and purpose, and would have taken over the more congenial language. Of course, if John had taken over the clearly Lukan characteristics, the case for his use of Luke would be clinched on redaction-critical grounds. Nevertheless, the degree to which Luke 24:12 is paralleled in the much more developed Johannine account by the addition of typically Johannine motifs is striking. Moreover, Neirynck points to a Lukan motif in John 20:9: Why is the disciple's not knowing the Scriptures mentioned?[32] It is unmotivated in John's account, but it may be motivated by Luke's, where the risen Jesus expounds the Scripture to his disciples, particularly as they pertain to his own resurrection (Luke 24:44–47). Given Luke's account, John's mentioning that the disciples did not know the Scriptures becomes immediately intelligible. (Of course, one should also consider the fact that according to the earliest kerygmatic formula of which we have knowledge, Jesus' resurrection was said to have taken place according to the Scriptures: 1 Cor. 15:4.)

As in the case of Boismard, we have only sketched the direction of Neirynck's arguments, without attempting to reproduce them completely. Nevertheless their character is clear. In effect, Neirynck asks how much is really necessary to explain John's text as it stands. It is a neat and, to Neirynck's mind, altogether appropriate application of Ockham's razor. Can one not make John's account intelligible on the working hypothesis that he simply knew Matthew and Luke? If so, would he not also have been motivated to conflate and, so to speak, reconcile these accounts to bring them into one whole, complete narrative? Thus Neirynck offers a succinct redaction-critical rationale to account for how John dealt with his synoptic sources. Increasingly, Neirynck and those who follow him in speaking of John's dependence upon and redaction of the Synoptic Gospels will find it incumbent upon themselves to offer such explanations.[33]

---

[32] Ibid., 177.

[33] Aside from Neirynck, Sabbe, and other Louvain colleagues, one notes the 1990 Louvain Colloquium Seminar Paper of Michael D. Goulder, "John 1, 1–2, 12 and the Synoptics," and the article of Thomas M. Dowell, "Jews and Christians in Conflict: Why the Fourth Gospel Changed the Synoptic Tradition," *Louvain Studies* 15 (1990): 19–37.

It is worth observing that before turning to the question of John and the Synoptics, Neirynck had made major contributions to synoptic criticism as an exponent of Markan priority. Especially important are his *Duality in Mark: Contributions to the Study of the Markan Redaction*, rev. ed., BETL 31 (Louvain: Louvain University Press, 1988), and *The Minor Agreements of Matthew and Luke against Mark with a Cumulative List*, in collaboration with Theo Hansen and Frans van Segbroeck, BETL 37 (Louvain University Press, 1974). In a recent article, "Introduction: The Two-Source Hypothesis," in *The Interrelations of the Gospels: A Symposium Led by M.-E. Boismard, W. R. Farmer, F. Neirynck, Jerusalem 1984*, edited by David L. Dungan, BETL 95 (Louvain: Louvain University Press, 1991), 3–22, Neirynck has eloquently summarized the case for the Markan hypothesis.

## JOHN AND LUKE AGAIN: ANTON DAUER
## AND HANS-PETER HEEKERENS

The discussion of the relationship between the Gospel of John and the Gospel of Luke has been carried forward in two recent works that belong in the post-consensus era: Anton Dauer, *Johannes und Lukas: Untersuchungen zu den johanneisch-lukanischen Parallelperikopen Joh 4,46–54/Lk 7,1–10—Joh 12,1–8/ Lk 7,36–50; 10,38–42—Joh 20,19–29/Lk 24,36–49*; and Hans-Peter Heekerens, *Die Zeichen-Quelle der johanneischen Redaktion: Ein Beitrag zur Entstehungs-geschichte des viertens Evangeliums.*[34] Although differing in perspective and very largely in results, they share two significant conclusions. First, both authors view the Johannine tradition or *Grundschrift* as independent of the Synoptic Gospels. But, second, both conclude that the final recension of John reflects knowledge not only of Lukan tradition but of the canonical form of the Gospel of Luke as well. It is worth noting that in these respects they agree with Boismard. They are also representive of the recent trend to look once again at the question of John and the Synoptics with a view to asking whether John does not show direct influence of, in this case, Luke. If not inspired by Neirynck, they are at least asking his question.

### Anton Dauer

Dauer's work extends the method and perspective that he developed in his inaugural dissertation on the Johannine passion narrative (see above, chap. 5) to the Johannine narratives with Lukan parallels (the healing of the official's son, the anointing of Jesus' feet, and the appearance of Jesus to the Twelve), and obtains remarkably similar results. In each instance the pericope in question betrays knowledge not only of Lukan tradition but of the Gospel of Luke itself. Yet John does not rely on Luke for his story, in the sense that he copied it from Luke. Rather, the original story came to him independently of Luke.

---

In this connection he writes (p. 5): "The basic conviction of the Markan hypothesis can be seen in the fact that the Gospel of Mark has so much in common with Matthew and Luke that a literary relationship, not only of individual pericopes but of the gospels as such, is undeniable and that the most adequate solution resulting from a comparative study of the language, the style and the content of the Synoptic Gospels is the use of Mark as a common source by Matthew and Luke." The case for Matthew's and Luke's independent use of Mark is often confirmed by redaction-critical analysis based on that premise. Will it be possible to say the same for John's use of Mark, or of either of the other Synoptics?

[34] Anton Dauer, *Johannes und Lukas,* Forschung zur Bibel 50 (Würzburg: Echter Verlag, 1984); and Hans-Peter Heekerens, *Die Zeichen-Quelle der johanneischen Redaktion,* SBS 113 (Stuttgart: Verlag Katholisches Bibelwerk, 1984).

In the form in which he received it, however, each story had already been influenced by Luke, not in the sense that some earlier author had known and copied Luke, but through the permeation of the available oral tradition by distinctly Lukan material including specifically Lukan redaction. Thus John does not know the Gospel of Luke, but, to put matters succinctly, John's source knew Luke. As in the case of the passion narrative, John's source is not Luke but an independent traditional source that nevertheless reflects knowledge of Luke. With this more recent work, Dauer in effect extends the scope of John's knowledge of the Synoptics.

Dauer rightly sees the problem as one of explaining the coexistence of widely acknowledged similarities and differences between John and Luke and observes that before Gardner-Smith wrote (1938), the vast majority of exegetes agreed that John knew one or more of the Synoptics.[35] (Dauer notes with interest that Schniewind believed the similarities between John and Luke were due to oral tradition without doubting that John had known Mark.[36]) Since Gardner-Smith, the situation has reversed itself, but within very recent years attempts to explain their relationship on a literary basis have once again risen. The judgments of critics as to whether John knew the Synoptics tend to be based on how heavily the individual critic weighs the similarities and differences and which of them are regarded as the problems to be explained. Since, in his earlier study, Dauer found a way out of the impasse by looking for traces of Lukan (and Matthean) redaction in John and asking whether such traces lay in Johannine redaction or in John's tradition or source, he now proposes to extend his method of questioning to these pericopes with Lukan parallels.

The first pericope with which Dauer deals, the healing of the centurion's servant or the official's son (John 4:46–54/Luke 7:1–10), will suffice to exhibit his method and results.[37] It has been worked over by numerous scholars and, of course, has a Matthean (8:5–13) and thus presumably a Q parallel. Dauer first establishes the similarities between John and Luke only, then the differences between John and Luke; then the agreements between John and Matthew only, then the differences.[38] This is followed by a wide-ranging sketch of the history of exegesis of the passage in modern research.[39] But the first major item of business is a tradition-historical or source-critical analysis of

---

[35] Dauer, *Johannes und Lukas*, 16–17.
[36] Ibid., 23.
[37] Ibid., 39–125.
[38] Ibid., 39–44.
[39] Ibid., 44–51.

the Johannine pericope in order to recover the underlying tradition or source. Here his footnotes indicate that Dauer is in continuous dialogue with predecessors such as Bultmann, Fortna, Schnackenburg, Lindars, and Boismard, among others. It is probably fair to say that his criteria are, with Fortna, primarily contexual and linguistic. A few examples will illustrate this state of affairs.

John 4:46a, which brings Jesus into Cana of Galilee and refers to the wine miracle there, is assigned to the evangelist. It locates the episode in Cana rather than Capernaum. The latter location is original, as the Q version shows, and the backward reference to a previous narrative or statement is typical of the evangelist. John 4:46b is the beginning of the traditional narrative in the source; it is all the story itself (as distinguished from the Johannine framework) needs to set the stage. It has parallels—setting the scene at Capernaum—in Matthew 8:5–6 and Luke 7:1–2. (Interestingly enough, Aland's *Synopsis* begins the Johannine narrative with 4:46b, with 4:46a separated by almost fifty pages.)

John 4:47a with its reference to Jesus' coming from Judea to Galilee is again redactional, for it brings the narrative into line with the overall Johannine framework.[40] The *akousas*, found both in John and in Luke 7:3, might be expected and does not require the knowledge of Luke's Gospel to be understood. John 4:47b (*apēlthen . . .*) is, however, necessary to the progress of the narrative and is assigned to the traditional source. Its use of *herōtan* agrees with Luke. Even though John's *hina katabē* seems to conform with John's geographical scheme, Dauer ultimately assigns it to the traditional source, noting its similarity to Luke (*hopōs elthōn*).[41] John 4:47's statement about the son's being at the point of death is very close to what is said in Luke 7:2 and is assigned to the source, to whose narrative thread it is integral.[42] Verses 48-49 are adjudged redactional in agreement with most recent exegesis (Bultmann, et al.), although the portrayal of Jesus' attitude toward signs may well be informed by tradition.[43] John 4:50a resumes the thread of the original account and is traditional, although v. 50b is redactional. Both the language and the theology of the latter are Johannine.

Ultimately, Dauer produces a source consisting of 2:12 (the source's redactional transition between 2:1–11 and 4:46, which originally followed immediately thereafter), 4:46b, and 47b (perhaps also traditional elements in

---

[40] Ibid., 55–56.
[41] Ibid., 58.
[42] Ibid., 58–59.
[43] Ibid., 59–63.

47a), 50a (perhaps also traditional elements in 50b: *ho anthrōpos eporeueto*), 51, 52 (minus certain Johannine touches, e.g., *oun* and *exthes*, the latter conforming to the Johannine time frame), most of v. 53 (minus the *ho huios sou zē*), and 54a.[44] John 54b, which qualifies the second sign as having been done after Jesus came from Judea into Galilee, is assigned to the Johannine redaction, in agreement with many analysts, as an awkward effort to conform the miracle story to the Johannine narrative scheme, in which it may be the second sign narrated but is certainly not the second sign mentioned. Dauer's reconstituted source is not dissimilar to Fortna's. Several elements in this source are held in common with Luke only, and to these Dauer will return.

Dauer then moves to an analysis of Luke 7:1–10, which naturally involves a consideration of Matthew 8:5–13 also.[45] The most notable difference between the synoptic versions (which are closer to each other than either is to John) is that in Matthew the petitioner approaches Jesus directly, whereas in Luke he employs mediators. Interestingly enough, the closest parallels between either of the synoptic stories and John lie in the beginnings and endings. Dauer scrutinizes the endings first.[46] He contends that Matthew 8:13 (particularly the *iathē ho pais [autou] en tē hōra ekeinē*) is redactional, and probably also the concluding formulation of Luke 7:10, in which the emissaries return to find the sick servant now well. The Q version was not a miracle story properly speaking at all but an apothegm, and both Matthew and Luke have suppressed an original ending formulation with their own. Luke's version is taken to be closer to the original, in part because of its affinities with Mark 7:30, a similar story, and in part because in healing stories Luke may be observed to transmit Mark (and therefore presumably other sources) more accurately than does Matthew.

The logion of Matthew 8:11–12 is a redactional insertion of Matthew.[47] (It appears in a different context in Luke.) Matthew 8:8–10 and Luke 7:6b–9 are, however, part of the common (Q) source, and the differences can be explained as the result of the evangelists' redaction. That the origin is Q is shown not only by verbatim agreements in this section but by their following closely upon the Sermon on the Mount/Plain in either Gospel. Moreover, the narrative framing of the stories, with the Capernaum setting and chief characters, in all probability belongs also to Q.[48] Although most exegetes view the

---

[44] Ibid., 72–73.
[45] Ibid., 76–116.
[46] Ibid., 78–84.
[47] Ibid., 84–87.
[48] Ibid., 87

Matthean version as more original, because it is simpler, Dauer does not entirely agree. Rather, he argues that the emissaries in Luke's version are original and have been eliminated in Matthew, as in John.[49]

While the Lukan version is closer to the original (Q), significant redactional elements of Luke are nevertheless present. Some of these also turn up in John, for example, the use of *herōtan* (Luke 7:3/John 4:47); *ēmellen teleutan* (redactional in Luke 7:2; cf. *ēmellen gar apothnēskein* in John 4:47). Characteristically, they lie in parts of the Johannine version that on other grounds Dauer has ascribed to the pre-Johannine source rather than to the fourth evangelist.[50] The obvious differences of the Johannine account are scarcely to be explained as the fourth evangelist's alterations of the Lukan narrative: the sickness is described differently; in Luke the sick person is the centurion's slave, in John the official's son; the centurion's approach to Jesus is through emissaries, the official's direct; John and Luke use different words for healing (*iasthai* and *diasōzein*); in John, Jesus utters a healing word, but not in Luke; and so forth.[51] The similarities of the Johannine and Matthean accounts in distinction from the Lukan are in some respects more striking; in both, *pais* is used of the sick person (cf. John 4:51; otherwise *huios*); in both, the point of time of the healing is noted, the moment Jesus spoke (John 4:50-53; Matt. 8:13); both use *iasthai* for the act of healing; both portray Jesus telling the petitioner to go, and in the immediate context the man's belief is noted (John 4:50; Matt. 8:13).[52] In fact, the affinities between the story's ending in John and Matthew (the reference to the hour of healing) are so striking as to suggest that John or John's source has been influenced by Matthew. The differences between John's and Matthew's versions are nevertheless real, for example, in John the *huios* lies near death of a fever, while in Matthew the *pais* is lame (paralyzed); in John, the official implores Jesus' help directly, in Matthew the centurion only speaks of his slave's deplorable condition; in John, the messengers inform the official of the healing, in Matthew (in contrast to John and Luke) there are no intermediaries at all and this episode is therefore lacking.[53]

What theory best explains these complex relationships, particularly that between John and Luke? Possibly a common oral tradition underlies John on the one hand and Luke as well as Matthew on the other, but this fails to account for the presence of Lukan redactional elements in the Johannine

---

[49] Ibid., 88–98, 99–107.
[50] Ibid., 117–20.
[51] Ibid., 40–41.
[52] Ibid., 42–43; cf. 108.
[53] Ibid., 43–44.

version. Moreover, there are important points of agreement between Matthew and the pre-Johannine version. More probably, thinks Dauer, the pre-Johannine story was a free rendition (*freie Wiedergabe*) of Matthew 8:5–13, which had already been influenced by Luke 7:1–10 before its incorporation into the canonical form of the Gospel. Thus John does not know Luke, but the pre-Johannine source knows both Matthew and Luke.[54]

The conclusions drawn about the other pericopes are similar, and for the same reason. A Johannine source betrays evidence of not only Luke, but Lukan redaction. Thus the original story of the anointing of Jesus' feet (John 12:1–8) was the product of the interweaving (*Ineinanderfliessen*) of the canonical form of Luke 7:36–50 and Mark 14:3–9 in the oral tradition John used.[55] John's similarities to both stories are thereby accounted for without having to suppose that the evangelist had the Lukan or Markan accounts before him.

For the appearance stories (John 20:19–29/Luke 24:36–49) the same solution is near to hand. Lukan redactional elements appear in John 20:19–29, proving that John reflects knowledge not only of Lukan tradition but of canonical Luke.[56] Yet the Johannine story also contains elements that are traditional, such as the closed doors, the showing of the hands and *side*, the formulation about forgiveness of sin, and the bestowal of the Spirit by Jesus. In important respects it is independent of Luke. Dauer's solution is no surprise. The pre-Johannine version of the story, while not derived from Luke, has been influenced by oral tradition based on Luke, presumably in the process of transmission.[57]

In conclusion, Dauer asks whether these three traditional units came to John the Evangelist separately or as part of a continuous source. He is inclined to favor the latter possibility in somewhat the form suggested by Robert T. Fortna (*The Gospel of Signs*).[58] That is, John knows an earlier narrative source that has already been influenced indirectly or through oral transmission by the Synoptic Gospels, particularly Matthew and Luke.

In this monograph Dauer comes closer to the view, hallowed by tradition of church and scholarship, that John knows and assumes the Synoptics. No wonder that Neirynck applauds his apparent move in that direction but points out that his stylistic grounds for not simply conceding John's direct use of

---

[54] Ibid., 120–25.
[55] Ibid., 204–6.
[56] Ibid., 285.
[57] Ibid., 287–288.
[58] Ibid., 299.

them as sources are far from ambiguous.[59] Yet with reason Dauer finds it difficult to understand the Johannine accounts redaction critically as derivative from the Synoptics in the way one can often perceive and understand Matthean or Lukan narratives as derivative from Mark. What is more, much if not most of John's Gospel, particularly outside the passion and resurrection narratives, is not based on the Synoptics in any obvious way. So, by declining to see the fourth evangelist as directly responsible for the affinities with the other Gospels, he avoids the not inconsiderable problem of explaining why John, if he knew the others, wrote such a very different gospel.

### Hans-Peter Heekerens

Heekerens's work[60] moves along lines rather different from Dauer's, even though it supports the same general conclusion, namely, that the Gospel of John somehow manifests knowledge of the Gospel of Luke, although its own narrative is basically independent of the synoptic. Heekerens presupposes the positions of his teacher Hartwig Thyen and Thyen's earlier student Wolfgang Langbrandtner. According to Langbrandtner, whose view is closely allied with Thyen's, the Gospel of John is based on a gnostic or proto-gnostic narrative source (*Grundschrift* = G).[61] The history of the Johannine community and its gospel was then a history of their moving from Gnosticism to a version of Christianity in closer accord with the Synoptics and the developing orthodoxy of the church. With this movement came knowledge of the Synoptics on the part of the final redactor, whom Thyen and his students would call the evangelist, for it is he who put the Gospel into its present canonical form, from which standpoint it should be interpreted.

Heekerens's distinctive thesis is that this redactor, who knew at least the Gospel of Luke, incorporated into the final recension of the Gospel a collection of miracle stories (*Zeichen-Quelle*) consisting of the narratives now found in 2:1–12; 4:46–54; and 21:1–14.[62] In this signs source, the present resurrection story of 21:1–14 was a miracle story of Jesus' ministry (cf. Luke 5:1–11 and

---

[59] Frans Neirynck, "John 4:46–54: Signs Source and/or Synoptic Gospels," *ETL* 60 (1984): 367–75.

[60] See n. 34 above.

[61] Langbrandtner, *Weltferner Gott oder Gott der Liebe.* Langbrandtner's work was inspired by his mentor Hartwig Thyen (pp. viii–ix). Cf. Thyen's earlier article, "Johannes 13 und die 'Kirchliche Redaktion' des vierten Evangeliums"; also Thyen's lengthy *Forschungsbericht,* "Aus der Literatur zum Johannesevangelium," *ThR* 39 (1974): 222–52, 289–330, which Langbrandtner cites, and *ThR* 42 (1977): 252, where Thyen cites Langbrandtner in succinctly stating his own position.

[62] Heekerens, *Die Zeichen-Quelle der johanneischen Redaktion,* 11–16.

the similar views of Fortna and Boismard). Significantly, Heekerens attacks the integrity of the signs-source hypothesis as set forth by Bultmann, Becker, Fortna, and Nicol.[63] No satisfactory explanation of why only the first two signs of the putative source are numbered is forthcoming, and the alleged stylistic unity of the source is questionable, as its critics have pointed out. Nevertheless the two (numbered) Cana miracles (John 2:1–11; 4:46–54) and John 21:1–14 are said to be remarkably free from specifically Johannine dialogue or discourse in which, typically, the meaning of the miracle just transpired is brought out.

If one excepts 2:1–11 and 4:46–54, one finds that three or four of the remaining five Johannine miracle stories in John 5; 6 (two); 9; and 11 have Markan parallels, depending on whether one allows the miracle of the resurrection of the young man in the fragment of the *Secret Gospel of Mark* (M. Smith) to count as a parallel to John 11.[64] Moreover, they appear in the same order as in Mark. Possibly at some point they belonged to a primitive miracle collection on which both Mark and John drew (Koester), although at this juncture it is difficult to say. Heekerens apparently regards this as more likely than that John knew Mark directly. In any case, his thesis regarding the other three miracle stories would not depend on this possibility.

Heekerens takes for granted Thyen's view that John (i.e., the final redactor = JR) knew at least the Gospel of Luke, simply referring to his teacher's "good arguments" in his lengthy *Forschungsbericht* in *Theologische Rundschau*.[65] When one looks those citations up, however, one finds that Thyen has only expressed his doubtless well informed judgment about the matter without mounting a sustained argument. (But the installment of the *Forschungsbericht* dealing with John and the Synoptics was finally not written by Thyen but by Jürgen Becker.) Heekerens' espousal of JR's knowledge of Luke does not end with this concurrence with Thyen's general position. Since JR knew Luke, Heekerens thinks the affinities with Luke in John 4:46–54 and 21:1–14 may well stem directly from the Gospel of Luke rather than the signs source, which was independent of the Synoptics.

For example, Heekerens suggests that JR has inserted the saying about a prophet having no honor in his own country (4:44) into the transition to 4:46–54 under the influence of Luke 4:24, where it is related to the two miracles of Elijah and Elisha performed in strange lands.[66] John's reflection

---

[63] Ibid., 17–43.
[64] Ibid., 42–43.
[65] Ibid., 50. Cf. Thyen, *ThR* 42 (1977): 238, 247, 251ff.
[66] Heekerens, *Die Zeichen-Quelle der johanneischen Redaktion*, 124–25.

on this saying (4:44), which is not actually quoted directly but referred to, is likewise related to Jesus' performance of a miracle in a strange land, Galilee. (Judea or Jerusalem is his *Heimat*, where he is without honor.) It is as if JR knows the Lukan narrative as he inserts the two Galilean miracles (2:1–11; 4:46–54) into G ( = *Grundschrift*) and comments on them with Jesus' famous saying about the prophet. Moreover, in Luke 4:25–26 the miracle of a gift of food is reported (cf. John 2:1–11), whereas in 4:27 it is a miracle of healing (cf. John 4:45–54). Also, the use of the story of the great catch of fish to introduce the concluding resurrection narrative (21:1–14) may even have been influenced by the presentation of Peter as fisher of men in the comparable Lukan account (Luke 5:1–11).

Heekerens's primary purpose is not to illumine John's relationship to the Synoptics, but it is nevertheless significant that he views the Fourth Gospel as based on independent sources while showing the influence of Luke. In both of these respects he agrees generally with Dauer. Yet in significant respects they also differ. For Dauer, the influence of Luke impinges upon John's source; for Heekerens, upon the redactor (or evangelist). Moreover, for Dauer that source seems to be a miracle source (or gospel) of a synoptic or pre-synoptic type, although he is wary of attempting to define the source precisely. For Heekerens it is a proto-gnostic document—in other words, a source of a different sort. Dauer then sees John's original tradition as closely related to the Synoptics, with the Johannine trajectory, so to speak, moving away from them. Heekerens sees John beginning in a very different traditional and theological milieu but being brought closer into line with the Synoptics by the work of the final redactor.

### Hartwig Thyen: A Note

As we have already noticed, both Heekerens's and Langbrandtner's positions have been worked out in conjunction with their mentor Hartwig Thyen's emerging view of the relationship of John to the Synoptics, particularly Luke. In that scholar's more recent utterances, he has made it unmistakably clear that he now not only believes that John knew Luke but fully embraces the results and perspective of Frans Neirynck, whose work he cites with hearty approval. Thus in his 1990 Louvain Colloquium paper, Thyen expresses himself as follows:

> As far as the relation of the Gospel of John to the Synoptics is concerned, I am, with the English commentators and especially the more recent works of F. Neirynck, M. Sabbe, F. Vouga, and many others, convinced that John knew not

only the tradition attested by our Synoptic Gospels, but these gospels themselves in their finished, literary form, and that in his own way he used them, indeed, all three of them.[67]

At the same time, Thyen disavows his own early literary or source-critical work, at least as a means or presupposition of interpretation. Of course, in that earlier work Thyen had already departed from his teacher Bultmann in declaring that, whatever the history of the Gospel's development, John was now to be read in light of chapter 21, which belongs to its latest redactional layer and is to be regarded as the work of the "evangelist" rather than of an eccesiastical redactor.[68] At that point Thyen was still working within the re-daction-critical perspective, which he later abandoned, assuming that a biblical work is to be read from the standpoint of its final redaction. He differed from Bultmann principally in the weight he attached to that redaction, at the same time believing it to be somewhat more extensive, or pervasive, than Bultmann had supposed. Inasmuch as for Thyen—as for Bultmann—the final redaction reflects knowledge of the Synoptics, Thyen's shift in nomenclature and exe-getical perspective meant that the Gospel itself should be interpreted with the Synoptics in view, something that Bultmann would have denied. This advance over Bultmann positioned him well for the next move, however—namely, away from redaction criticism or any mode of interpretation that grants to the hypothetical situation, layers, and development of a text the decisive voice in the interpretation of that text. Thyen's move aligns him with the literary-critical approaches to, or readings of, biblical texts now so much in vogue on the American scene, except that while that American enterprise has been largely secular or atheological, Thyen's is quite theological in intention and purpose.

There is an interesting parallel between Thyen's shift of ground and the movement of R. Alan Culpepper from *The Johannine School* (which, along with the Johannine circle or the Johannine church, Thyen now abjures) to the *Anatomy of the Fourth Gospel*, whose overall purpose and perspective Thyen generally approves.[69] Thyen is much more explicitly negative about the earlier

---

[67] Hartwig Thyen, "Johannes und die Synoptiker—Auf der Suche nach einem neuen Paradigm zur Beschreibung ihrer Beziehungen anhand von Beobachtungen an Passions-und Osterer-zählungen," to be published in the proceedings of the meeting in BETL (translation mine). On Thyen's position on John's knowledge of the Synoptic Gospels, see also his article "Johannes-evangelium," in *Theologische Realenzyklopädie*, vol. 17 (Berlin: Walter de Gruyter, 1988), 200–25, esp. 202–3, 205–8 (where Thyen discusses Bultmann's source theory), and 215 (where knowledge of Luke provides the *terminus a quo* for dating the Fourth Gospel).

[68] See n. 61 above.

[69] R. Alan Culpepper, *The Johannine School: An Evaluation of the Johannine School Hypothesis Based on an Investigation of the Nature of Ancient Schools*, SBLDS 26 (Missoula, Mont.: Scholars Press, 1975). See n. 3 above.

stops on his journey than Culpepper would be, but the common movement and direction are clear enough. We have already noted that, for Culpepper, John's knowledge of the gospel story is evident in a number of ways. That is, the evangelist (and the implied author) knows this story, and probably the intended reader (certainly the implied reader) knows it too. Yet Culpepper does not find it necessary to take a position on the question of whether John actually knew the Synoptics in the form we have them. It remains a question whether for the kind of intertextual interpretation that Thyen now strongly espouses it is necessary to believe that John knew the Synoptics. Of course, Thyen may well believe that on other grounds, as his recent endorsement of the work of Neirynck and others would indicate. At the same time, it is worth pointing out that to assume that such conscious intention on the part of the actual author is a prerequisite for intertextual reading is to remain within the assumptions of the older redaction criticism, for which the putative intention of the author was of decisive significance.

In any event, with his decision to regard the present, canonical text as the work of the evangelist rather than a secondary redactor, Thyen already reopened, at least for himself, the question of the relation of the Gospel as the evangelist composed it, to the other Gospels, since the final redaction reflects familiarity with one or more of the Synoptics. As Thyen's exegetical work continues and his hermeneutical horizon changes, the Fourth Gospel's relation to the Synoptics becomes more and more important.

## BRUNO DE SOLAGES

Finally, we turn to Bruno de Solages's *Jean et les synoptiques*, published the same year (1979) as Neirynck's critique of Boismard issued under the same title.[70] The two books could scarcely differ more, especially when one considers that they are about the same subject and contain remarkably similar conclusions: John knows and uses the Synoptic Gospels. De Solages's work is a wonderful combination of complexity and simplicity. The complexity of the book consists in his effort to marshal and measure the actual extent of the agreement between John and the Synoptics, both over the extent of the Gospels and in individual pericopes; the simplicity in his explanation of why, if John knew the other Gospels, he did not use them as sources. Unlike Neirynck, who engages in intense discussion and debate with other scholars, de Solages

---

[70] Mgr. [Bruno] de Solages, *Jean et les synoptiques* (Leiden: E. J. Brill, 1979).

by and large goes his own way, rarely citing the work of colleagues. De Solages's book can therefore scarcely be considered the culmination of a newer trend in scholarship. It was, however, a work that clearly signaled the end of the old consensus on John's independence and the reopening of the question of John and the Synoptics. Particularly significant is the author's effort to quantify the relationship of the content of John to that of the Synoptics and to compare and contrast that relationship with those which exist among the Synoptic Gospels. In attempting to do this, de Solages has performed a useful service to gospel scholarship, for the kind of work he accomplished could afford an important basis for any further discussion of the problem of John and the Synoptics.

Part One, entitled "Jean n'utilise pas les synoptiques comme source," begins with an effort simply to identify those verses of John which may reasonably be said to be paralleled in the Synoptics. These are displayed in a table of columns in which every verse of John is given in the left-hand column and every synoptic verse that could be considered a parallel is noted in its respective gospel column opposite the Johannine verse.[71] Only correspondences between verses are recorded. Thus where there are only broad parallels (John 21) nothing is noted in the Synoptic columns.

Often the corresponding verses of the Synoptics are bracketed or framed to indicate they do not have the same wording or are not in the same order as their synoptic counterparts. It is not surprising that until the passion many pages are largely blank. De Solages observes that one cannot fail to be struck by the relative paucity of such correspondences as compared with those among the Synoptic Gospels.[72] Moreover, such correspondences as exist are usually isolated rather than continuous. Totaling the corresponding verses, the author concludes that of John's 868 verses, 153 (or 17.6 percent) have synoptic counterparts.[73] He might have noted that this would compare with upward of 90 percent of Markan verses that have Matthean counterparts.[74] Even such a figure as he proposes for John and the Synoptics is really not comparable to the figures for Mark and Matthew, however, for even in parallel pericopes the incidence of verbatim agreement or near-agreement is much greater among the Synoptics than between John and any one of them. Nevertheless de Solages performs a useful service in quantifying Johannine-synoptic relationships in

---

[71] Ibid., 4–20. See the sample chart following in the text, taken from p. 20.

[72] Ibid., 21.

[73] Ibid., 22.

[74] Allan Barr, *A Diagram of Synoptic Relationships* (Edinburgh: T. & T. Clark, 1938), 3, calculates that 609 of Mark's 662 verses have Matthean counterparts.

| | John 20 | Lk. | Mk. | Mt. | | John 21 | Lk. | Mk. | Mt. |
|---|---|---|---|---|---|---|---|---|---|
| 1 | Mary Magdalene at the tomb | " | $16,1^b+$ 2-4 | " | 1 | | | | |
| 2 | She goes to make the announcement to Peter and John | " | 16,8 | " | 2 | | | | |
| 3 | | | | | 3 | | | | |
| 4 | | | | | 4 | | | | |
| 5 | Peter and John at the tomb | | | | 5 | | | | |
| 6 | | 24,12 | | | 6 | | | | |
| 7 | | | | | 7 | | | | |
| 8 | | | | | 8 | | | | |
| 9 | | | | | 9 | | | | |
| 10 | | | | | 10 | | | | |
| 11 | | | | | 11 | | | | |
| 12 | Mary Magdalene sees two angels | $24,4^b$ | $16,15^b$ | " | 12 | | | | |
| 13 | | | | | 13 | | | | |
| 14 | | | | | 14 | | | | |
| 15 | "Go speak to my brothers" | | | $28,9\text{-}10^a$ | 15 | | | | |
| 16 | | | | | 16 | | | | |
| 17 | | | | | 17 | | | | |
| 18 | | | | | 18 | | | | |
| 19 | | | | | 19 | | | | |
| 20 | | | | | 20 | | | | |
| 21 | Apparition to the Twelve | 24,36-41 | | | 21 | | | | |
| 22 | | + 47 | | | 22 | | | | |
| 23 | | | | 18, 18 | 23 | | | | |
| 24 | | | | | 24 | | | | |
| 25 | | | | | 25 | | | | |
| 26 | | | | | | | | | |
| 27 | | | | | | | | | |
| 28 | | | | | | | | | |
| 29 | | | | | | | | | |
| 30 | | | | | | | | | |
| 31 | | | | | | | | | |

A TYPICAL DISPLAY OF JOHANNINE-SYNOPTIC
PARALLELS FROM DE SOLAGES

this way. He dramatizes the obvious but significant fact that most of what John contains is simply not found in the Synoptics and vice versa.

Particularly useful is de Solages's effort to quantify, that is, set a percentage value on, the extent of verbal agreements between John and the Synoptics in the passion narrative, John 6, and certain common logia.[75] To spread the linguistic net as wide as possible, de Solages uses three categories of agreement: verbatim agreement (abbreviated I); equivalent words (i.e., same root, but different inflexion; abbreviated E); and synonyms (abbreviated Σ). He finds, for example, that through John's entire passion narrative (John 18–19) there is a 15.5 percent agreement with Mark (i.e., the total agreement comprising categories I, E, and Σ). That percentage of agreement rises to 33.3 percent if only the corresponding verses are considered.[76] This figure compares with Luke's percentages of 65.2 in relation to Mark for the entire passion and 66.6 for the corresponding passages or verses. With Matthew/Mark, those percentages are 65.2 for the passion as a whole and 70.0 for the corresponding verses. In the case of traditions within the Synoptics known to be independent of each other (e.g., the Beelzebul accusation of Luke 11:14–15, 17–23, from Q; and Mark 3:21–30) the percentages of agreement are, on the same terms, somewhat higher than those between the passion narratives of Mark and John. De Solages can think of no better proof of the independence of the Johannine and synoptic passion traditions.[77]

As a test case, de Solages conducts an extensive comparison of the wording of John 6:1–21 (feeding and walking on the water) and the corresponding synoptic passages,[78] which constitute the longest continuous parallels outside the passion. Among other things, de Solages finds a maximal 27.2 percent agreement (I, E, and Σ) between John and Mark (expressed as a percentage of John) throughout the passage, somewhat lower than in the corresponding parts of the passion. The percentage of identical agreement (I) is only 13.9 percent. The identical agreement is only a little more than one half of the broader agreement, and both are relatively low. This is exactly what one would expect to find in independent but parallel traditions. Moreover, the verbatim relationship of Matthew or Luke to Mark is generally more than twice as strong as the verbatim relationship of either Matthew or Luke to John, again a token of the independence of the Johannine traditions.[79]

---

[75] De Solages, *Jean et les synoptiques,* 27–66.
[76] Ibid., 27.
[77] Ibid., 28: "Il est difficile d'imaginer meilleure preuve de l'independance de leurs traditions."
[78] Ibid., 30–49.
[79] Ibid., 50.

The comparison of a series of Johannine logia of Jesus with synoptic counterparts (John 4:44; 5:23b, 29; 6:51; 8:51[52]; 12:23b, 25, 26; 13:16, 20; 14:25–26, 31; 15:19b, 20a, 20b–21, 26, 27; 16:23) yields similar results.[80] None of them occurs in the same context in John and Mark, an indication that John does not follow Mark. In those cases in which the verbal correspondence seems quite high (e.g., John 13:20 and Mark 9:37), the logia are relatively brief, the correspondences might easily result from memory, and in any event are not sufficient to prove literary dependence.

De Solages begins the second part of his work ("Jean connait la tradition synoptique")[81] with the confident assertion that although John does not use the Synoptics as sources, he nevertheless knows the synoptic tradition (and, indeed, the Synoptic Gospels). Because the percentage of resemblance is usually stronger between John and Mark than between John and the other Synoptics, and because Mark as the most ancient gospel could scarcely have been ignored by John, de Solages first studies the relation between John and Mark. Despite the fact that the overall percentages of verbal agreement between John and Mark are not great, there are some pericopes in which they are sufficiently high to be difficult to explain apart from John's knowledge of Mark. Already the higher percentage of agreement in the corresponding passages of the passion has been noted. In several episodes within the passion the degree of agreement rises even higher: the mocking of Jesus (John 19:2–3 = Mark 15:16–19); the crucifixion (John 19:16–19 = Mark 15:15b, 20b–22, 24a, 26–27); the cleansing of the temple (esp. John 2:13, 15, 16, 18, 19 = Mark 11:15–17, 28; 14:58); the anointing at Bethany (John 12:1–8 = Mark 14:3–9).[82] The percentage of total agreement $(I + E + \Sigma)$ between John and Mark in these passages ranges between the upper 40s and the lower 60s, that is, closer to the percentages between Mark and Matthew or Luke in corresponding passages of the Synoptics than to the much lower percentages of the independent traditions as represented by the Beelzebul accusation in Mark 3:21–30 and Luke 11:14–15, 17–23 (Q).[83] With some justification, de Solages concludes that such passages as these reflect John's direct knowledge of Mark. Looking again at the feeding stories of Mark and John, which on grounds of wording did not seem to require a literary relationship, de Solages observes that they contain exactly the same numbers: two hundred denarii,

[80] Ibid., 50–66.
[81] Ibid., 67–185.
[82] Ibid., 69–96 passim.
[83] Ibid., 97.

five loaves and two fish, five thousand men, twelve baskets.[84] He again concludes that this agreement indicates John's knowledge of Mark.

Comparisons of data or material held in common between Matthew and John and Luke and John[85] lead de Solages to the conclusion that John did not write with the text of either before him, although the affinities with Luke are acknowledged to be more numerous than those with Matthew. The story of the official's son (John 4:46–53 = Luke 7:1–10/Matt. 8:5–10, 13) is, however, taken to be an adequate indication that John knew Q, a conclusion that the few logia held in common would not suffice to demonstrate.

What, then, is John's attitude toward the synoptic tradition?[86] Although John knew at least Mark,[87] unless he had specific reason for taking up synoptic episodes he avoided repeating them. Thus he omits some essential episodes like the baptism of Jesus. He repeats others when necessary, for example, the temple cleansing. (His moving it forward from the passion to the beginning of the story is sufficient reason to repeat it.) In general, his use of the synoptic material indicates that he affirmed its validity.[88] He completes the synoptic tradition, adding, for example, episodes of Jesus' ministry in Judea, and clarifies it, giving the circumstances of Jesus' word about the destruction of the temple (i.e., John 2:18–22; the cleansing of the temple) reported at the Markan trial (Mark 14:53–59).[89] At points he corrects the Synoptics,[90] particularly with regard to the general temporal and geographic framework of Jesus' ministry, but also in such relatively minor details as Jesus' carrying his own cross to the place of crucifixion. (In affirming John's approval and positive use of the Synoptics, the supplementation theory, de Solages does not mention Windisch's arguments against it.)

Finally, the crucial question: How could the fourth evangelist, who knew such an important source as Mark, which was used by Matthew and Luke, largely ignore it? Because, according to de Solages, he was himself the Beloved Disciple, an eyewitness, as 21:24 (written by a later hand) avers. As such, he was an independent authority. Chapter 21 as a whole is taken to be substantially authentic, that is, from the same author who composed the rest of the Gospel, and a long chapter is devoted to demonstrating that it is stylistically

---

[84] Ibid., 98–99.
[85] Ibid., 99–113 and 113–58, respectively.
[86] Ibid., 170–85.
[87] Ibid., 170.
[88] Ibid., 172–73.
[89] Ibid., 174–75.
[90] Ibid., 182–85.

almost as close to chapters 1–20 as chapter 20 to chapters 1–19, and much closer to those chapters of John than to Luke 1–24.[91]

The claim that the author was an eyewitness is supported by the Gospel's precision about geographical locations and dates. Moreover, the Gospel gives the impression of "things seen" (details such as six water pots, the whip of cords, Jesus' fatigue at the well, and others). But what of the discourses?[92] De Solages faces this problem head-on, acknowledging in view of the Synoptics the difficulty of taking them as verbatim reports of what Jesus said on the occasions reported. Yet their nuclear historical basis is supported by elements within them familiar from the Synoptics (e.g., John 5:29 = Matt. 25:46) and by the way they are bound to traditional, and presumably historical, narratives. Who was the author?[93] The ancient tradition that the Beloved Disciple was John the son of Zebedee is embraced. After Peter, John is mentioned more often in the Synoptics than any disciple,[94] and in the list of Acts 1:13 he has moved up to second place among the Twelve from fourth, where he is found in Luke 6:13–16. The almost total silence of the Gospel about the son of Zebedee is taken to support the traditional view. John was not, however, written much earlier than the end of the first century, if then. John lived, as tradition (or legend!) has it, until the time of Trajan.

If the evangelist was John the son of Zebedee, an original disciple and an apostle, a number of characteristics are explained: the precision with which facts are reported; the independence toward the Synoptics, which he sometimes neglects and sometimes corrects; the relative paucity of traces of Luke and Matthew, whose authors he knew were not eyewitnesses; acquaintanceship with Q (probably the logia of Matthew). The unique connections with Luke are to be explained by the latter's having inquired of eyewitnesses (such as John) in composing his gospel.[95]

Interestingly enough, de Solages shares common ground with both Windisch and Büchsel, although he cites neither. That is, like them he finds it necessary to explain the evangelist's purpose or intention, and also his lofty attitude, in dealing with the other Gospels. With Windisch, de Solages would agree that John manifests a certain feeling of superiority (*Superioritätsgefühl*). But he would not agree that he intended to suppress or displace the other Gospels in church usage. As we have seen, de Solages once more calls upon

---

[91] Ibid., 189–236.
[92] Ibid., 248–57.
[93] Ibid., 258–66.
[94] Ibid., 259–60.
[95] Ibid., 267.

the venerable supplementation and correction theory. On this point he would stand in sharp tension with both Windisch and Büchsel, for the latter accepted Windisch's demonstration of the untenability of that position. Yet de Solages would agree with Büchsel, in contradistinction to Windisch, that the authoritative stance John manifests vis-à-vis the other Gospels is based on a sense of superior eyewitness authority. Both de Solages and Büchsel would, however, grant that John wrote something more, or other, than history in the everyday sense of the word. Thus, neither would be disposed to defend John's rendition of the discourses as reports of what Jesus actually said on a given occasion.

The diligence of de Solages and the complexity of his linguistic-statistical work are matched by the simplicity of the solution that he proposes. It is not difficult to take issue with his conclusions, whether with regard to John's knowledge and use of the Synoptics or the explanation of the relationship that he proposes. Yet he has made a significant contribution just in trying to quantify the degrees of similarity and difference of language and content between John and the Synoptics. Two sets of facts, the sheer divergence of content between John and the Synoptics and the much lower level of verbatim agreement where they correspond, have impressed de Solages and he has performed a useful service in setting forth these differences in ways that can be measured, and if necessary corrected.

De Solages's view that John knew the Synoptics, or at least Mark, but did not use them as sources makes a certain sense of the data, although it does not necessarily follow from it. The explanation that this state of affairs results from the author's having been not only eyewitness to the events he describes but one of the Twelve has, however, a wondrous simplicity about it. Yet de Solages makes no attempt to meet the objections that have been mounted against this view. Indeed, he scarcely seems aware of them. Moreover, although the supplementation theory, which de Solages represents as basically explaining John's treatment, or omission, of the greater part of the synoptic material, may seem satisfactory as a general theory of their relationship, when one examines individual cases or pericopes in order to assess how well they may actually be explained or interpreted on this basis, many questions remain, as Windisch has indeed shown. While de Solages's simple solution may seem as plausible as many a more complicated and sophisticated treatment of the perplexing data of the Johannine and synoptic texts, it presents its own problems and really does not arise inexorably out of the data that he presents. Rather, the author seems to have grasped the opportunity to correlate the data with the ancient tradition of the church.

# 7

# *Retrospect and Prospect*

Our survey of the problem of John and the Synoptics in the twentieth century has had two goals. First, in the course of our discussion the character of any comparison between John and the Synoptics should have become clearer. Second, in our description of the development of scholarship in this century the various possibilities for explaining the relationship of John to the Synoptic Gospels have been explored, and perhaps exhausted.

## THE CHARACTER OF THE COMPARISON

First, there is a general and comparable similarity of content: both John and the Synoptics are narratives of the ministry of Jesus that portray him engaging in similar activities and finally dying on a cross. Thus they are of the same or similar genre. We are not comparing John with Romans; we are comparing similar documents. Beyond this, there are more specific grounds for comparison. As in the case of the synoptic problem, the hardest or clearest evidence is of two basic sorts: order of episodes or material and wording. The synoptic problem centers upon the fact that in both aspects there is an interrelationship of the Gospels that cries out for a literary-critical solution. That is, both Matthew and Luke frequently agree with each other and with Mark, or the one agrees with Mark and the other departs from Mark. Where the three Gospels cover parallel material, one does not usually find agreement of Matthew and Luke against Mark. Mark is in this sense the middle term between Matthew and Luke. (There are, of course, the so-called minor agreements in wording between Matthew and Luke, which are usually explained by coincidence or textual assimilation.[1]) It is difficult to imagine an explanation of these relationships, as extensive and close as they are, that does not involve direct knowledge and use of the one Gospel (Mark) by the other two, the use of those two (Matthew and Luke) by Mark, or some variation of these basic alternatives. In the one case we have the critically orthodox Markan hypothesis, in the other the Griesbach-Farmer hypothesis.[2] While the Griesbach-Farmer hypothesis remains a logical possibility, most scholars continue to favor the Markan hypothesis for reasons best described as redaction-critical. That is, given the Markan text, it is usually possible to understand, in terms of literary method and early Christian history and doctrine, how the other evangelists were using Mark. On the other hand, given the existence of Matthew and Luke, Mark's redactional purpose and policy are exceedingly hard to fathom.

When one turns to the Gospel of John, relationships with the Synoptics are much more complicated, rarer, and more difficult to state. It will be useful to summarize the evidence, as it appears on the basis of our survey, but not so much as assured results as *dicta probantia*. The simple and neat pattern of a middle term (Mark) with two closely related variables (Matthew and Luke) fades away. John seems, by general consensus, most closely related to Mark, but there are affinities or similarities unique to Matthew and, especially, to Luke.

As to verbatim agreement, there are, as we have seen, verbatim parallels, agreements in wording involving clauses or sentences, between John and especially Mark, but these are relatively rare in comparison with those among any of the Synoptic Gospels. In those cases the extent of agreement with Mark is usually somewhat greater than with Matthew or Luke. In the latter case, the agreement is often greater with Matthew than with Luke, Matthew's wording being much closer to Mark's than to Luke's. (On the Markan hypothesis, Luke is rewriting Mark much more extensively than is Matthew.) Nevertheless there are instances in which there is distinctive verbatim agreement between John and either Matthew or Luke. In other words, it is not clear that John is related to Matthew and Luke only through Mark, even

---

[1] See Streeter, *The Four Gospels*, 295–331.

[2] For William R. Farmer's basic position, see his book *The Synoptic Problem: A Critical Analysis* (New York: Macmillan Co., 1964). The debate has continued in the aftermath of this book. C. M. Tuckett, ed., *Synoptic Studies: The Ampleford Conferences of 1982 and 1983* (Sheffield, England: JSOT Press, 1984), provides perspective on the continuing debate between the advocates of the Griesbach hypothesis and the majority of scholars who still defend Markan priority.

though such agreement in wording as is found seems on the whole stronger with Mark than with either of the other two.

A similar proposition applies also to the order of episodes or materials. One generally observes that the Markan material, when found at all in John (and more often than not it simply does not appear in John) is found in the same order as in Mark. This is particularly striking in the parallel episodes of the feeding of the five thousand, Jesus' walking on the water, and related matters, which are found in John 6 and Mark 6 and 8 as well as in the passion narratives. In Mark, of course, they appear as a kind of doublet (feeding of five thousand, feeding of four thousand), while in John there is a single instance. Nevertheless here and elsewhere, where parallel episodes appear in John and Mark they are most often in the same order. The same is generally true of John and the other Synoptics, except that there are, in the passion narrative particularly, departures from the Markan order that appear to be parallel to, or correlated with, similar departures in Luke, suggesting that John knows not only Mark but Luke. As we earlier observed, the phenomenon of Luke's departures from Matthew and Mark so frequently paralleling John has prompted at least one scholar to suggest that Luke knew John and shows the latter's influence precisely at the points at which he (Luke) departs from Mark (and Matthew).

The nature of the agreements of wording and order has led eminent and careful scholars such as Barrett and Kümmel to the conclusion that John knew the Synoptics, certainly Mark, probably Luke, and possibly Matthew. This is, on the face of it, a reasonable conclusion.

The evidence for John's relationship to, and possible knowledge of, the Synoptics is not, however, limited to matters of wording and order per se. Whether these agreements occur in redactional or traditional material is deemed important. Does John take up synoptic matter that belongs to tradition or to synoptic redaction? Insofar as the latter may be the case, John's knowledge of the Synoptic Gospels themselves must be reckoned with. On the other side, is such synoptic matter, whether redactional or traditional, found in Johannine redactional or compositional materials, or in material likely drawn from tradition? The question here is, of course, the point at which synoptic influence impinges upon the Gospel of John.

Inasmuch as the narrative order of the Synoptics is now taken to be largely redactional, John's agreement with that order implies his knowledge and use of the Synoptics, particularly Mark. On the Markan hypothesis, of course, Matthew's and Luke's agreement with Mark in order implies their adoption of the Markan redactional framework. This being the case, why should there be any doubt that John knew one of the Synoptics, probably Mark? Room for doubt appears at two points. First, John's overall outline or itinerary of

Jesus' ministry differs widely from the Synoptics. Second, exactly to the degree that elements of Mark's order can be judged traditional rather than redactional, John's similarity need not be derived from it or from any of the Synoptics. In the passion narrative the traditional nature of the order of events could be assumed as long as the postulate of an early, traditional, pre-Markan (or pre-gospel) passion narrative was granted. (Even if such a postulate were not granted, however, one could argue that the events of the passion imply and require a certain order.) John 6 poses a similar problem. Insofar as its order can be regarded as traditional, there is no necessity of postulating John's use of Mark (or Matthew; because of its omission of Jesus' walking on the water, Luke falls out of the picture). There is, however, less intrinsic reason for supposing that there existed such a traditional cluster, centering on the feeding, than for supposing there was a traditional passion narrative. The argument for tradition must in this case show the difficulty of deriving the Johannine rendition from the Markan-Matthean account.

The scholarly discussion has, however, turned up types of evidence other than order and wording. These range from the general consideration that John presupposes—and presupposes for his reader—knowledge of the gospel story, which the Synoptics also tell, to specific instances in which John seems to presuppose or share some bit of information that we derive from the Synoptics. Often this latter sort of agreement occurs between John and Luke. For example, John seems to presuppose, or otherwise reflect, knowledge of such personalities as Mary, her sister Martha, and their brother Lazarus, as well as the village in which they live; all of which he shares with Luke only. But there are distinctive agreements with Matthew as well: for example, the saying of Jesus in John 13:20 is closer to that in Matthew 10:40 than to the (possible Q) parallel in Luke 10:16. This last instance is representative of a number of sayings parallels between John and one or more of the Synoptics. It is interesting, and probably significant, that such parallel sayings as are not embedded in (probably traditional) narratives (e.g., "One of you will betray me"; "Are you the King of the Jews?") are in John almost invariably found in contexts different from the Synoptics, even as many Q parallels are found in different contexts in Matthew and Luke. But the difference of setting in John is more pronounced.

## POSSIBILITIES FOR EXPLAINING
## THE RELATIONSHIP

Such different sorts of relationships as we have instanced obviously point in different directions, some in the direction of John's dependence on the Synoptics and others against it. In the twentieth-century discussion of the question of John and the Synoptics, the basic possibilities for explaining these relationships have been explored and perhaps exhausted. Generally speaking, the question has been put in terms of John's independence of, or dependence on, the Synoptic Gospels, not the other way around! That is, the view that John was known to the synoptic writers is usually ruled out because of John's more explicitly developed theology, expressed not just in the editorial framework but on the lips of Jesus himself. Nevertheless it is sometimes suggested that in specific areas or respects John attests an earlier tradition or point of view; for example, in dating the Last Supper on the night before, rather than the night of, the Passover feast, John may represent an earlier, historically accurate, tradition.

That John knew the Synoptic Gospels was the position of the ancient church, and indeed of most Christian exegesis down through the centuries. Of course, until the rise of critical scholarship in the nineteenth century, the Gospel of John was taken to be the work of John the son of Zebedee, the disciple of Jesus. When that traditional consensus broke up, most critical scholarship continued to affirm John's knowledge and positive use of the Synoptics, but scholars like Benjamin W. Bacon were disposed to disallow much if any historicity in the Johannine narrative. John departed from the Synoptics in the direction of theology and away from history. Bacon's view of John's position vis-à-vis the Synoptics in the early twentieth century now seems rather closely paralleled by Frans Neirynck and the Louvain School. Insofar as John departs from the Synoptics his redaction is original, his own composition, and serves a theological rather than historical purpose.

As we have already observed, in his major departure from the view that John used the Synoptics with a positive purpose, Hans Windisch (1926) continued to embrace the traditional position that John knew them. What Windisch strongly contested, and set out to refute, was the accompanying assumption that the fourth evangelist had written in order to supplement, interpret, or mildly correct and improve upon his predecessors. Rather, he wrote a gospel which he hoped would displace the others in the general usage of the church. At best the Synoptics inadequately represented Christian truth in the face of Jewish and gnostic opposition and challenges. Thus the evangelist put the true and proper Christology on Jesus' lips, at the risk of undercutting historical verisimilitude, which mattered little to him in any event. It is interesting that in his recent work on the Gospel of John Martin Hengel takes the position that John must have known the Synoptics when he wrote. Nevertheless, John set about to write a more adequate gospel, and thus in effect rejected, or sought to supersede, the works of his predecessors. In taking this position, Hengel sees its implications quite clearly, and cites Windisch in a positive light as the proponent of this position.[3]

The view that John wrote without knowledge of the Synoptics, of course, obviates the position of Windisch and Hengel, for as Bultmann aptly put it in his review of Windisch, one does not set out to displace what one does not know. As the chief and original English-speaking proponent of John's independence in the twentieth century, Percival Gardner-Smith (1938) had a broad and continuing influence. Because he found it more difficult to explain John's differences from the Synoptics on the assumption of the fourth evangelist's knowledge and use of them than to explain the similarities on the assumption of his independence, Gardner-Smith chose the alternative of independence and, in doing so, made much of the newly discovered importance of oral tradition in the primitive church. After World War II, C. H. Dodd and Ernst Haenchen expressed basic agreement with Gardner-Smith, and Bultmann's position (1941), worked out quite independently, lent further support. Thus it became the consensus position of the 1960s and 1970s. Yet while there was a consensus that John did not use the Synoptics, but other, related tradition, there was less agreement on the nature or form of that tradition. On the one hand, Gardner-Smith and Dodd thought in terms of a still oral tradition, since both were deeply influenced by form criticism. On the other hand, Bultmann, although a founder of form criticism, discerned behind the Fourth Gospel several written sources. His source-critical work then became the source of inspiration for further attempts to recover the narrative source(s) of John, particularly Fortna's.

Parallel to this general consensus on John's disuse of the Synoptics there developed a particular consensus on John's relationship to Luke. As we observed, scholars from Schniewind to Maddox declined to grant John's knowledge or use of the present form of the Gospel of Luke. Despite many points of contact, John seems not to know or reflect precisely the special Lukan material. Nevertheless, John and Luke share distinctive knowledge or insights, frequently in contradiction or competition with Mark and Matthew. Thus perhaps not surprisingly Cribbs proposed that Luke's departures from Mark and Matthew at many of those points where John sharply disagreed with them strongly suggested Luke's knowledge of the Gospel of John, or at least of Johannine traditions or sources. But moving in another direction, Dauer

---

[3] Martin Hengel, *The Johannine Question*, trans. John Bowden (London: SCM Press, 1989), 194 n. 8: "H. Windisch's account of the relationship between the Fourth Evangelist and the Synoptics is still the best."

extended his previous research on the passion by arguing that oral tradition emanating from Luke had influenced narrative sources used by the fourth evangelist and thus explained their affinities. Again, consensus on John's not having used Luke directly did not lead to agreement on how their relationship was to be explained.

Indeed, the consensus with regard to John's independence of the Synoptics was at best confined to the origin of the Johannine tradition or the original Gospel and did not extend uniformly to the Gospel of John in its present form. Thus both Bultmann and, a quarter of a century later, Raymond E. Brown (1966), in their respective commentaries, found evidence in the Gospel of John of knowledge of the Synoptics at a late, redactional stage. Neither ascribed that knowledge to the evangelist himself but rather to a later and final redactor. (Albeit in Bultmann's view his redaction sought to correct the Fourth Gospel and bring it into line with a developing ecclesiastical orthodoxy, while in Brown's the redaction represented a more positive construction of the original Johannine line.) A decade after Brown, M.-E. Boismard, taking an essentially similar view, pushed knowledge of the Synoptics back to the stage of the evangelist's own final redaction of his material. Thus, for him, John himself actually knew the Synoptics, although his narrative is not based on them.

Whether Boismard already felt the weight of Neirynck's rejection of the consensus in favor of independence is difficult to say. It is clear enough, however, that Neirynck was not satisfied with Boismard's concession that John the evangelist knew the Synoptics only at the last stage of his developing the form of the Gospel. (Actually, in Boismard's view also, the canonical form of the Gospel is the product of a final redaction by another hand, as is the case with Bultmann and Brown.) In Neirynck's view, the concession that the evangelist's knowledge of the Synoptics cannot be denied raises in an urgent way the question of whether that knowledge need be confined to a later redactional level. Does it not really remove the need to postulate hypothetical written sources other than the Synoptics?

Obviously, for Neirynck the application of Ockham's razor in order to dispense with hypothetical sources is an attractive possibility, one that counts on the side of seeing the Johannine narrative as derivative from the Synoptics. The persuasiveness of this position, as distinguished from its neatness, depends largely upon how well it works in exegesis. To what extent does John unmistakably reveal knowledge of the Synoptics? How well can his departures from the synoptic baseline then be understood? If telltale verbal, structural, and substantial elements of the Synoptics can be found in the Fourth Gospel, why indeed have recourse to hypothetical sources? At this point, how one envisions earliest Christianity and its transmission and dissemination of the

gospel tradition becomes a major consideration. To what extent do the canonical Gospels represent that tradition? Exhaustively, or only partially? If
only partially, the door is open to the possibility that John's points of contact
with the Synoptics were mediated through other sources and traditions no
longer extant. Although the evidence for early extracanonical documents and
sources may be scanty, their existence cannot be ruled out.[4]

Nevertheless, Neirynck's intensive search for traces of John's knowledge of
the Synoptics, indeed, of synoptic redaction, has attracted the favorable attention of a number of scholars, including Hartwig Thyen of Heidelberg, one
of Bultmann's last students. As we have seen, Thyen expresses agreement
with Neirynck and "the English commentators" on the question of John's use
of the Synoptics. (Presumably he refers here not only to C. K. Barrett, who
continued to hold out for the older, traditional position against the newer
consensus, but also to R. H. Lightfoot and Edwyn Hoskyns.) Hoskyns in
particular made a great deal of John's knowledge of the substance of the
Synoptic Gospels and the theological issues they raise. In a very real sense,
Hoskyns stood in the tradition of Clement of Alexandria and of John Calvin.
John is the interpreter of the synoptic tradition. Although Hoskyns avoided
tying his own position too closely to the view that John knew the Synoptic
Gospels in the form we have them, the burden of his position is clear.

Mgr. de Solages took a somewhat different position, believing that John
knew the Synoptics but that his wide departures from them indicate that it
is inaccurate to speak of his use of them. At some points (e.g., John 6) the
fourth evangelist may have used them, but more often he went his own way
in relative or complete independence of them. His apostolic eyewitness carries
its own authority. With de Solages we run the gamut of scholarly opinion

---

[4] See the seminal essay of George Kennedy, "Classical and Christian Source Criticism," in *The
Relationships Among the Gospels: An Interdisciplinary Dialogue*, ed. William O. Walker, Jr. (San
Antonio, Tex.: Trinity University Press, 1978), 125–55. Kennedy points out that note making
or note taking was common in antiquity, especially in anticipation of composing a larger document
(pp. 136–37) and that such a procedure is likely reflected in Papias's description of how Mark
composed his Gospel on the basis of Peter's preaching (Kennedy refers to Eusebius, *Ecclesiastical
History* 3.39.15–16). Wayne A. Meeks, "Response," Walker, *Relationships*, 157–72, is appreciative;
esp. 159–60 on note taking. Reginald H. Fuller refers back to this suggestion in a positive way
in his seminar report (Walker, *Relationships*, 178–80).

The comments of Kennedy about oral tradition in antiquity (Walker, *Relationships*, 142–
43), suggest that such traditions may have attained an extensive and relatively fixed form. The
same point is also made by Albert B. Lord, "The Gospels as Oral Traditional Literature" (Walker,
*Relationships*, 33–91), although he emphasizes and explains the variations that normally occur
in such materials. Lord compares synoptic texts only, but it would be worth asking whether the
kinds of variations he finds in known oral literature are not more like variations between John
and the Synoptics where they are parallel.

and find a scholar who embraces both ends of the dilemma, so to speak, in that he affirms that John knew the Synoptics but for the most part denies that he used them. Nevertheless he does not reject them, but by and large confirms them. It is not too much to say that we hear once again in de Solages, who in his book never cites another scholar on specific points or issues, the voice of the exegesis of the ancient church.

The twentieth century has seen a variety of positions on the relationship of John and the Synoptics emerge. That John knew the Synoptic Gospels was, of course, first assumed. Then the discussion reached an opposite pole, so that John's independence could be taken for granted, but, as we have noted, there was something less than unanimity on how to account for John's uniqueness in terms of sources and traditions, whether written or oral. Synoptic influence continued to be granted, if minimally, but was accounted for in various ways: parallel, but related, tradition; the influence of the Synoptic Gospels per se on John's sources—perhaps through the influence of continuing oral tradition; later redactional efforts to bring the Fourth Gospel into line with the Synoptics, whether by the original author or a later hand. Behind such consensus as existed there lay a plethora of different opinions and modes of explanation, and Boismard's comprehensive theory is a truly amazing attempt to incorporate, or accommodate, as many of them as possible. In contrast to Boismard's brave effort, Neirynck represents a call to return to simplicity and, as he thinks, cleanness and clarity: John's principal sources were the Synoptic Gospels which we know from the New Testament. Yet, as we have seen, the new, and also ancient, defense of John's knowledge and use of the Synoptics encounters rough sailing when one asks why, if John knew those other Gospels, he treated them as he did.

Thus our survey of the question of John and the Synoptics ends on an ambiguous note, which represents quite accurately the present divided state of scholarly opinion. We have seen how the older assumption that John knew, used, and approved of the Synoptic Gospels broke down in the face of challenges from the one side by Hans Windisch and from the other by Gardner-Smith. If for a while a consensus in favor of John's independence seemed to reign, beginning shortly after World War II and extending into the 1970s, by the end of that decade serious challenges had been mounted against it, and there was a variety of opinion about whether John knew the other gospels and, particularly, about the point in the development of the Fourth Gospel at which the Synoptics were known or used. A substantial body of opinion was returning to positions held at the beginning of this century, but the movement was by no means universal.

# HANS WEDER AND
# KARL THEODOR KLEINKNECHT

The divided state of scholarship is well illustrated by two articles that appeared back to back in the 1985 volume of the *Zeitschrift für Theologie und Kirche*, one on John 6 by Hans Weder, the other on John 13 by Karl Theodor Kleinknecht.[5] Each deals with a Johannine text that has significant synoptic parallels; each is endeavoring to make theological sense of the respective passage against the background of the tradition John employed. Indeed, the two texts are related, because in John 6 we find the most explicit Johannine exposition of the Eucharist, which in the other Gospels is, of course, found at the Last Supper (cf. John 13).

While recognizing the similarities of John 6 to the feeding and other materials of Mark 6 and 8, Weder does not attribute them to John's use of Mark. The feeding of the multitude and the walking on the sea have already coalesced in the pre-Johannine tradition, which also contained other elements found in the Synoptics, such as the demand for a sign and the confession of Peter. In all likelihood, John's distinctive tradition is early, presumably antedating the doubling that produced two feedings in Mark.[6] Form-critical and motif analysis of the Johannine miracle stories generally shows that they have greater affinities with each other than with other parts of the Gospel, a finding that

---

[5] Hans Weder, "Die Menschwerdung Gottes: Überlegungen zur Auslegungsproblematik des Johannesevangeliums am Beispiel von Joh 6," *ZTK* 82 (1985): 325–60; and Karl Theodor Kleinknecht, "Johannes 13, die Synoptiker und die 'Methode' der johanneischen Evangelienüberlieferung," *ZTK* 82 (1985): 361–88.

Only after this book was in the hands of the publisher was I able to read the articles by Peder Borgen and Frans Neirynck in *The Interrelationships of the Gospels: A Symposium Led by M.-E. Boismard, W. R. Farmer, F. Neirynck, Jerusalem 1984*, ed. David L. Dungan, BETL 95 (Louvain: Louvain University Press, 1990), which similarly illustrate the present situation. Borgen's article, "John and the Synoptics" (pp. 408–37), is followed by a response by Neirynck (pp. 438–50) and, in turn, by Borgen's response to Neirynck (pp. 451–58). Borgen discusses the Pauline and Markan parallels to John 6:51–58 (cf. 1. Cor. 10:3–4, 16, 17, 21; 11:23–29 and Mark 14:22–25), as well as synoptic parallels to John 5:1–18 and 2:13–22, and concludes that there are more Johannine parallels with the Pauline passages cited than with any of the synoptic. This finding bespeaks the use of common oral traditions rather than any literary relationship. Neirynck objects that the eucharistic texts and traditions Borgen adduces constitute a special case, and in the other instances points to parallels that Borgen is said to have ignored. In making his rejoinder Borgen maintains (p. 456) that "Neirynck has not clarified the Fourth Evangelist's method, the form used in his treatment of Mk, his understanding of Mk (and tradition), or how and why his readers would find his treatment of Mk acceptable and authoritative." Their interchange represents quite well the present divided state of opinion, in which the once-reigning consensus of John's independence has been challenged on the basis of putative points of contact within the texts, while its defenders object that John's redactional use of Mark (or other synoptics) cannot be explained adequately, and other possibilities for understanding the relationship are not explored.

[6] Weder, "Die Menschwerdung Gottes," 330.

suggests that they stem from a common source. Presumably the miracle source had already some theological stature, as a signs source, within the Johannine community. Characteristically, John develops stories from this source, through Jesus' dialogues, to express his theology, which is not unrelated to that of the source. Here Weder cites with appreciation and agreement the work of Robert T. Fortna.

Moreover, such an origin of the Johannine material fits the concept of a Johannine school or community, which Weder finds persuasive. The text of the Gospel did not develop overnight. "It is the result of a long reception- and traditioning process. Also the Gospel of John must be regarded as a product of intensive theological work, taking place over a considerable length of time, possibly in a school, in any event in a theological collective."[7] Within such a setting a signs source developed and was propagated.

Kleinknecht would fully agree with such a general appraisal of the milieu of the Fourth Gospel, but his assessment of the relationship of the Gospel of John to the Synoptics differs. At the outset Kleinknecht indicates agreement with M. Sabbe that John 13 probably betrays knowledge of the Synoptics, particularly Mark 14 and Luke 22.[8] He seems guarded in his endorsement of this position; nevertheless the number of parallels or points of contact would otherwise be difficult to account for as coincidental. Some knowledge of Mark and Luke seems to be required to explain the structure of the Johannine text, which can be closely correlated with those Gospels. It is, in fact, the structure that carries the case. (There are not sufficient verbal or verbatim parallels alone to warrant this view.) John 13 does not contain a good bit of what is found in Mark 14, and vice versa. Yet what John has in common with Mark, or items comparable to Mark, usually appear in John in the same order as in Mark.[9] (Kleinknecht presents a two-page chart to demonstrate these rela-tionships.) Moreover, when John departs from Mark's order, his departure is characteristically related to a departure of Luke from that order. Thus when Luke reports the prediction of the betrayal of Judas after, rather than before, the words of institution (against Mark and Matthew), John takes the oppor-tunity to insert the foot washing (his equivalent of the Eucharist) immediately before the prediction of betrayal. John seems to take his cue to depart from Matthew and Mark from Luke.[10] Moreover, Luke has positioned Jesus' words

---

[7] Ibid., 326.

[8] Kleinknecht, "Johannes 13," 363. The reference is to M. Sabbe, "The Footwashing in Jn 13 and Its Relation to the Synoptic Gospels," *ETL* 58 (1982): 279–308.

[9] Kleinknecht, "Johannes 13," 364, 372. See the chart on pp. 370–71.

[10] Ibid., 372, 373–80.

about service, found in the public ministry in Mark (10:45) in the brief discourse of Jesus after the prophecy of betrayal. John has then concretized these words in Jesus' act of washing of the disciples' feet. John thus takes Luke a step further, so to speak.[11] It is interesting that Jesus then commands his disciples to do to each other as he has done in John (13:15), whereas in Luke only among the Gospels (cf. Paul) does Jesus specifically instruct the disciples to "do this" after the words of institution. Moreover, the same salvific significance is assigned to the foot washing (13:8) as to the Eucharist (6:53) in John, another indication that John has intentionally put the foot washing in place of the Eucharist at the Last Supper and moved the latter forward into the public ministry (John 6), probably because it was a point of conflict between Jesus' followers and their Jewish foes.

In a curious way, the results of Kleinknecht's exegesis put him in agreement with de Solages, in that John knows and reflects the synoptic narratives, but they are hardly his sources in the usual sense.[12] John is very different from Mark, or the Synoptics, because of his distinct theological purpose; his intention was by no means to harmonize his account with theirs. If in John 13 the evangelist used the synoptic materials, "this use has a character wholly different from that found in the province of the Synoptics, which can be reconstructed by means of redaction criticism."[13]

We see then in Weder the continuing vitality of the most recent consensus, and this is all the more important in that Weder is at work on a major new commentary on John (Evangelisch-Katholischer Kommentar). Weder will apparently stand in the tradition of most commentaries of recent decades, which do not assume John's knowledge and use of the Synoptics as a premise for exegesis. In Kleinknecht, on the other hand, we find a version of the newer, revisionist view: after all, John knows the Synoptic Gospels. Yet to say that is not to solve a problem so much as to state one. Given John's knowledge of the Synoptics, how may his appropriation or use of them be understood and described? Sabbe's conclusions, in line with Neirynck's, are in a sense Kleinknecht's beginning point. As far as Kleinknecht is concerned, John's knowledge of the Synoptics would not in principle exclude his use of other tradition as well. In fact, if his gospel is representative of a school or circle of early Christianity, as Kleinknecht also thinks, that is what one would expect. In that case, the suggestion of Kleinknecht is not necessarily in conflict with the classical source-critical position represented by Weder. But this is not a

---

[11] Ibid., 376.
[12] Ibid., 383.
[13] Ibid., 382. (My translation.)

matter to be resolved by compromise, so to speak, but in the exegesis of the Gospel.

At the beginning of the century, the exegete or commentator could safely assume John's knowledge of the Synoptics. We then passed through a period of a quarter of a century or more (1955–80) in which the opposite assumption was the safer one: John was perhaps ignorant of the Synoptics, certainly independent of them. We have now reached a point at which neither assumption is safe, that is, neither can be taken for granted. Any exegete must argue the case afresh on its merits, and in different ways the articles of Weder and Kleinknecht signal this new situation. Yet John's independence still finds many defenders, and precisely Kleinknecht, who believes that John in all probability knew Mark and Luke, is careful to assign a dominant role to the evangelist's own distinct theological purpose and method. Apart from its ancient, canonical setting, John's independence is obvious enough. The problem is how to understand and articulate it.

## TEXT AND CANON

To speak of John's canonical setting suggests two other dimensions or aspects of the problem of John and the Synoptics that would bear further reflection and investigation. These may be brought under the traditional scholarly rubrics of text and canon.

As we have noted, in his study of Luke and John, F. C. Grant made far-reaching and somewhat speculative suggestions about the interrelationship of Luke and John in the Jerusalem resurrection narratives of the two gospels, proposing that the gospel texts have been assimilated to each other, specifically, Luke to John. The most famous and typical example is Luke 24:12, the summary report of Peter's visit to the empty tomb, which parallels John 20:3–10. In the twenty-fifth edition of Nestle-Aland, Luke 24:12 had been relegated to the apparatus with the implied judgment that it was not a part of the original text. Its absence in Codex Bezae and the Old Latin tradition puts it into the category of Westcott and Hort's "western non-interpolations," to which they ascribed a high value. Other omission variants in Luke 24 fall into the same category (i.e., vv. 36c, 40).[14] The same could be said of the famous

---

[14] Bruce M. Metzger, *A Textual Commentary on the Greek New Testament* (London and New York: United Bible Societies, 1971), 184, 186–87, assigns all three readings, which are retained in the UBS text, as in Aland's twenty-sixth edition, a D rating, indicating that the highest degree of doubt attaches to them.

saying about the poor in John's account of the anointing of Jesus (12:8), which is unattested in Bezae and the Sinaitic Syriac. (Indeed, 12:8b is missing even in the most ancient P[75].) Moreover, in the same pericope the curious expression concerning the costly ointment of pure nard is omitted in Bezae on the Markan side (14:3). In the present, twenty-sixth edition, such readings now stand in the resultant text. We have seen, moreover, that both Boismard and Neirynck accept Luke 24:12 as an authentic part of the Gospel of Luke, although they construe the significance of that fact in different ways. Grant, on the other hand, took such omissions in but a few manuscripts such as Bezae as evidence for an earlier, unassimilated stage of the Lukan, Johannine, and Markan texts. In fact, he proposed Lukan assimilations to John in chapter 24 for which there is no manuscript evidence, inferring them from the evidence that does exist and from the known fluidity of the text in the second century.

There is a danger that text-critical judgments may become, like patriotism in Dr. Johnson's famous saying, the last refuge of scoundrels, or those who doubt John's use of Synoptic Gospels. In fact, in his 1990 Louvain *Forschungsbericht* Neirynck issued such a warning, albeit couched in somewhat gentler terms. When we speak of the gospel text in the second century, however, we are venturing into the unknown. Admittedly, the "western non-interpolations" of which we have just spoken are not represented in the most ancient papyrus witnesses, notably P[75], which dates from the close of the second century or the beginning of the third. Such evidence doubtless weighed heavily in the judgments embodied in the twenty-sixth edition of the Nestle-Aland text. One does not lightly take issue with the experts who are in control of the evidence. Yet it is precisely the case that we lack the relevant evidence for the text in the second century.[15] From the evident stability of the text in the period of more than a century between P[75] and Codex Valentinus one may perhaps infer its stability in the preceding, second century, but for the present at least the inference cannot be widely substantiated. Insofar as the gospels in question

---

[15] Kurt Aland, "Der Text des Johannes–Evangelium im 2. Jahrhundert," in *Studien zum Text und zur Ethik des Neuen Testament: Festschrift zum 80. Geburtstag von Heinrich Greeven*, ed. Wolfgang Schrage (Berlin: Walter de Gruyter, 1986), 1–10, emphasizes the stability of the text of John reaching back into the second century. The second-century fragments (P[52], P[90], P[66]) attest John 18:31—19:7 impressively, although a number of lacunae must be supplied in each of the fragments. From this evidence the stability of the rest of the text is to be inferred. Somewhat different implications might be drawn, however, from Hans-Werner Bartsch, "Über den Umgang der frühen Christenheit mit dem Text der Evangelien: Das Beispiel des Codex Bezae Cantabrigiensis," *NTS* 29 (1983): 167–82. See esp. p. 180: "As already the collecting of the stories about Jesus by the synoptic writers shows, the Gospels were not for early Christianity a 'holy text' whose authenticity had to be affirmed. Rather, the process of development and unfolding of the text went further, if in limited measure." (Translation mine.) Because of the lack of manuscript evidence, neither the affirmation of Aland nor the inference of Bartsch can be proved.

were not yet regarded as canonical, their texts would have been subject to more variation or alteration than would have been the case in later years. Helmut Koester's comments on this point are pertinent and significant:

> The problems for the reconstruction of the textual history of the canonical Gospels in the first century of transmission are immense. The assumption that the reconstruction of the best archetype for the manuscript tradition is more or less identical with the assumed autograph is precarious. The oldest known manuscript archetypes are separated from the autographs by more than a century. Textual critics of classical texts know that the first century of their transmission is the period in which the most serious corruptions occur. Textual critics of the New Testament writings have been surprisingly naive in this respect.[16]

The canonical, or noncanonical, status of the Gospels in the second century and even earlier is relevant to our problem in another way. Inevitably, the fact that the Gospel of John now stands in a canon of Scripture with the three other Gospels, partly parallel and partly quite different, affects our view of their relationship. Since the late second century, comparison has taken place in what we might call a canonical context, and this is natural enough. The canonical gospels invite comparison with one another, and their contrasting differences raise problems and questions. This is especially the case with any comparison involving the Gospel of John. Probably the differences between John and the Synoptics were a problem in the formation of the canon and had something to do with the apparent hesitancy among some second-century, and later, Christians to accept the Fourth Gospel alongside the other three.

The apocryphal gospels, whether those attested by the church fathers and extant only in fragmentary quotations (e.g., *Hebrews, Ebionites, Nazarenes, Egyptians*) or those which have turned up in modern times (*Thomas, Peter, Secret Mark,* Egerton Papyrus 2), were all written during the second century, if some or parts of them did not originate even earlier. They shed significant light on the problem of John and the Synoptics in the period of their origin and earliest transmission. It is quite clear that the apocryphal gospels do not attest a controlling influence of the Synoptic Gospels, or of the four that were to become canonical, even if for the most part they reflect knowledge of them. The customary dating of these apocryphal gospels at mid-second century or later is in large measure a corollary of the assumption that where they are

---

[16] Helmut Koester, "The Text of the Synoptic Gospels in the Second Century," in *Gospel Traditions in the Second Century: Origins, Recensions, Text, and Transmission,* ed. William L. Petersen, Christianity and Judaism in Antiquity 3 (Notre Dame, Ind.: University of Notre Dame Press, 1989), 19.

parallel to the synoptic or canonical Gospels they are derivative from them. To a considerable measure they may well be, although this whole question has recently become the subject of serious debate.[17] What is not debatable, however, is the extent to which the apocryphal gospels diverge from the synoptic or canonical counterparts. Such divergences, even if late (indeed, particularly if late), show that the synoptic and canonical gospels still were not exercising the kind of authority and control they have exercised since. After the second century the writing of such gospels gradually ceased or became the province of heretical groups. In the inchoate period of the second century, however, precisely the identification of heretical groups was a matter of conflict and debate. How then does this situation shed light on the question of John and the Synoptics?

One must say simply that what was true of the relationship of the so-called apocryphal gospels to the Synoptics, and to the canonical four, even in the mid-second century, would have been all the more true of the relationship of John to the Synoptics at the end of the first century and the very beginning of the second. Somewhat the same sort of independence that is suggested by what we know of the apocryphal gospels is to be found also in the Gospel of John. Neither John any more than the apocryphal gospels seems to have been composed under some sort of canonical constraint, even though both attest knowledge of synoptic material, whether based on synoptic tradition or one or more of the Synoptic Gospels themselves. This state of affairs is very important for our assessment of Johannine-synoptic relationships. It is all too easy and natural to make the canonical assumption, and therefore to treat John as if the author must have known the Synoptics, and, if he did, to assume that he would have written his own gospel out of some dominant relationship to them, whether one of interpretation, supplementation, or opposition. John's wide divergences from the Synoptics are, on the other hand, construable as indications of the author's ignorance of them, since, it is assumed, had he known them, he would have conformed his narrative more closely to them. None of these assumptions is, however, necessary, or necessarily true.

Modern views of the relationship between John and the Synoptics are thus all too easily determined by their canonical status. Moreover, another, more modern, canon of judgment may also come into play. Matthew and Luke apparently knew and used Mark independently of each other, and used Mark

---

[17] See, e.g., Crossan, *Four Other Gospels;* Koester, "Apocryphal and Canonical Gospels," *HTR* 73 (1980): 105–30; also D. Moody Smith, "The Problem of John and the Synoptics in Light of the Relation Between Apocryphal and Canonical Gospels," in the proceedings of the 1990 Louvain Colloquium, *John and the Synoptic,* ed. Denaux, where relevant literature is cited.

in such a way that much of the content and order of Mark was taken up into each of them. Was Mark canonical for Matthew and Luke, but not for John? That is, of course, to put the question anachronistically, but perhaps not unhelpfully. Matthew and Luke are to a considerable degree patterned upon Mark, and where they have Mark, follow Mark. Of course, neither adheres slavishly to Mark; they add to Mark, change his wording, rearrange his order. But they also again and again return to Mark. Is it a safe assumption that any first-century (or second-century) Christian who undertook to write a gospel would have felt it necessary to follow Mark to the extent that Matthew and Luke did? In the light of our knowledge of the apocryphal gospels, a negative answer seems to follow, which would apply directly in the case of the Gospel of John.[18] As we have already observed, given the existence of Mark or the Synoptic Gospels, and even the probability that one or more of them was known to the fourth evangelist, it does not necessarily follow that he would have felt constrained by them. Indeed, it is the relationship among the Synoptic Gospels that is remarkable and even unique.

In that the Gospel of Mark supplies the basis for the Gospels of Matthew and Luke it marks an early stage in the development of a gospel canon, which eventually grows to include the Gospel of John. But only after overcoming some resistance does the Gospel of John come in, and none of the other non-Markan gospels follow it. The emerging gospel, and New Testament, canon bends to accommodate the Gospel of John and in doing so deepens and changes its character. The Gospel of John, whether or not it was written with the others in view, now inevitably colors the way they are received and read and in turn is colored by them. Their coexistence in the Christian canon of Scripture modifies and mollifies the sharpness of their juxtaposition, a sharpness that has been established and perhaps accentuated by historical-critical readings. At the level of such reading and exegesis, the questions of John's knowledge and use of the Synoptics remains a vexing, critical one. At the same time, the whole question of their points of contact and the tensions between them, if it has not been resolved by their inclusion in the same New Testament, has been moved to the level of theological discussion and inter-textual relationships.

---

[18] See D. Moody Smith, "The Problem of John and the Synoptics."

# Selected Bibliography

Only works bearing directly upon the relationship of the Fourth Gospel to other gospels are included. With the exception of a few representative and important books, commentaries and introductions have been omitted. For further bibliographical help, the author index may be consulted.

Bacon, Benjamin W. *The Fourth Gospel in Research and Debate.* New York: Moffatt, Yard & Co., 1910.

———. *The Gospel of the Hellenists.* Edited by Carl H. Kraeling. New York: Henry Holt, 1933.

Bailey, J. A. *The Traditions Common to the Gospels of Luke and John.* NovtSup 7. Leiden: E. J. Brill, 1963.

Barrett, C. K. *The Gospel According to St. John: An Introduction with Commentary and Notes on the Greek Text.* London: SPCK, 1956. 2d ed. Philadelphia: Westminster Press, 1978.

———. "John and the Synoptic Gospels." *Expository Times* 85 (1974): 228–33.

Baum-Bodenbender, Rosel. *Hoheit in Niedrigkeit: Johanneische Christologie im Prozess Jesu vor Pilatus (Joh 18, 28—19, 16a).* Forschung zur Bibel 49. Würzburg: Echter Verlag, 1984.

Becker, Jürgen. "Wunder und Christologie: Zum literarkritischen und christologischen Problem der Wunder im Johannesevangelium." *NTS* 16 (1969–70): 130–48.

———. "Aus der Literatur zum Johannesevangelium (1978–1980)." *ThR* 47 (1982): 279–301, 305–47.

Blinzler, Josef. *Johannes und die Synoptiker: Ein Forschungsbericht.* SBS 5. Stuttgart: Verlag Katholisches Bibelwerk, 1965.

Boismard, M.-E., and A. Lamouille, with the collaboration of G. Rochais. *L'Evangile de Jean: Commentaire.* Volume 3 of *Synopse des quatre Evangiles en français.* Paris: Editions du Cerf, 1977.

Borgen, Peder. "John and the Synoptics in the Passion Narrative." *NTS* 5 (1958–59): 246–59.

———. "John and the Synoptics." In *The Interrelations of the Gospels: A Symposium Led by M.-E. Boismard, W. R. Farmer, F. Neirynck, Jerusalem, 1984.* Edited by David L. Dungan, 408–37. BETL 95. Louvain: Louvain University Press, 1990.

Brown, Raymond E. "Incidents That Are Units in the Synoptic Gospels But Dispersed in St. John." *CBQ* 23 (1961): 143–60.

———. *The Gospel According to John.* 2 vols. Anchor Bible 29, 29A. Garden City, N.Y.: Doubleday & Co., 1966, 1970.

Büchsel, Friedrich. "Johannes und die Synoptiker." *Zeitschrift für systematische Theologie* 4 (1926): 240–65.

Bultmann, Rudolf. *The Gospel of John: A Commentary.* Translated by George R. Beasley-Murray, R. W. N. Hoare, and J. K. Riches. Philadelphia: Westminster Press, 1971.

Carson, Donald A. "Historical Tradition in the Fourth Gospel: After Dodd, What?" In *Gospel Perspectives,* vol. 2: *Studies of History and Tradition in the Four Gospels.* Edited by R. T. France and David Wenham, 83–145. Sheffield: JSOT Press, 1981.

———. *The Gospel According to John.* Grand Rapids: Wm. B. Eerdmans Publishing Co., 1991.

Colwell, Ernest C. *John Defends the Gospel.* Chicago: Willet, Clark & Co., 1936.

Cribbs, F. Lamar. "St. Luke and the Johannine Tradition." *JBL* 90 (1971): 422–50.

———. "A Study of the Contacts That Exist Between St. Luke and St. John." *Society of Biblical Literature: 1973 Seminar Papers.* Edited by George MacRae, 2:1–93. Cambridge, Mass.: Society of Biblical Literature, 1973.

———. "The Agreements That Exist Between Luke and John." *Society of Biblical Literature: 1979 Seminar Papers.* Edited by Paul J. Achtemeier, 1:215–61. Missoula, Mont.: Scholars Press, 1979.

Crossan, John Dominic. *Four Other Gospels: Shadows on the Contours of the Canon.* Minneapolis: Seabury/Winston, 1985.

———. *The Cross That Spoke: The Origins of the Passion Narrative.* San Francisco: Harper & Row, 1988.

Culpepper, R. Alan. *Anatomy of the Fourth Gospel: A Study in Literary Design.* New Testament Foundations and Facets. Philadelphia: Fortress Press, 1983.

Dauer, Anton. *Die Passionsgeschichte im Johannesevangelium: Eine traditions-geschichtliche und theologische Untersuchung zu Joh 18,1–19,30.* SANT 30. Munich: Kösel-Verlag, 1972.

————. *Johannes und Lukas: Untersuchungen zu den johanneisch-lukanischen Parallelperikopen Joh 4,46–54/Lk 7,1–10—Joh 12,1–8/Lk 7,36–50; 10,38– 42—Joh 20,19–29/Lk 24,36–49.* Forschung zur Bibel 50. Würzburg: Echter Verlag, 1984.

Denaux, A. ed., *John and the Synoptics* (Proceedings of the 1990 Louvain Colloquium). BETL. Louvain: Louvain University Press, 1992.

de Solages, Mgr. [Bruno]. *Jean et les synoptiques.* Leiden: E. J. Brill, 1979.

Dodd, C. H. *Historical Tradition in the Fourth Gospel.* Cambridge: Cambridge University Press, 1963.

Dungan, David L., ed. *The Interrelation of the Gospels: A Symposium led by M.-E. Boismard, W. R. Farmer, F. Neirynck, Jerusalem, 1984.* BETL 95. Louvain: Louvain University Press, 1990.

Fortna, Robert Tomson. *The Gospel of Signs: A Reconstruction of the Narrative Source Underlying the Fourth Gospel.* SNTSMS 11. Cambridge: Cambridge University Press, 1970.

————. "Jesus and Peter at the High Priest's House: A Test Case for the Relation Between Mark's and John's Gospels." *NTS* 24 (1977–78): 371–83.

————. *The Fourth Gospel and Its Predecessors: From Narrative Source to Present Gospel.* Philadelphia: Fortress Press, 1988.

Gardner-Smith, Percival. *Saint John and the Synoptic Gospels.* Cambridge: Cambridge University Press, 1938.

Glusman, Jr. Edward Francis. "The Shape of Mark and John: A Primitive Gospel Outline," Ph.D. diss., Duke University, 1977.

Goodenough, Erwin R. "John a Primitive Gospel." *JBL* 64 (1945): 145–82.

Goodwin, Charles. "How Did John Treat His Sources?" *JBL* 73 (1954): 61– 75.

Grant, F. C. "Was the Author of John Dependent Upon the Gospel of Luke?" *JBL* 56 (1937): 285–307.

Green, Joel B. *The Death of Jesus: Tradition and Interpretation in the Passion Narrative.* WUNT 33. Tübingen: J. C. B. Mohr (Paul Siebeck), 1988.

Haenchen, Ernst. "Johanneische Probleme." *ZTK* 56 (1959): 19–54. Republished in Haenchen's *Gott und Mensch: Gesammelte Aufsätze.* Tübingen: J. C. B. Mohr (Paul Siebeck), 1965.

————. "Historie und Geschichte in den johanneischen Passionsberichten." In *Die Bibel und wir: Gesammelte Aufsätze,* 2:182–207. Tübingen: J.C.B. Mohr (Paul Siebeck), 1968.

————. *John 1* and *John 2*. Edited by Ulrich Busse and Robert W. Funk; translated by Robert W. Funk. Hermeneia. Philadelphia: Fortress Press, 1984.

Hahn, Ferdinand. "Der Prozess Jesu nach dem Johannesevangelium." In *Evangelisch-Katholischer Kommentar zum Neuen Testament, Vorarbeiten*, 2:23–96. Neukirchen-Vluyn: Neukirchener Verlag, 1970.

Heekerens, Hans-Peter. *Die Zeichen-Quelle der johanneischen Redaktion: Ein Beitrag zur Entstehungsgeschichte des vierten Evangeliums*. SBS 113. Stuttgart: Verlag Katholisches Bibelwerk, 1984.

Hoskyns, Edwyn C. *The Fourth Gospel*. Edited by F. N. Davey. 2d ed. London: Faber & Faber, 1947.

Howard, W. F. *The Fourth Gospel in Recent Criticism and Interpretation*. Revised by C. K. Barrett. London: Epworth Press, 1955.

Kelber, Werner H., ed. *The Passion in Mark*. Philadelphia: Fortress Press, 1976.

Klein, Hans. "Die lukanisch-johanneische Passionstradition." *ZNW* 67 (1976): 155–86.

Kleinknecht, Karl Theodor. "Johannes 13, die Synoptiker und die 'Methode' der johanneischen Evangelienüberlieferung." *ZTK* 82 (1985): 361–88.

Koester, Helmut. *Synoptische Überlieferung bei den apostolischen Vätern*. TU 65. Berlin: Akademie Verlag, 1957.

————. *History and Literature of Early Christianity*. Vol. 2, *Introduction to the New Testament*. Philadelphia: Fortress Press, 1982.

————. *Ancient Christian Gospels: Their History and Development*. Philadelphia: Trinity Press International, 1990.

Kümmel, Werner Georg. *Introduction to the New Testament*. Rev. ed. Translated by Howard Clark Kee. Nashville: Abingdon Press, 1975.

Kysar, Robert. *The Fourth Evangelist and His Gospel: An Examination of Contemporary Scholarship*. Minneapolis: Augsburg Publishing House, 1975.

————. "The Gospel of John in Current Research." *RSR* 9 (1983): 314–23.

————. "The Fourth Gospel: A Report on Recent Research." In *Aufstieg und Niedergang der römischen Welt*. Edited by H. Temporini and W. Hasse, II.25.3 (1985), 2389–2480. Berlin: Walter de Gruyter.

Langbrandtner, Wolfgang. *Weltferner Gott oder Gott der Liebe: Der Ketzerstreit in der johanneischen Kirche: Eine exegetisch-religionsgeschichtliche Untersuchung mit Berücksichtigung der koptisch-gnostischen Texte aus Nag-Hammadi*. BBET 6. Frankfurt Am Main: Peter Lang, 1977.

Lindars, Barnabas. *Behind the Fourth Gospel*. Studies in Creative Criticism 3. London: SPCK, 1971.

————. *The Gospel of John*. New Century Bible Commentary. Grand Rapids: Wm. B. Eerdmans Publishing Co., 1972.

Maddox, Robert. *The Purpose of Luke-Acts.* FRLANT 126. Göttingen: Vanden-hoeck & Ruprecht, 1982.

Mohr, Till Arend. *Markus- und Johannespassion: Redaktions- und traditions-geschichtliche Untersuchung der markinischen und johanneischen Passionstra-dition.* ATANT 70. Zurich: Theologischer Verlag, 1982.

Morris, Leon. "The Relationship of the Fourth Gospel to the Synoptics." In *Studies in the Fourth Gospel,* 15–63. Grand Rapids: Wm. B. Eerdmans Pub-lishing Co., 1969.

Neirynck, Frans. "John and the Synoptics." In *L'Evangile de Jean: Sources, rédaction, théologie,* 73–106. Edited by M. de Jonge. BETL 44. Louvain: Louvain University Press, 1977.

———. "John and the Synoptics: The Empty Tomb Stories." *NTS* 30 (1984): 161–87.

———. "John 21." *NTS* 36 (1990): 321–36.

———. "John and the Synoptics: 1975–1990." In *John and the Synoptics.* Edited by A. Denaux. BETL. Louvain: Louvain University Press, 1992.

———, with the collaboration of Joël Delobel et al. *Jean et les synoptiques: Examen critique de l'exégèse de M.-E. Boismard.* BETL 49. Louvain: Louvain University Press, 1979.

Nicol, N. *The Sēmeia in the Fourth Gospel: Tradition and Redaction.* NovtSup 32. Leiden: E. J. Brill, 1972.

Noack, Bent. *Zur johanneischen Tradition: Beiträge zur Kritik an der literar-kritischen Analyse des vierten Evangeliums.* Copenhagen: Rosenkilde og Bag-ger, 1954.

Onuki, Takashi. "Die johanneischen Abschiedsreden und die synoptische Tra-dition: Eine traditionskritische und traditionsgeschichtliche Untersuchung." *Annual of the Japanese Biblical Institute* (1977): 157–268. Tokyo: Yamamoto Shoten.

Osty, E. "Les points de contact entre le récit de la passion dans Saint Luc et dans Saint Jean." In *Mélanges J. Lebreton, RSR* 39 (1951): 146–51.

Perrin, Norman. *The New Testament, An Introduction: Proclamation and Parenesis, Myth and History.* Rev. ed. Dennis C. Duling. New York: Harcourt Brace Jovanovich, 1982.

Pharr, Philip Allen, "The Passion Narrative of the Fourth Gospel: A Study of Sources in John 18:1–19:42," Ph.D. diss., Duke University, 1972.

Reim, Günter. *Studien zum alttestamentlichen Hintergrund des Johannes-evangeliums.* SNTSMS 22. Cambridge: Cambridge University Press, 1974.

Robinson, James M. "The Johannine Trajectory." In *Trajectories Through Early Christianity,* James M. Robinson, with Helmut Koester, 232–68. Philadel-phia: Fortress Press, 1971.

Robinson, John A. T. *The Priority of John.* Edited by J. F. Coakley. London: SCM Press, 1985; Oak Park, Ill.: Meyer-Stone Books, 1987.

Sabbe, M. "The Footwashing in Jn 13 and Its Relation to the Synoptic Gospels." *ETL* 58 (1982): 279–308.

Schnackenburg, Rudolf. *The Gospel According to St. John.* Trans. Kevin Smyth et al., 3 vols., New York: Crossroad, 1968–82.

Schniewind, Julius. *Die Parallelperikopen bei Lukas und Johannes.* Hildesheim: G. Olms, 1958.

Sigge, Timotheus. *Das Johannesevangelium und die Synoptiker: Eine Untersuchung seiner Selbständigkeit und der gegenseitigen Beziehungen.* Neutestamentliche Abhandlungen 16, 2/3. Münster: Aschendorff, 1935.

Smith, D. Moody. "The Sources of the Gospel of John: An Assessment of the Present State of the Problem." *NTS* 10 (1963–64): 336–51.

———. *The Composition and Order of the Fourth Gospel: Bultmann's Literary Theory.* Yale Publications in Religion 10. New Haven and London: Yale University Press, 1965.

———. *Johannine Christianity: Essays on Its Setting, Sources, and Theology.* Columbia, S.C.: University of South Carolina Press, 1984.

———. "The Problem of John and the Synoptics in Light of the Relation Between Apocryphal and Canonical Gospels." In *John and the Synoptics.* Edited by A. Denaux. BETL. Louvain, Louvain University Press, 1992.

Smith, Joseph Daniel, Jr. "Gaius and the Controversy Over the Johannine Literature." Ph.D. diss., Yale University, 1979.

Streeter, B. H. *The Four Gospels: A Study of Origins.* London: Macmillan & Co., 1936.

Teeple, Howard. *The Literary Origin of the Gospel of John.* Evanston, Ill.: Religion and Ethics Institute, 1974.

Thyen, Hartwig. "Johannes und die Synoptiker—Auf der Suche nach einem neuen Paradigm zur Beschreibung ihrer Beziehungen anhand von Beobachtungen an Passions-und Ostererzählungen." In *John and the Synoptics.* Edited by A. Denaux. BETL. Louvain: Louvain University Press, 1992.

Trocmé, Etienne. *The Passion as Liturgy: A Study in the Origin of the Passion Narratives in the Four Gospels.* London: SCM Press, 1983.

Wahlde, Urban C. von. *The Earliest Version of John's Gospel: Recovering the Gospel of Signs.* Wilmington, Del.: Michael Glazier, 1989.

Weder, Hans. "Die Menschwerdung Gottes: Überlegungen zur Auslegungsproblematik des Johannesevangeliums am Beispiel von Joh 6." *ZTK* 82 (1985): 326–60.

Windisch, Hans. "Die Absolutheit des Johannesevangeliums." *Zeitschrift für systematische Theologie* 5 (1927): 3–54.

————. *Johannes und die Synoptiker: Wollte der vierte Evangelist die älteren Evangelien ergänzen oder ersetzen?* Untersuchungen zum Neuen Testament 12. Leipzig: J. C. Hinrichs'sche Buchhandlung, 1926.

Worsley, F. W. *The Fourth Gospel and the Synoptists: Being a Contribution to the Study of the Johannine Problem.* Edinburgh: T. & T. Clark, 1909.

# Index of Scripture and Ancient Sources

# Index of Modern Authors